CW00495789

LOOKING FOR THEOPHRASTUS

Also by Laura Beatty

Lost Property
Darkling
Lillie Langtry
Pollard

LOOKING FOR THEOPHRASTUS

Travels in Search of a Lost Philosopher

LAURA BEATTY

Atlantic Books
London

First published in hardback in Great Britain in 2022 by
Atlantic Books, an imprint of Atlantic Books Ltd.

With thanks to Cambridge University Press for permission to
quote from *Theophrastus: Characters*, translation by James Diggle.

1 2 3 4 5 6 7 8 9

A CIP catalogue record for this book is available from the British
Library.

Hardback ISBN: 978 1 83895 436 9
EBook ISBN: 978 1 83895 437 6

Design www.benstudios.co.uk

Printed in Great Britain by TJ Books Ltd

Atlantic Books
An imprint of Atlantic Books Ltd
Ormond House
26–27 Boswell Street
London
WC1N 3JZ

www.atlantic-books.co.uk

To Rupert

And might it not be… that we also have appointments to keep in the past, in what has gone before and is for the most part extinguished, and must go there in search of places and people who have some connection with us on the far side of time, so to speak?

W.G. Sebald, *Austerlitz*

I

The Man

If it happened, then someone must have seen it. A fisherman coming home across an evening sea, one early star burning on the horizon and the sky still light. There, ahead of him, something bobbing on the water – the head, a little pale balloon with its ribbon of blood unwinding behind it all the way to the horizon.

Or maybe it wasn't like that. Maybe the fisherman heard it before he saw it; first thinking it a seagull's cry, but then thinking, no – it isn't that, someone is singing. So he looked around to see where it came from, this strong, unearthly song. Could it be coming from there, that little collection of flotsam? It is likely that there was other detritus from the murder. The flesh and bones, the coils of things normally hidden and now spilled out, floating on the sea's surface, rising and falling with the swell. There, in the middle of it all, would have been the head, singing. Because that is the important point – not the murder, not the women tearing him apart with maddened hands, but the fact that the song refused to die. It went on unchanged, pouring out of the dismembered man's mouth as if nothing had happened, on and on, all the way down the Hebros river and out across the sea, until the head landed, still singing, on a beach on the island of Lesbos. That was the greatest outrage, that one human being's song could do that, cheat time – that Orpheus' music was so free it was death-proof.

*

It is evening, October and windy; I'm standing at the rail of a ship, a ferry, waiting to leave Piraeus for Lesbos, where the head of Orpheus came to rest. Below me, on the empty quayside, one or two cars are parked, men are set up for fishing over propped rods. The dark is fast coming down. Somewhere there is music playing – Greek music, with its strange running and halting rhythms. I lean and listen to the tune, now fast, now slow, now fast again, on its endless, trance-inducing round.

At the dock's abrupt edge, a family, with a set of white plastic tables and chairs, dines quietly, as if they were in their own home. The music is coming from the open window of their parked car, as they pass each other salads in little Tupperware dishes. Above them, the ferry – which is in proportion to the sea not the land – bulks gigantic against the dock. It is not human in scale, so what on earth kind of journey are you taking, I find myself thinking, if this is your vehicle of choice?

I'm going a long way – much further than the 143 or so nautical miles between Athens and Lesbos. I'm going back about 2,400 years to find someone, a philosopher whose work once burned itself across the sky of Western thought, and then somehow fell into darkness and was gone.

A forgotten philosopher? Why on earth would we need one of those, let alone one from so impenetrably far back in human history? Well, because this one is different: less titanic perhaps but more modern in his thinking, more recognizable and therefore more relevant to now. For a start, he comes not from the grandeur and confidence of classical Greece, but from the moment of muddle and compromise just after it, when Athens' grip on its own world was slipping and the dream of democracy was dying.

I was familiar enough with classical Greece, with its myths and its poetry, its confident statues and its architecturally astonishing temples. I knew it first, as a child, in its mythic mode, as a place of slippage – a Narnia for grown-ups, whose woods were full of centaurs and whose people turned into trees, or stones. Then, later, I knew it in its heroic and tragic mode, as a place of grandeur and clanging bronze, governed by fate and made of gold, very, very far back in time and unassailable in its almost perfection. What it never was, or what I could never see, was its ordinary mode, its day to day.

Then, about ten years ago, I came across something else, something very unexpected. It was a little green book of character sketches and the sketches were of ordinary people – people like the Chatterbox, *who sits next to a stranger he's never met before and first launches into singing his own wife's praises, then recounts the dream he had last night, then describes in every detail what he had for dinner. Then, as no one has managed to stop him, he carries right on saying things like, 'People nowadays are far less well-behaved than in the olden days... The city is crammed with foreigners. A little more rain would be good for the crops.'*

These people were out and about in the marketplace, in and out of each other's houses for dinner. They were gossips and flatterers, and farmers, and city boys, all talking in their own ordinary voices, in their ordinary clothes, among the clutter of their ordinary possessions.

How could something so long ago feel so immediately present? It was as if all the previously invisible, unmentioned and unimaginable humdrum of unassailable Athens had catapulted itself suddenly into my writing room. I didn't know what to make of it. Where, in the canon, did it fit? It was so different. It read like something out of a novel but it was two thousand years too early. I looked again at the name on the cover: Theophrastus. It wasn't like anything else I'd ever read. I sat holding the book in my hands and wondering about its author.

How do you know how to do this, Theophrastus? What is this? I've been reading for years and I've never even heard of you. Who exactly are you?

Very little has survived to answer my questions but I started to see what I could find. I picked through the fragments and soon, like catching sight of someone out of the corner of your eye, always just as they disappear, I began to glimpse a man who seemed always intent, who looked at everything with focused attention, no matter how big or small. Someone who asked, in between his researches into metaphysics, philosophy, law and logic, what are these tiny creatures? What are these flowers at my feet, up again out of the dead ground? What are these stones, these storms, these winds that walk in on us out of the horizon with such devastating authority? He was one of the first to hold conversation with the world and, with no instruments to help him other than his own mind, to try to write down how it works, how it started.

'Theophrastus who?' people say, when I mention him. 'Never heard of him,' and 'Bless you!' one person says, thinking his name is the sound of a sneeze.

So I'm going to fetch him and bring him back. I'm going to the place where he's still dimly present, living out a shadow-life in the monochrome underworld of written memory – hence Orpheus. The point about Orpheus is that he doesn't just look nostalgically back to a better time – he goes and fetches the past, with his music, and brings it forwards; and that, to me, has always seemed a more useful direction. I will need a song, perhaps, like the one playing below me, or something else from Orpheus' armoury. Either way, I'm going to look for Theophrastus in all the places where he lived and then lead him forwards into the present, so that his life can run again across our own time, if only for a moment.

Below me, on the dock, the family's quickening music mixes with the sound of the sea – the changing rhythms of a Greek dance, which, in its circularity, is another thing that is unending. And that would be another way to enter the Underworld: dancing. That would be a good way to bring someone back from the dead. I've seen the Greeks on ancient pots, even before Theophrastus' time, dancing just the same as they do now, with their arms round each other's shoulders, circling and circling as if, between then and now, the running, halting rhythms continually unwind and check and change but never stop. That's all I need, something to hold time up for long enough to get there, and then to get back, something to change time's insistent linearity, its always forward motion, something to hold it in place.

Out beyond the harbour, the sea has turned heaving and poisonous, although the crew don't seem to have noticed. Have they not seen? Because already the gangplank is lifting. Up and down its rising incline the men in boilersuits run reckless, while the walkie-talkies in their pockets crackle like fireworks. I look at the land behind; the little lights coming on in the houses. I've changed my mind. I want to get off. But the ropes are flung back to the loosened ship and already the anchor chain runs rattling home. It is too late. I am committed. Above me the foghorn sounds twice and, in a foulness of fuel and churning water, the ferry eases back, and abandons itself to the sea and the coming dark.

Behind us as we slide away, the few people on the shore stand motionless and only half watching. With unfocused eyes, they witness the ferry dwindle until it's just a chock rolling in a waste of waters.

An hour or so later, it is fully dark when I look through the porthole. Black mountains of water heap and slide. Anything could be happening out there. Somewhere on the same waterway – but in a smaller vessel, one that bucks in the waves like a pony – Theophrastus crosses and re-crosses, still passing swiftly by, now on the landward side, now on the seaward. Or he chases behind us, on one of his journeys, making for Athens, or Lesbos, or Anatolia – perhaps the first time he made the journey to Athens, impatient, on his way to Plato's Academy, leaning his body into the wind in excitement, while the ropes sing and the water slaps over the side. He is watching with screwed-up eyes for the first sign: the sight of Athene's bronze crest, her spear-tip flashing in the light, a thirty-foot metal woman brooding over the city that took her name. Look for it as soon as you pass the temple at Cape Sounion. That's what he's been told. That is where it's first visible. And then the Athenians on the trading ship pointing her out with shouts, recognizing home.

I too look out for Cape Sounion, illuminated now by electric light, its frail skeleton put down on the hilltop like something forgotten. Odd and ancient and without use any more, while the Aegean slides by in the dark, and all night the ferry rolls, blunt and dogged, persisting through heavy seas. Intermittently, because I can't sleep, I peer through the porthole at the mountains made of water. I think of Theophrastus braving the sea back and forth in his smaller, engine-less boat. You are far less fearful than me. The ship descends and rises, occasionally hitting a wave face-on with a juddering smack. Tens of feet up from the waterline, I watch the spray shoot up against the glass. I will pray to anyone who will prevent my shipwreck. And I mean anyone.

*

In the morning, I come up on deck like someone stunned, to find a different world, the ferry easing through blue seas, under an open sky. We're coming into port. Here is Mytilene, Lesbos' capital city, with the sweet curve of its harbour, its dome and its gracious looks, doubling itself in glassy waters. I totter down the gangplank and along the waterfront as far as a coffee house. I've arrived.

The coffee house has a high ceiling, and turn-of-the-century grandeur. Huge arched windows look out at the harbour. It is so light, and it is so big that it runs the length of the block, its far end opening onto the shopping street behind. You can order a latte here, which comes in a cup like a bowl, accompanied by two mysterious, powdery, half-sweet biscuits; you can balance out your tiredness with caffeine and you can adjust. There is plenty to look at. Everyone, it seems, is passing through. Everyone is talking. They look like people from Theophrastus' *Characters*. Old ladies whose bodies have melted downwards into bulging ankles. Young men with slicked-back looks who whistle through their teeth and hurry by. Men with stomachs like footballs and light-coloured shoes; and men shuffling by in vests and braces, their hands holding plastic bags stuffed with what seem to be dock-leaves. I nest myself in this hubbub. I listen to the gulls crying, the foreign conversations, the foreign traffic noise – different horns, different sirens, scooters. I put my hands around the cup and look at the pale coffee and think of the distances I've travelled – of the long miles and the long, long time that there have been things to look at and people present to do the looking. And I'm looking, myself, for the man who started it all, who taught us first how to do it, how to use our eyes.

Only he isn't here. I'm imagining him in the boat that crossed my path in the night. I'm imagining him, arriving at his own destination, in his own morning, approaching Piraeus, which I have long left. Slower because he is under sail – and in the shadow of triremes, the famous Greek fighter ships with their three banks of oars, turning and manoeuvring, out on exercise in the water beyond the harbour. Close to, on the seaward side as the little vessel nears land, a trireme, perhaps in the process of swinging round, holds itself steady for a moment, as if catching its breath. Then comes the roar, *O opop, O opop*, as the rowing chant breaks out again and 170 oarsmen bend and pull and the ship leaps forward like a fighting dog.

On the little merchant vessel, they stand at the gunwale, turning their heads in admiration as it shoots past. The speed of it! The oars hissing in the water like heated knives and the metalled prow flashing. The noise and the force of it, as it slices through the water with its painted eye staring, and on the deck of the merchant vessel the watchers suck in their breath and shiver because this is the power of Athens.

Then into the harbour itself, in a glitter of water, between boats that jostle and bob at several commercial jetties. On the quay, where a family is perhaps picnicking, cargoes are unloaded and it is noisy – shouts, whistles, gulls crying. Crates and sacks stacked. Grain from the Black Sea and the Nile delta, Egyptian slaves, the cloth that Theophrastus' father finishes, terracotta, and garum (a condiment made from fish guts that is Lesbos' most prized export). In the naval harbour, the warships coming in are hauled up the slipways into the ship-sheds to another shouted chant, and the oarsmen stand, massive, and walk to and fro, among piles of ship's tackle. Here and there, the city's notables, the men who finance the triremes, hold conversation with their captains, rings flashing on their hands as they point and talk.

And Theophrastus would have come down the gangplank into all this hubbub for the first time, aged about seventeen, as disoriented as I am in Mytilene. His possessions thrown down to the quay and the noise rising up around him and the strange feeling of standing on solid ground after so long on the rocking deck of a ship. It is roughly 355 BCE. He has come to Athens so he can study under Plato. Is he met by someone? Does he have a contact or a friend of his father's to guide him, or does he just shoulder his bundles and set out alone, in the shadow of Themistocles' walls, to travel the four and a half miles or so from Piraeus to Athens? Either way, his shoulders and the back of his head are visible only for a short while before he is lost among the steady traffic between the two towns, dust permanently raised in the wake of wagons. And when he arrives finally and passes through the Piraean Gate and into the muddle of streets beyond, if he hesitates at any point, if he stops to ask directions, he speaks in dialect, with a giveaway accent. He too is a foreigner.

For me, in my café, there are the soft, dropping sounds of Modern Greek, because Greek is a language made of 'l's and 'k's and softened 'd's, whispered and stopped at the front of the palate, like water running away over leaves and stones. '*Poli kala*', the people say to each other repeatedly. '*Oreia*'. And they gather their bags and rise from their tables, or put their bags down and stop and talk, or start off again, doing whatever it is that people do in Greece, and which, whatever it is, looks better, or more mysterious, or more significant than anything I might have been doing, at this sort of time, ordinarily, in England.

And then, after a while, I leave. I go out into streets bright with striped light to find somewhere to stay, discovering by accident, up a side-street, the Hotel Alkaios, named after an ancient poet, with a courtyard full of trees covered in ripe pomegranates and red-shuttered windows to match. In a solidly furnished room, I flop onto a bed at last and stare at the ceiling, and ask myself how on earth you go about finding a man who has been dead for over two thousand years.

Orpheus, who is now known only for taking his wife back from the dead, may actually have existed, in some far distant past, as a Thracian philosopher and musician, but whether he did or whether he didn't, a myth grew up about him. In Homer, 'mythos' simply means 'word', or 'speech' or 'spoken account', without distinguishing between truth or falsehood. Our modern meaning, which is a response to the idea of myth as story, is unhelpful in that it only represents untruth. It has forgotten its original purpose, which was to explain. In the beginning, myths were an attempt to answer our first question: why? They were the product of a powerful crossover between metaphysical thought and close observation: narratives that grew out of an attempt to understand an essential truth. They tried to explain why the world works as it does.

The myth that grew up around Orpheus is, among other things, an explanation of the nature of music. It is interested in how music relates to death and, in particular, how it relates to death's servant, time. As we know, it tells how a musician, who had lost his wife, was allowed – alive – down to the Underworld to take her back, on the single condition that, as she followed him up, he did not once stop or look behind him, and how, just as he reached the lip of the world, he failed. He turned round and Eurydice dispersed before his eyes as if made of mist. It tells how Orpheus mourned Eurydice for the rest of his life and how finally he was torn apart by cultic women, some say for his rejection of their advances and some say just because the burden of his sorrowing was too great.

In other words, music creates its own conditions. It catches time into its own measure and makes it keep a different beat, and it catches up emotion and memory and holds them safe without our knowing. In music, we travel back to places or people that existed before – to a memory, or to a whole set of feelings – of first love, say, or first loss

– under which conditions an eighty year old might find themselves dropped sheer over the cliff of being twenty again, or a man might find his dead wife alive. So long as Orpheus keeps moving forwards through his song, so long as he doesn't either break or stop, Eurydice will be there.

I first read this myth as a child. I remember I read it several times, somehow hoping each time that between readings the ending might have changed – that Orpheus might, this time, have come to his senses and followed the simple instruction. Why was he so stupid? Why didn't he do as I would have done – because I, as a child, had answers. I would have reached behind me, without looking, to hold her hand, to know that she was safe. I read it again. Why did Orpheus always look back?

I know now, of course. He looked back because he was grown-up. It is only as children that we live in a seemingly endless present, a place of waiting, in which we lean into the future, impatient, through the decades of snail-paced birthdays. We measure how much our feet have grown, how far we can spit, how tall we are, in a world where bigger is better. And then one day, who knows why, we turn round and look back.

*

Lying on my hotel bed, thinking about the Orpheus myth, about what the truth at its centre might be, I make my own journey backwards, to the self I lost at the edge of childhood, to the place where it all started. I remember the moment, in my own life, when I first turned round and saw my childhood self, pale as a ghost on the lip of the world, and thought it irretrievably lost. I was eleven and we'd just moved house. Under the wide, freewheeling skies and through the sugar-beet fields and among the woods and streams of Nottinghamshire, I'd had a wild, wide-ranging childhood. Then we moved to Reading, where I woke up, on the threshold of adolescence, boxed into a terraced house on the side of a busy road.

The town was hard, and the town was grey. Its pavements were grey and its buildings were grey and the birds that blew about its streets like litter – the gulls and the pigeons – were grey, as was my new school uniform. Reading closed itself around me with its always-indoors places. Even the sky was small and hemmed in, and at night it had to be lit up, as if it too was indoors; the soft silver of its own scattered lights swallowed in sodium glow.

We weren't allowed to roam around. It was dangerous. It wasn't clear how. At night, outside my bedroom, there was a drunk – was it just once, or every night? – staggering and groaning in the street below my window. Perhaps he was the danger. I didn't know. In the mornings, I bicycled down the hill, past the sterile cherry blossom – not grey but so pink it might have been plastic – on my boy's bike, on my way to my girls' school.

I missed the stream, where we used to play. I missed the skies and the whirling winds. I missed the fields where the owl passed, white-faced, before bedtime, and his hollow hoot in the dark. I missed the world that had seemed to match my restlessness with its own, always changing, always turning through the circle of its seasons. But looking back now, I can see that what the move really marked was the end of childhood, the end of a particular way of being. It closed me into my body, and my body had become a place I did not want to be. I didn't want this unstoppable plumping. I didn't want this clock inside me, telling me monthly that I was now a woman. I wanted my old unbounded self. Where was the girlboy, fishbird, fluid thing I'd been before? How would I ever get used to this lesser, more restricted me?

Where could I go, now I couldn't leave my own body? Where could I roam, wide and wild, like I always had before?

*

I was twelve when I discovered ancient Greece. It was brightly lit, the Greece I first encountered, running with water, flickering with spirits and fluttering with draperies, a place where everything was fluid and shape-shifting. Its people were often only half-human, or human only half the time. They were half-god, half-goat or half-horse. In this respect, it restored the world I'd known in childhood, a wild and flowing world where everything was alive, where mind and body were yet undivided, the mind soaking up the world through the body, as if the two were unbounded and equal, the one shot through with the other, like a piece of cloth.

Instinctively, perhaps, when this was lost to me, I followed Orpheus back into myth, to where girls can become reeds or streams or deer, and where no boundary of time or species is so fixed it can't be crossed. It was perhaps an odd choice for a child in Reading but I just liked what I'd glimpsed of the freedom and strangeness of the ancient world. It was a place I often went to with my questions, so it was no surprise that an answer should come from another story about Greece: Leonard Cottrell's *The Bull of Minos*. I can't now remember why I picked it up. It was a paperback, in an edition called Pan Piper Illustrated. There was something exotic-sounding about that. It had black and gold lettering on its red and white cover, the whole of the rest of which was filled with a black bull's head: strange and savage-looking. It had a gold rosette on its forehead and long and finely tapering golden horns between which the title was caught. Something about it matched how I felt.

I'd never seen anything like it before but I recognized it immediately, like something I had lost.

It is the account of three archaeological excavations, at Mycenae, the Minoan palace at Knossos, and ancient Troy. That makes it sound dry. It isn't dry. It's full of light and full of gold and both of those were the opposite of grey. More than that though, it is the story of the passionate exploration of a ruined civilization by two men who believed that the great myths they'd been told as children were historically true. I too knew the stories of Troy and its wooden horse, of Agamemnon and his terrible murder, and of King Minos and his labyrinth. I'd read them as stories, not as histories. If I had an instinctive feeling that myths existed to explain the nature of life, that didn't mean I took them to be factual accounts. It had never occurred to me that there might be real places where, at some distant time, these things (or versions of them) had truly happened. So I followed Cottrell, as he followed his chosen archaeologists; he was often tired and disoriented by travel, often disappointed, often alone, as here, on a train at nightfall:

> Glancing up when the train had been halted for nearly a
> minute I happened to see a station name-board in the yellow
> light of an oil lamp. It was Mycenae. Even as I snatched
> my bag from the rack and scrambled out of the carriage
> the absurdity of the situation struck me. To see the name
> of Agamemnon's proud citadel, Homer's 'Mycenae, rich in
> gold', the scene of Aeschylus's epic tragedy, stuck on a station
> platform, was too bizarre. And yet there it was. And there was
> I, the sole occupant of the platform, watching the red rear-
> light of the little train as it slowly receded into the night.

For some reason, this was the paragraph that caught me – the idea that stories could be true, that a book could open like a door onto a real place, existing both now in the present, and also as it was in some other distant time. I loved the blurring of the edges of history, fiction and reality. I loved the slippage of travelling in three dimensions at once, through time, across geographical space and into story. And there was so much detail. There was this whole country where I'd never been – the drama of the digging, and the waiting and working, and the impossible dream of gold. There was the first breath-stopping glint of it, those long-lost possessions of kings lying, battered but intact, in the mud. But there was also the ordinariness of stations and grubby carriages and train lights. I was caught among the moonlit olive trees as Cottrell set out to walk to his lodgings, with his suitcase in his hand and the ancient stories in his head.

Behind him, my little box room in Reading forgotten, I too was setting out on that midnight road, free and fierce with intent, and with the glamour of the Greek myths moving like great shadowing clouds, somewhere in the air above me.

Over a lifetime, I've gone on reading these stories and histories and poems. They have represented to me something true but long lost, a way of relating to the world through the body as well as the mind, more than animal, a kind of mineral belonging, a communion in the fullest sense. More than that, in the case of Orpheus, they give me hope that if one can find a way around the instructions, some parallel means, then it might still be possible to get back what is lost.

*

So Orpheus' story tells us how impossible we find it, not to look back with longing for what is gone; but while it shows us the trap we are caught in, it also gives us the key. It shows us the conditions under which the lost thing can be raised and re-lived, even if only for a while. In song, in music and in story, we are sidestepping time. That is what reading is. You can slip into a book like you slip into water and whatever you find there – just like whatever you find underwater – is a different but unquestionable reality. It lasts as long as it takes to read and you live it alongside your own life. What's more, if it's powerful enough, something of its atmosphere will remain, like silt from a risen river, to change the contours of your inner world, to colour your mind.

Theophrastus wasn't his real name. He was born Tyrtamos, the son of a rich man, at Eresos on the western end of the south coast of Lesbos, in 372 BCE, or thereabouts.

Picture the island in the fourth century BCE, wide and fertile and well watered, folded protectively around two sea gulfs which loop up to its centre, full of fish and cuttlefish, and with birds circling overhead. It has been inhabited for several millennia already. It grows vines and olives, oak trees, walnuts, planes with their mosaic shade. It has boiling springs that fizz up out of volcanic rock to meet the sea in a hiss of steam. It has rivers and reedy flats and sudden streams and soft valleys and rugged, volcanic mountains. It has flowers in variety and profusion, a fallen forest of petrified trees. It is both one of the largest and one of the most topographically varied of the Greek islands.

All this is divided between five competing cities – Mytilene, Methymna, Antissa, Eresos and Pyrrha – each of which has its own distinct identity and each of which is reluctant to cede control to any other. The cities trade independently with the rest of the Greek world and as far afield as Egypt, often founding colonies along the way, at Assos on the coast of Anatolia for instance, or at the mouth of the Hebros river where Orpheus was dismembered, or on the Hellespont. Mytilene, which in Theophrastus' time has sprawled to roughly the same size as Athens, has two harbours, one military and one mercantile, and is part of a powerful twelve-city trading cooperative that has a permanent emporium at Naucratis, on the Nile. The island exports many things: wine and alum and oil, textiles, terracotta and garum. Lesbos is rich.

It also prides itself on its cultural standing. Theophrastus would have grown up knowing that he came from the island where Orpheus' severed head washed up, still singing, on the beach at Antissa. Both Achilles and Odysseus are supposed to have landed here. So, an island fixed in myth, blessed with poetry and music. By Theophrastus' time it had already produced four of the great founding lyric poets of Greek tradition: Arion, Sappho, Alkaios and Terpander.

Theophrastus' father was a fuller. He had a business cleaning woollen cloth, both in the process of making the fabric and afterwards, when it had become whatever it became – cloaks, blankets, tunics. Once, when asked who his friends were, Theophrastus answered quickly, *How would I know? I am rich.* Everyone had clothes that needed cleaning, after all. This was done by treading or pounding the cloth in a bath which contained a whitening agent, so for this reason Theophrastus' father may also have traded in gypsum, which was the substance most commonly used. This was mined further south, on the islands of Samos and Melos. In an otherwise dry and impenetrable treatise on stones, Theophrastus wrote a description of the mines on Samos that is so precise, so detailed and so vivid that it has to be first hand. He must have seen the mines himself, I'm sure of it. And this is how one might follow him, sifting through what's left of his writing, picking up the little details, like clues, as if tracking an animal by its spoor:

> *It is not possible to stand upright while digging in the pits of Samos, but a man has to lie on his back or his side. The vein stretches for a long way and is about two feet in height, though much greater in depth. It is surrounded on both sides by stone and is taken out of the space between… The earth is used mainly or solely for clothes.*

So here Theophrastus is, so interested, so observant, that he notes the height of the seam, its length and depth. He compares it to gypsum from Melos, where it seems he has also been. Samian gypsum is *beautiful… greasy, dense and smooth.* How old is he? Still a boy, having made the trip down the coast of Asia Minor with his father, being shown the world of trade for the first time. And when they arrive at the quarry, watching in fierce sunlight and gypsum-dust while the men, caked white like ghosts, work the seam on their backs, it must have been hoped he would follow in the family business.

But he didn't. Something else happened. Somewhere in spaces I can't imagine: In a room? In an open space? In cool colonnades, or a garden, in a grove of trees, or under the shade of a single, spreading plane? I don't know, but somewhere, Theophrastus was educated. Democracy demanded a literate population and Lesbos, at least while Theophrastus was growing up, was democratic. In Athens, all schedules of taxes, all legal cases and all new legislation had to be written up on white tablets and publicly exhibited, for everyone to read. So it follows that enough people were able to do so. In fact, it seems, from inscriptions found in the surrounding countryside, that even the shepherds may have been educated to some degree. Alphabets have been found carved into the rocks, in jumbled order, as though by someone practising – αβλ, where it should read αβγ, for instance – and in one place, the inscription, 'I am bored watching sheep.'

Theophrastus' teacher was called Alcippus, and from Alcippus he learned mathematics; he learned how to read, and how to write, holding a stylus and scratching his letters into a wax-covered tablet or writing passages out in ink. In one speech by the great orator Demosthenes, which attacks an opponent's back-street upbringing, there is a snatched insight into the atmosphere of Ancient Greek schooling which makes it sound oddly Victorian:

But do you—you who are so proud and so contemptuous of others—compare your fortune with mine. In your childhood you were reared in abject poverty. You helped your father in the drudgery of a grammar-school, grinding the ink, sponging the benches, and sweeping the school-room, holding the position of a menial, not of a free-born boy.

From Alcippus, Theophrastus also learned poetry and systems of government. He learned the rhythm of reading a scroll using sticks to hold and unroll it to the length of a page at a time. One stick for the top of the roll and one for the bottom. At the end of the page length, he learned to allow the top of the scroll to roll down, trapping both sticks at the bottom as place marks. Then he'd push the whole scroll up the desk and roll down a page length again. Up, down, slide, up, down, slide, working the sticks in a kind of reading dance. Most of all, because scrolls were rare and precious, he learned to absorb information by ear, keep it, memorize it, organize it, frame and formulate his thoughts about it, and then to speak those thoughts out loud. Information was most quickly and widely transferred in speech, as if the transition from an oral to a literate society wasn't something that simply switched from one to the other with the invention of writing but took place very slowly over a long period. In many ways, in Theophrastus' time, Greece was still an oral culture. The ability to speak off the cuff, in public, was an essential skill.

So he learned how to speak formally, in passages, as we would now write, measuring his audience as he went. He learned how to catch attention – with words and with gesture. And how to use his voice itself – its range, its rise and fall – and then how to fit, in the flash of an instant, his thoughts into sounding words. He found that, together, speech and thought could combine, like a weight of water, could lift an audience and sweep it away. Why would you want to clean cloaks, or count money, or watch dust-caked slaves at a rock-face if you could do that?

*

He didn't. He thought about it, what he might do. A soft and susceptible boy, the kind of boy who might have told himself secretly: what great thing I might one day be. A boy who laid out his collections of things, the carefully noticed same types of shell, the little lumps of minerals, and all the types of gypsum his father brought him. A boy who, when he undressed at night, quietly folded his clothes.

So, when the time came, he chose his moment and he faced his father and told him something of the dreams that were beating in his chest. How he wanted to learn, and to learn philosophy. How in Athens they were solving the nature of the world. They were going to be able to understand what it was, how it worked. They were going to think it out. How he must be there because, maybe, if he studied, he could make a difference. His mind was good and he felt so strongly the mystery of all these things. It must be possible, surely, with time and application, to understand how they work, what their principle of organization or purpose might be. He might just be the man to do it. Alcippus believed in him. If he could have this one chance, he might be another Plato.

Presumably Alcippus, who had studied at the Academy himself, put the idea into his head. The fulling business, so hopefully built up for Theophrastus' future, was put to use funding his studies instead and off he went to the Academy at Athens, to study under Plato.

Plato was in his early seventies, working on the *Timaeus*, his attempt to describe the nature of the physical world. How can we know what we know, he was still asking, as he had been for years. How can we possibly trust our senses when they are so deeply subjective? But by now his thinking had become mathematical – numbers contained the only certainties he could trust.

Maybe Theophrastus had already heard of Plato's image of perception, or maybe he heard it for the first time in Athens, listening in his new surroundings, electric with attention. How, according to Plato, we are in a place of darkness, sitting chained in a cave, with our backs to a high wall which partially blocks the cave's only entrance. Along the top of the wall, people and animals are walking in front of a bright fire. It is their shadows that we watch, wavering and flickering in front of us, across the walls of the cave. That, Plato says, is what we think is real. If we could break the chains and walk up and out, and if we could recover from the blinding light of reality that would hit us as we emerged, we would see the things themselves, not just their shadows. They would be essential and absolute, not changing, not variable, not endlessly and puzzlingly different in small and pointless ways – we'd be able to see the blueprint (to use a modern term) that determines the water-ness of water, the tree-ness of a tree, or the cup-ness of a cup. These things are Plato's ideal forms and they have the pure, irrefutable truth of mathematics. They *are*. And we will only reach them, Plato taught, through abstract calculation and through thought.

Imagine Theophrastus listening and thinking. Trying Plato's ideas out for himself. Information pours into him all the time, through all his senses. There are five in total – as if for the purpose of corroboration – are we really to mistrust them all? Beside him some Athenian stranger shifts. He can see the youth's tunic. He knows the nodding blue flower from which its fibres are made. He knows the wool of his cloak, how it's shorn, spun, woven, carded, dyed and cleaned. If he picks up two stones and holds them in his hand he feels their weight. If he closes his fist on them he feels them grind against each other. If he looks at them they appear as different from each other as two people.

Shadows in a cave? He puts down the stones, looks back at Plato, who is still talking.

So Theophrastus had got what he wanted. He had made it to the Academy but nevertheless, these first days of his arrival in Athens couldn't have been easy. Life must have been both the same and very different from how he had dreamed it would be: the stylized discipline, the lectures that were as much display as they were learning, the rhetoric, the theatricality of Academic performance, the elegant leisure, the heightened atmosphere, the emphasis on exercise of mind and body, the dining clubs.

The boys of his own age, those who were the children of Athenian citizens on both sides, were all doing their two years' military training. He would have seen them, parading around in their cloaks and their newly instituted manhood. Known as the Ephebes, they lived in garrisons at Piraeus, received a wage of four obols a day and were taught how to fight with sword and spear, how to use catapults and how to shoot. Meanwhile, he was an outsider to all of that. So he sat in the Academy instead, listening to the ideas and the famous names arguing and wondered where to align himself. There was Plato, with his poetry and his entitlement and his former athleticism like a faint echo in the way he sat and the way he moved, holding court – should Theophrastus follow him? Or should he take a different tack? Should he follow someone more extreme, someone who was from outside, like himself, whose ideas were less elegant? Because, among the philosophers in Athens at that time, there were others whose thought was less abstract: Diogenes the Cynic, for example, exiled from his native town on the Black Sea, so it was said, for counterfeiting money. Nothing is left of his writings but his thinking was exemplified in the way he chose to live. The legend is that he lived in a barrel, or an amphora turned on its side, and he spent his days in the marketplace, deliberately shocking Athens by eating, shitting and occasionally masturbating in public. For this last offence, when called to account, he is supposed to have answered that he wished it were possible so easily to relieve hunger by rubbing the belly. Otherwise, he lived an ascetic life, routinely exposing himself to physical hardship in order to toughen himself up and routinely challenging his contemporaries for their moral and intellectual decadence. When the philosophers were dining, he would arrive dishevelled and stinking and pour scorn on Plato's doctrine. 'As Plato was conversing about Forms', so the story goes, 'and using the words "tablehood" and "cuphood", Diogenes said, "table and cup I see but your tablehood and cuphood, Plato, I can no wise see". "That's easily accounted for," said Plato, "for you have the eyes to see the visible table and cup but not the understanding by which tablehood and cuphood are discerned."'

These are the types of conversation that the young Theophrastus would have witnessed, as he learned to eat and drink in the Academy style, reclining on a bench in a graceful manner, listening to the talk and to the music which punctuated it for entertainment. Athenian society was varied, sociable, stylized, ornate and tolerant. The whole pageant of eating was important, from the water brought in for hand-washing, in silver ewers, to the garlands of flowers for the guests' heads. One directive went:

Be sure and have the second course quite neat,
Adorn it with all kinds of rich confections,
Perfumes, and garlands, aye, and frankincense,
And girls to play the flute.

We know something too of what Theophrastus himself heard and thought, since among the writings of the Arabic scholars there are records of some of his own sayings. These too are very much later, probably written in Baghdad in the tenth century AD by Arabic Aristotelians, part of a cycle of texts called the Siwān al-Hikma, or the Vessel of Knowledge. Here we catch tiny glimpses of how these evenings with Plato went. 'Theophrastus said that when Plato sat down to drink he would say to the musician, "sing to us of three things: of the First Good, of the secondary coming into being, and of the manifestation of things".' That is, sing of first principles, of their causes and of their manifestation in the world. So, the philosophical arguments and discussions weren't limited to the daytime teachings of the Academy but went on far into the night.

All of this, for the young Theophrastus, was heady and exhilarating, but as might have been expected, there were also difficulties. However great Plato and the other thinkers might have been, Athenian society was both competitive and snobbish. Theophrastus was not an Athenian so he had no rights in Athens. Here he was a small fish, whereas on Lesbos he had felt big. He was inferior, a metic or resident alien, and, as such, he couldn't hope to own property ever, or take part in the city-state's democracy. He had to pay an annual foreigner's tax. Whenever there were public processions, he had to walk with the other metics, carrying one of the special bowls that identified each one of them as outsiders. Besides all of which, he would not have spoken Attic Greek, but a dialect with an accent that betrayed his island origins. He learned fast. He learned to speak perfect Attic Greek and he was to spend all of his later life in Athens. But even with all of this, still something always gave him away. Bargaining, in his fifties, with a stall-holder in the market, he was piqued by the old woman addressing him dismissively as 'Stranger'. Something marked him out. 'Stranger, it is not possible to sell these more cheaply.' He was, and would always remain, less than an old market woman born in the city.

*

There was someone else who must have been immediately noticeable to Theophrastus, as he sat, meditating on his outsider status and wondering whose ideas to choose. There was another metic of great significance in Athens at this time – Aristotle, who came from Stagira in Chalkidiki, that little claw that reaches out into the Aegean at the top of Greece. In 355 BCE, Aristotle was roughly twenty-nine, so thirteen years older than Theophrastus and forty-four years younger than Plato. And in the hothouse atmosphere of the Academy, Aristotle was Plato's favourite pupil.

Aristotle – what was he like? Not the name behind a monumental architecture of thought. Not just the symbol of an intellectual system, a system that can outlast millennia. Neither of those, but Aristotle the man, as he was then, with the itch of his great work still to do, making his way in the pride and din of Athens at its toppling peak, walking about the streets, and going to the dinners, and answering Diogenes or Plato with his own quick ideas. The Arabs preserved so much of Aristotle's thought and tradition, and there are, among their writings, and in the *Lives of the Philosophers* (written, confusingly, by a different Diogenes), many descriptions of what Aristotle was like – but it is difficult to see a consistent, let alone a real person among the different accounts. He seems to have generated particularly strong and diverse reactions. Which to believe? Some are all idealization and mythologizing, some are almost savagely offensive. Aristotle was the kind of man who, for instance:

> … was an avid reader of books and a prodigious worker. He
> shunned empty talk, weighing every word before answering
> a question. He liked music and preferred the company of
> mathematicians and logicians. He was a most eloquent man, a
> most distinguished author and, after Plato, the most eminent

among Greek philosophers. At the same time he was a good man… displaying a genuine interest in the problems of his fellow men. He was modest, unassuming and considerate, and he was moderate in his habits and restrained in his emotions. Aristotle was fair, a little bald-headed, of good figure and rather bony. He had small blueish eyes, an aquiline nose, a small mouth, a broad chest and a thick beard.

Or, he was a trivial man who 'tied his shoes in an extravagant fashion' and 'spent part of the day in the fields or by the rivers'.

Or, he was vicious and scornful and made money as a quack; a man physically 'small, bald, stuttering, lustful and with a hanging paunch'.

Or, 'his calves were slender, his eyes small, and he was conspicuous by his attire, his rings and the cut of his hair'.

Or, he was 'white-skinned, a little bald, of small stature and strong bones, with small eyes, a thick beard, blue-black eyes, an aquiline nose, a small mouth and a small chest'.

Only sometimes, in the maze of words, is it possible to catch sight of a real person. Sometimes you can see him, as Theophrastus must first have done; like someone appearing momentarily among a crowd, for a split second he is looking straight at you – a man who is small, sparse-haired and with blue eyes of great penetration. Was that…? Over there, I thought I saw… Did you see? And then he's gone. But there is something else – something that lasts after the crowd has swallowed him and he's lost. His blue eyes, when they lock their gaze onto yours, are vivid with power: Aristotle is charismatic.

At any rate, Plato loved Aristotle for his quickness of mind, for his boundlessness and perhaps also for his difficulty, his refusal of intellectual control. He called him 'the Reader', or sometimes 'the Mind'. According to the Arabic scholars, Plato habitually refused to begin his lectures if Aristotle was absent. 'The audience is deaf,' he would say, sitting in silence while his audience shifted. He would wait. And then only once Aristotle had appeared would he begin, saying as he did, 'the audience is complete', or, 'begin to recite – the Mind is present'. So, to the young Theophrastus, Aristotle must have seemed a rising star, the man to watch, and of course, like Theophrastus himself, the Mind was an outsider.

But the Mind was restless. For his own part, sitting in the audience, listening, as he did every day, and feeling his thoughts turn, Aristotle must sometimes have felt frustration. He was young and, while Plato's great work was done, his was still to do. It wasn't so much his aims; they were broadly the same. His thinking was grounded in Plato's, but increasingly now he found himself wanting to take a different direction. The ideal forms for instance – however much he loved and revered his master, he couldn't make them fit his own understanding of life.

Didn't anyone share his unease? Plato's eager-faced disciples, just lapping it all up, complacent as cats, no questions asked.

But the world! The world was so fickle, so subject to change, so enthrallingly complex. What could it possibly have to do with something as static as an ideal form? And why not try to understand the nature of things as they are before looking for the essences they'd borrowed from elsewhere?

Plato's lecture continued. His thought tended always towards the grandeur and dependability of absolutes. 'If we are ever to know anything absolutely we must be free from the body and must behold the actual realities with the eye of the soul alone.' So understanding is to be achieved only through abstraction, through pure definition.

And all the time, although he started from the same place and with the same aims, Aristotle's mind pulled in the opposite direction.

'Wonder' is what starts the philosopher off, Plato says, and there they are in agreement. Aristotle believed, as Plato did, that it was this feeling of wonder at the world that drove philosophical enquiry, and which might, in different men, have produced poetry, or myth. Indeed, in some of their predecessors, it had produced a combination of all three – such as Parmenides, an early pre-Socratic philosopher who explained the workings of the moon as 'a torch which round the earth by night/Does bear about a borrowed light'.

'It is owing to their feelings of wonder,' Aristotle would later echo, 'that men now begin, as at first they ever began, to philosophise.' For 'wonder is what a philosopher feels and philosophy begins in wonder'.

Both Plato and Aristotle use the word '*thaumazein*', which can simply mean to wonder why – in other words, to think about something – but which can also mean to marvel at, to honour, or even to worship. Later, Aristotle would formulate wonder, a natural response to the world of things, as something that branched in one of two directions: either into intuitive understanding, which produced myth, or into rational understanding, which produced the disciplines of science and philosophy. The important question, for those who chose philosophy, then became which way your wonder took you: up, like Plato, away from the constantly changing muddle of the physical world, into something pure and abstract; or down, like Aristotle, because the pull of the physical world is so potent, so mysterious, that understanding how it works is the thing that matters.

Aristotle's love for the world of things was religious in its intensity. He felt its power to be immanent. He just couldn't figure out where it was or how exactly it worked and he couldn't lift his attention free from the phenomenological until he'd solved that problem. He couldn't be sure that the world his senses saw was just some diminishment from the ideal. Shifting uneasily in Plato's audience, his mind pulled away. Why disregard matter? Surely knowledge could, and should, be built up from real evidence provided by your senses at work in the world. What he wanted to try to do was gather up as much detail, as much information and understanding as possible, and only then, across all the collected evidence, begin to look for the pattern that might direct it, in all its great weight and variety and quantity, back towards some abstract origin, some single, prime cause.

Why did none of these boys seem to see things as he did? Why did none of them question, or differ in approach?

Or did they?

Imagine how it must have been for Aristotle the first time he heard Theophrastus speak. Sitting, unsuspecting, listening to the lecture. Today the same as yesterday. The same as the day before, in the heat, with his restless mind pulling and the swallows scooping by at speed. Above him, when he looked away, crows cocking their heads in the trees as if they too were listening, but for what? The usual crowd of boys among Plato's audience. The usual turns of phrase. The intellectual posing. How that one turns his hands while he speaks. How this one smooths at his cloak and thrusts forwards with his chin. The familiar rehearsal of the familiar dialectic. And then suddenly this one he hasn't noticed before stands up to answer; this well-dressed boy speaking Attic Greek with an accent, and Aristotle's face looking up in sudden astonishment: Who is *this*? As if a change of light had swept the auditorium. Who is this stranger that I've never seen before? Because of the flair, the elegant, effortless passages pouring from his eighteen-year-old mouth. Your memory, Theophrastus. Your confidence. The brilliance of your improvised, off-the-cuff thought.

Aristotle, with his ears pricked and his breath held, as alert as a stalking fox. Now, here was something he could work with. At last.

Or was it the other way around? Was it Theophrastus with his instinctive eye for detail who recognized in Aristotle's questions the pull of a different direction, something he could follow? When Aristotle sat down, having addressed his audience, did Theophrastus master his nerves and rise in reply? Or did he wait and catch him among the crowd streaming out to go home? Did he fall into step and quiz him about his position? What did Aristotle make of the Forms, for instance? What did he think about the world that the senses perceive? Was it not challenging in its mysteriousness – I mean Change – wasn't Change a problem? Because Change seemed to Theophrastus, as it did to Aristotle, to characterize the phenomenological world. And Change couldn't be compatible with fixed forms, could it? Did character count for nothing? And the world, in its strangeness, and variety and changeability, was it not important enough in its own right, worthy of study? Should it not be explored and understood before it was rejected in favour of something more lofty?

May I be your pupil?

It was a significant moment when Theophrastus, so young, looked for the first time through the keyhole of those blue eyes and found himself falling, with the great spaces of Aristotle's mind opening out before him. It must have been dizzying. They couldn't have known it at the time but Aristotle and Theophrastus would spend almost all of the rest of their lives working together, from that moment onwards, only separating when Aristotle left Athens in self-imposed exile, to die. It was Aristotle, struck by the astonishing eloquence of the boy called Tyrtamos from Lesbos, who named him first Euphrastus (well spoken) and then Theophrastus – divinely spoken – the name by which he has always been remembered.

*

In Theophrastus' case, the biographical details are consistent. He was a soft man, all the sources agree, 'above all ever ready to do a kindness and with a fondness for discussion'. He was sociable, beloved by his many friends. 'A man of gentleness and naturally of erotic bent.' It's hard to know exactly what is meant by that. I take it to mean that his affections weren't domestic. His recorded loves are his pupils and the son Aristotle left in his care. The Greeks had a pragmatic approach to the power of love; you learnt faster and better if you were enthralled, whether mentally or physically – it didn't matter. Just as, for the Thebans, you fought better and harder if you were side by side with your lover, so, among the philosophy schools, the relationship between master and pupil was intense, often tipping over into the sexual. There's no point looking at this through modern eyes. It was simply different.

What else? He thought kindness was a better way to deal with the world than being brusque or high-handed. For instance, *Intelligent tax collectors,* he once observed, *manage to collect more by mild methods than they would manage to collect by harsh and violent ones, just as the leech gets more blood without causing pain or making a sound than the mosquito with its sharp sting and awful noise.* But if he was gentle and pragmatic in his relations with people, his mind, his tongue and his sense of humour were extremely sharp. 'Theophrastus was quick witted, learned, proficient, and meant for this career', 'a man of remarkable intelligence and industry'. Also, he never wasted time. He felt it was in short supply. *An intelligent person,* he is supposed to have said, *ought to deal with time as gently as a non-swimmer who has fallen into a flowing stream deals with the water.* That is to say he should flail at it desperately, energetically and without ceasing, until it stops.

He and Aristotle were matched in their work ethic. And they were matched in their outlook, equal in their thrall to the workings of the world of things, in their determination to know it and to understand. Perhaps they began to form a clique of like-minded students. Perhaps they questioned more than they should have done, or perhaps Aristotle did, because he was disliked, whether for what was seen as ingratitude to his old and failing teacher, or for something more personal. Some of the accounts suggest that towards the end of Plato's life something went wrong for Aristotle in Athens; something that shook him from his position of security at the Academy.

Some say there was a bitter difference of opinion and that Aristotle, having gathered around him a group of followers of his own – perhaps including Theophrastus – insulted Plato in public, making fun of his age and his failing powers. Some say that Plato was not pleased with Aristotle's lifestyle. Some say he didn't like the way Aristotle dressed:

> Aristotle did in fact give a lot of attention to his clothes and his shoes. He also kept his hair trimmed, quite an unusual thing in Plato's eyes. He likewise took pride in all the rings he wore. Aristotle had a kind of mocking expression on his face. And when he spoke the ill-timed, gossipy, and chatterbox tone in his voice suggested that this too was part of his character. Clearly all of these qualities were unbefitting a philosopher so when Plato observed them he did not take a liking to Aristotle but preferred Xenocrates, Speusippus and others before him.

As is always the case, these are partisan accounts, written after the event, to explain the fact that Athens seemed to reject Aristotle the moment that Plato was no longer there to protect him with his favour. When Plato died, it happened that Aristotle was away from

Athens. In his absence, Plato's relative, Speusippus, was appointed head of the Academy, and when Aristotle returned he found himself passed over. Speusippus was a pleasure-loving man of legendary bad temper and with little self-control. He was the kind of man who came home in a fury once and, seeing his favourite dog lying peacefully in the courtyard, snatched it up and hurled it into the well, and then continued to be angry all the long time it took for the dog to drown. Some say that Aristotle, piqued at Speusippus' appointment, turned straight round and left Athens again, this time for the long term.

That is possible. He was Plato's favourite after all, and he was by far the most capable candidate, so he might have naturally expected to step into his shoes. The fact is that Aristotle was too complex a character to be universally liked. It's possible that some of his evident philosophical difference from Plato got interpreted emotionally and then retrofitted to explain biographical events, like why he left Athens. It's more likely that the choice was made against him for the prosaic reason that Aristotle, as a metic, was debarred from owning property in Athens. He couldn't, therefore, have inherited the Academy. If he was disappointed, that was only natural. Two things point to his continuing love and reverence for his former master. The first is the elegy he wrote on Plato's death. The second is that when he left he took with him Xenocrates, Plato's most solidly conventional disciple. Xenocrates was not just intellectually aligned with Plato, he was loyal to him, like a dog. He was a man of such integrity that he was the only person, whenever called as witness, who was never put on oath. If Aristotle had differences intellectually, in terms of where he wanted to take philosophy, he must still have remained Platonic in the basis of his thinking, otherwise he would surely not have taken Xenocrates with him.

Whatever personal reasons Aristotle might or might not have had for departure, there were other, bigger changes afoot that might have tipped his decision. Up in the north, in Macedonia, a new threat was building. If Athens was as yet unconcerned, Aristotle, who came from Chalkidiki, on Macedonia's south-eastern border, would have been receiving messages and letters from home that kept him abreast of the changes coming. It was perhaps nothing to do with Plato's death – not philosophy at all, but politics that sent Aristotle scurrying for Asia Minor. Perhaps he could see what was coming.

Already, some of the more paranoid – or just more forward-thinking – Athenian speakers were agitating in the Assembly over Philip of Macedon's hunger for land. But for most people, long in the habit of looking south or east for danger, it was hard to know whether or not to worry. Chalkidiki was a long way away. Just as someone might see thunderclouds standing waiting on the line of the horizon, on an otherwise clear day, and think, 'Oh!', then forget about it because there are things to do near at hand and clouds often move on, or come to nothing, so no need to worry; not yet, at least.

That's how it must have felt when Philip started straining against his borders, feeling them too tight. People were slow. Athens was surely too far away and too powerful to be troubled. But for Aristotle, who knew Philip personally, it must all have looked very different. If Athens squared up to Philip, Aristotle was an outsider. Might he be identified as pro-Macedonian? His father had been the court doctor to Philip's father, Amyntas. Yet, at the same time, Aristotle's home town of Stagira was threatened. If Philip pressed on and conquered the various city-states of Chalkidiki, how would Aristotle stand in Athens? And how would he stand in his home town, if he maintained his relations with its conqueror? He was in a very difficult position.

Chalkidiki was full of anxious rumour. What was coming? Something was coming. Something was not right, even though in theory the cities currently had an alliance with Macedonia. Philip seemed so restless, his appetite for land suddenly so apparent. What was his army doing so far west of its border? What if he couldn't be trusted? Chalkidiki's most thoughtful citizens looked at the livestock grazing. If only their pastures could look less fertile; their cattle less fat; their ports less busy and thriving.

Months passed and Philip's army seemed to be gathering. What was happening now? Neighbouring cities, like Olynthus, havered about their loyalties – who to trust? In panic, the people of Olynthus changed sides. They made a new alliance. They crossed over to Athens. And then, just as they had feared, in 349 BCE the storm burst. Philip, who now had betrayal as an excuse, laid siege to the city of Olynthus. Messengers were somehow smuggled out, hurrying south to their new ally. Help us. Please help us. Grant us military aid.

And in Athens, the stately progress of democracy. Speeches to the Assembly, in the freshness of early summer, by men for whom the threat was a question of politics, just the exercise of opinion or an opportunity to improve their own standing. Demosthenes, Athens' most famous orator, rounding out his great sentences to an admiring audience. Nothing happened. Debating, this way and that. On the one hand… And, if there is one hand, there must always be another. While in the north Philip sat breathing on the city walls, and the people of Olynthus felt themselves surrounded, like a hare hiding in grass.

Waiting.

Please, Athens. Please hurry. We are in great danger.

Waiting.

Still nothing. And now the summer gales, the Etesian winds, are blowing hard from the north so nothing will come by sea. Which, in fact, is just what happened: the military detachment that Athens had finally voted to send in support was unable to set out. Hanging about at Piraeus watching a whipped-up sea, the soldiers argued, kicking at stones in the harbour, they, too, waiting.

Not that it would have made any difference even if the winds hadn't arrived, because there are other weapons than those made of steel and Philip makes use of all of them. In Olynthus, the people are now doubly uneasy. Something feels wrong on the inside, some disorder among themselves, as if a disease were moving unseen through the city, although everyone looks healthy. Odd things are happening. Someone of the highest importance is re-roofing his house with Macedonian timber. Did you notice? Someone else, it is rumoured, has magically acquired a herd of cattle. Round the city go the whispers. They've been seen grazing in the pastures, glossy with health. Someone told someone, who told someone. Someone else who previously always went on foot now comes strutting and prancing on horseback. Is that even the same horse as yesterday? I don't know, it somehow looks fitter, finer.

In the autumn of 348 BCE Olynthus fell to Philip. He had managed to bribe some of the chief magistrates into betraying their city. No one was spared. The city was rubbled and all the inhabitants sold into slavery. Let that be a lesson to the city and its bribable people – but a lesson to Athens, too, with all its ornate process, its money, its defensive league and its dreams of military might.

And now for Aristotle there is the unease of rumour. Was that the word 'spy' being swallowed just as he entered the room? Why did everyone suddenly fall silent? His father had been court physician. Aristotle himself was personally known to Philip. Were these things whispered against him in the streets, when the shocking news of Olynthus made its way back to Athens, when Demosthenes whipped

Athens into an anti-Macedonian frenzy? Was this perhaps a better reason than the headship of the Academy for leaving the city?

Whatever the reason, Aristotle left. As well as Xenocrates he took with him his own favourite, and his own favourite was Theophrastus, who by now was twenty-five. They were headed for Assos, on the coast of Asia Minor, at the invitation of a petty tyrant called Hermias, and they were going to start a philosophical school of their own.

Modern Mytilene is a surprising place – or am I tired, or just credulous? My own senses don't feel particularly reliable. According to the guidebook I have with me, Ermou Street, the main shopping street – a very concrete place of dust and coins and little shops crammed shoulder to shoulder, a place shadowed by striped awnings, selling mops, brooms, rugs, fruit, fish, nylon dresses, trousers, sheets and swimming goggles – was once, until it silted up, a canal: the Euripos. It connected the military harbour on the north side with a quick passage southwards, separating the old acropolis of Mytilene from the later commercial centre. I'm walking on what was once water when I walk along the street.

At its far end I stop and eat supper in a taverna with a piratical patron who calls himself George Copperfield. He has a bandanna tied round his head and a number of earrings and he hovers around the table, doing magic tricks. I wear my scientific face but the truth is I can see through none of them. Into my spare hand he presses a dirty pink foam ball covered with white polka dots. I am to crush it tight in my fist while he makes abracadabra noises and several flashy passes with his ringed hands. I do as he asks. When I open my fist there are two pink balls lying innocent in my palm.

All the way home I look hard at Ermou Street under my feet. I've changed my mind. I am no longer thrilled by its former life as water. Don't turn into the Euripos now, I tell it, tiptoeing along in uncertainty.

*

The next morning is concrete again. I go slowly past the sun-struck shop windows to the archaeology museums: the stylish new one and an old one, housed in a villa that stands in its own dusty garden dotted with the spoils of ancient buildings.

In the silence of an empty room in the museum, I look carefully at lumps of terracotta. I peer into clouded cases at flints and bones from the island's beginnings. They have the look of flies trussed and abandoned in old webs. They seem irretrievably dead. There is more time between Theophrastus and these than there is between me and him. This is good news. I do my best to puzzle over the small tickets below each case but it is hard work. They are almost bleached of information. Soon they will need a ticket for the tickets.

Behind me, all the while, a uniformed museum guard hovers. I am the only person visiting so she follows me from case to case, room to room. Then she follows me out again through the entrance hall and up a grand but sombre staircase. Her footsteps are my echo as I climb. She is as bored as I am. Both of us resolutely persist in our separate duty, I to muster interest, to gather information, she to keep up the mixture of suspicion and mistrust with which she must watch me watching the exhibits, vigilant, as if my glance might disintegrate some valuable find, or in case I should decide to use my camera. I don't want to use my camera. Nevertheless, she must maintain a passionate insistence that I don't photograph these little pieces of pot, these indecipherable lumps of what? These trussed-up flies. It is odd, being watched, watching.

Nothing much here to help me with my search. Except, at the top of the stairs, in an upright case, there is a small fifth-century terracotta acrobat, so small you might easily miss it, strung, springing forever in an arc of performance. I stop. She looks so light, so live; little traces of paint still ornamenting her. She comes from a grave at Pyrrha, a town that used to lie looking out on the Gulf of Kalloni, but which doesn't exist any more. It suffered the opposite fate to the Euripos; it got swallowed by water. But Theophrastus and Aristotle stayed there.

It isn't a connection really but still, in this game of fishing, I throw out my line. I move slowly on. I go into other rooms.

But if the little acrobat had come from the end of the fifth century, say, where it tipped into the fourth, she would only be thirty-odd years from Theophrastus' birth. Only sixty from when he and Aristotle were living and working at Pyrrha itself. I retrace my steps to look at it again, hurrying through room after room of pots and utensils, out to the top of the staircase, and here it is. So small a thing but still alive. Behind me the attendant shifts, clears her throat. She stares at the back of my head. I stare at the acrobat. The acrobat goes on oblivious, abandoning herself to her backwards fling. The relationship between the three of us clicks suddenly to life as my hand reaches instinctively for my phone. Now this, I would take. This I would photograph if I could. Here is something that will lead me back.

Lesbos, in ancient times, was famous for its terracotta. The acrobat on its own, in its museum case, looks rare, so exceptional, but little figures like this, to bury with your dead, were once common, sold in the market or at the stalls in the shopping street, or packed up for export, stacked in crates like the ones Theophrastus saw unloaded at Piraeus.

Theophrastus as a child, passing on his way here or there on an errand, and if the dates did coincide, and even if the objects were so common as to command no particular attention, that restless gaze once glancing over, just touching the acrobat briefly, running across its surfaces like a caress. And away again, to the face of a friend or a bird turning in the sky. Did he even notice that he'd seen it – if he even did?

It's not impossible. And if it's not impossible, then it's a point of contact. You can draw a line of connection, dot to dot, from your eye to the object and on, however far back, to anyone else also looking.

You can make a kind of continuity through sight, and you can establish a community, an agreement that you are in the same place and that the place you are in is made up of certain things. That is all I'm doing at the moment, just touching something that his gaze might have touched, just reaching back.

After a while, I walk out and on up the street to the new museum. There are fewer people here, away from the harbour and the shopping streets, just the occasional old man or dog, easing along on stiff legs, all belly and scrotum. I stand in the sun, thinking about the acrobat. There is another museum and I should go to it. But I am very bored by dead things. I'm looking for something alive. Around me, in various doorways, sit other women, in headscarves. They too seem to be watching for something, though it's difficult to tell what. If I could find a doorstep. If I were just to sit myself in it and wait, eyes squinted at this dust-whitened road, would he come along it? If I waited long enough, still enough to be dead myself, trussed in black clothes like these, with only my eyes alive, might it be possible to wait as long, backwards, as the museum stones have waited forwards?

*

Dutifully, I go to the museum. Here, there is a different problem. The interesting objects are all later, long after Theophrastus was dead and buried. There are mosaics from the Roman occupation, for instance. Here is Orpheus, with his head restored to his shoulders, playing his lyre to an audience of animals. Around him, the island's abundant wildlife is recorded in still-bright detail. The Romans were around centuries after Theophrastus, but still I can see how Lesbos was. I can see that there were partridges, stepping gingerly on pointed toes, storks making their legs last longer by using only one at a time, fish of many different kinds, duck, delicate doves, green turtles, flowers and dappled deer, loops of ivy, wild boar, grapes, spotted snakes and olives. Further on, in the centre of another mosaic, is the personification of the Euripos canal before it became a street: a boy with his head sprouting claws and pincers, as if, like the channel he represents, he might at any moment change shape altogether. Caught as he slips across the species divide, midway, half-man, half-lobster. I can't help thinking – remembering my walk up Ermou – that there is this slippage, in the ancient imagination, which we have forgotten about. I knew this as a child and I can't help feeling that the myths contain a truth that we are only now on the brink of rediscovering: that things are more fleeting, less fixed inside their taxonomic boundaries than we like to think. They are, in fact, often so closely connected that the edges blur. Think of trees and their 'wood-wide web' of fungus. If the fungus penetrates the tree's root-hairs – not just winding itself between the building blocks of the cells but passing right through and into the heart of the cell itself – then where does the tree stop and the fungus start? And what is the tree when it ends? Things are always growing, fading, flowing, changing. And what do you become, if the sea canal that you once were suddenly fixes itself in silt and stone and asphalt?

For the second time, as I move from room to room, I am shadowed by an attendant whose heels click like a clock down the passages behind me. We are opposed. She is keeping time and I am bent on breaking it, not least because again I am the only visitor. The museum closes at three and I'm aware I am taking too long. But in the next room there is one more thing. Out goes the line to the past again, another small connection. Here are mosaic floors that show characters from Menander's plays all grouped around a portrait of Menander himself. It was made years after Menander's death, so the portrait is imaginary. It is based on whatever statues there were that would have been done in his lifetime. But even so, it is Menander. Every philosopher has a famous pupil, someone who takes their thinking and moves it into something new, something ground-breaking. Menander is Theophrastus' most famous pupil. He was a playwright, known for being the father of Athenian New Comedy. To the guard's alarm I lean over the rail. The mosaic is faithful to the busts of him from Ephesus. I know; I have done my homework. I have studied the Google images. Menander has slightly staring eyes, slicked-back hair and a full mouth. He looks glamorous in an anachronistic way. He looks, in fact, like someone from *The Godfather*. He lived with his mistress at Piraeus, that place of comings and goings, until he died at fifty-two, drowned in the waters of the harbour where he happened to be swimming. I would like to say I told you so – I knew that sea was dangerous. 'Hello,' I say to him under my breath instead. 'I'm looking for Theophrastus.' Menander doesn't answer.

I walk back to the hotel thinking over my day of small connections; the little, scattered smithereens of a life long ago. These details that I'm gathering together – I don't know whether any of them reveal anything. It's impossible to tell at this distance. Everything in this shifting, ancient place echoes something else. Nothing stays what it seems. It changes, comes in and out of focus. Time stretches endlessly out and then suddenly collapses in on itself, confusingly relative, at no notice. Even things as fixed and solid as landmass behave the same way. Some days, for instance, when you look out at the nearest stretch of land it is crystal clear, the texture of the islands fuzzed like velveteen under the light. Other times they are shadowy or disguised as clouds. Sometimes they are simply not there at all. That's how it feels. Just like that. Theophrastus and his world materializes and dematerializes in just the same way.

They would have gone down to Piraeus, these two outsiders, master and pupil, Aristotle and Theophrastus, and taken a boat, and they would have loaded it with everything they needed for an extended stay. And with them went solemn and morose Xenocrates, a man of legendary sobriety, loyalty and ponderousness of mind, in mourning for his friend and teacher Plato. The boat pulled slowly away from the Greek mainland, struggling against an onshore wind, and out into open water, while Xenocrates sat in its stern, huddled into his cloak, feeling old, feeling pained, puzzling over the energy of these younger men – these fidget-brains, with their quickness and high spirits and their insatiable appetite for information. All their ambition. All their endless ideas. Xenocrates' intelligence is slower, a huge but almost motionless force that even Plato lost patience with from time to time. 'What an ass and a horse I have to yoke together,' he is supposed to have said, unkindly comparing him with Aristotle. 'One needed a bridle and the other a spur.' That's a hurtful thing to remember.

Maybe too he is remembering another such expedition, years ago, with Plato. When his own beloved master (Socrates) was killed, Plato had left Athens in disgust and embarked on a period of travel that lasted twelve years and ended in Sicily. There he met Dion, brother-in-law to the tyrant of Syracuse at the time, who became his pupil and devoted follower. Dion was quick and intelligent and particularly susceptible to Plato's ideals about good governance. He took Plato to meet his brother-in-law. But Plato, bruised and broken by Athens' various failures of government, wasn't diplomatic enough about his political opinions, in particular his opinion of tyranny. He found himself, at the tyrant's order, for sale in the slave market, where he was bought by a crew of pirates.

Despite this, his friendship with Dion survived over the years, and when Dion was, in turn, made tyrant, he wrote to Plato begging him to come back. He was worried, he wrote. Syracusan society was dissipated and losing itself in hedonism. No one thought about the good life. There were appetite-driven dissolutes everywhere he looked and his own son, Dionysius, was young and impressionable; please, if Plato would only talk to him as he'd talked to Dion all those years before, then something might change. This time it might work.

Plato was by now in his sixties. The decision was a painfully difficult one and in his own letters we can watch the process. 'I considered and debated whether I should hearken and go, or what I should do.' He wasn't a fool. 'Young men have sudden impulses, often quite contradictory ones.' To go all that way, at his age, and put himself in danger for an uncertain outcome. He was so comfortable in Athens, in his school. But his duty to his ideals won out. 'I ought to go,' he decided, 'if ever anyone were to attempt to realise my ideals in regard to laws and government, now was the time for the trial.'

Bravely, Plato set off for Sicily a second time, and with him, for support, he took Xenocrates. As he'd feared, it was at best a wild hope. The young Dionysius didn't have Dion's abilities or his susceptibility to the idea of goodness as the only possible route to a happy life. He preferred a quicker fix. Plato made two separate and heroic attempts but the project failed.

So Xenocrates doesn't know why he is here, now, in this boat in the cold dawn, with Aristotle, nor what exactly the point of this is, now Plato is gone. But perhaps, unbeknown to him, he has some currency for these two younger men, some experience that explains his presence on this ship – Sicily, for instance. Perhaps this tyrant they're now headed to, Hermias, will be more tractable. Or perhaps the reason is something else altogether. There are some who suggest that the passing of the Academy to Plato's nephew, Speusippus, was a handover of the building and grounds only; that the spirit of the

Academy has been left unhoused; that this is the purpose of the voyage. Together, Plato's most loyal and his most favoured pupil are carrying it – the spirit – like a precious little flame, to Assos.

You can get to Assos on a day trip nowadays, by boat from Mytilene, crossing into Turkish waters that are green like glass, where visible fish mouth at the surface scum. Stillness. No wind today. Just these bare lozenges of land as you approach, golden-coloured, like something half-dissolved, floating in undifferentiated sky and sea. And somewhere at the back of it all lurk the ghosts of giant mountains: Turkey and all the expanse of the eastern continent, stretching invisible beyond. I can't tell if this feeling of a vast unseen landmass is something I truly sense or simply the product of modern knowledge. Would it feel different if I hadn't seen a map?

Assos, when I reach it, seems small. The little rocky outcrop of its acropolis, its ruined temple with fat, flat-topped pillars looking back at Lesbos lying quiet in the sea. It seems provincial. Did it seem so to you, Theophrastus? Did you compare its lumpy buildings with the airy architecture of Athens? Did you notice its slightly crooked, big-stoned street, or its theatre? And if I sit here, for instance, facing the ruined stage, is my body occupying the shadow of yours? Am I sitting anywhere near where you once sat? No – the guidebook says, the way guidebooks do – the theatre most likely post-dates Theophrastus.

At any rate, this is the place where the three philosophers came. Hermias, the tyrant who ruled at the time, lived further down the coast from Assos, at Atarneus, controlling his portion of Asia Minor with an army of his own mercenaries. He seems a vivid choice as patron of a philosophical community. He was, by some accounts, a Bithynian Greek who had attended the Academy himself; by others, he was the former slave, and possibly eunuch, of a corrupt banker called Eubulus. In this latter story, he was either given his freedom on his master's death, or took over Eubulus' occupation, having first killed him. Whatever he was, he generated very divided opinions. Theopompus, a sour Sophist and the author of the version that had him down as a murderer, wrote a scornful letter to Philip of Macedon reporting that Hermias, 'though a barbarian, philosophises with Platonists. Though he has been a slave he competes with costly chariots at the meetings.'

He did indeed philosophize with Platonists and may have studied under Plato himself for a time. Plato certainly knew and thought well of him. Years before the arrival of Aristotle, Theophrastus and Xenocrates, two other Academicians, Erastus and Coriscus, returning to Coriscus' home town of Scepsis, further up towards the Black Sea, had carried with them a letter of introduction from Plato recommending them to Hermias, for protection. Plato writes:

> For you are living as neighbours to one another and each of
> you needs what the others can best supply. Hermias should
> know that his power for all purposes, has its greatest support,
> not in the number of his horses, or in other equipment of
> war, nor in the gold he adds to his treasury, but in steadfast
> friends of solid character. And to Erastus and Coriscus I say,
> old as I am, that they need to supplement their knowledge
> of the Ideas – that noble doctrine – with the knowledge and
> capacity to protect themselves against wicked and unjust
> men.

Here is Plato's prototype for how philosophy should be integrated into the life of power and government. He is not just asking for protection for his friends, although he admits that they are unused to the ways of the world, living as they have been in a philosophical community. Erastus and Coriscus 'are inexperienced, since they have spent a great part of their lives with us, among men of moderation and good will', but their need for protection is balanced, in Plato's eyes, by power's need of wisdom. He isn't envisaging a short-term connection. He is imagining a long and mutually beneficial association whose survival is important enough for Plato and the Academy to mediate in the case of any disagreement. Plato asks:

> What is the point of these remarks? To you, Hermias, since I have known Erastus and Coriscus longer than you have, I solemnly declare… that you will not easily find more trustworthy characters than these neighbours of yours, and I therefore advise you to make it a matter of central importance to attach yourself to them by every honourable means. Coriscus and Erastus in their turn I advise to hold fast to Hermias and to try to develop this mutual alliance into a bond of friendship. If ever any one of you should seem to be weakening this union (for nothing human is altogether secure), send a letter to me and my friends declaring the grievance; for unless the injury be very grave, I believe your sense of justice and your respect for us will make the words that we may send more efficacious than any incantation would be in binding up the wound and causing you to grow together again into friendship and fellowship as before.

The introduction was successful. The ground had been well prepared. When Aristotle, Theophrastus and Xenocrates arrived, they were assured of a welcome, and a community was soon established, joined by Neleus, the son of Coriscus. In fact, Aristotle then linked himself even more closely to Hermias – he married Hermias' niece, Pythias, who by some accounts was educated. I've seen her referred to as a 'biologist' but since biologists hadn't been invented yet that definition is problematic. At any rate, for a while, the new community was tight, harmonious and noticeably effective. One contemporary account has it:

> Hence all these men lived with Hermias… He listened to them… He gave them gifts… he actually changed the tyranny into a milder rule. Therefore he also came to rule over all the neighbouring country as far as Assos, and then being exceedingly pleased with the said philosophers he allotted them the city of Assos. He accepted Aristotle most of all of them and was very intimate with him.

In some ways, the dissemination of the Academy's philosophers is similar to the voyages of conversion made by the early monks, men like Cuthbert or Augustine; Socrates' ideal of the good life, as formulated by Plato, was being brought to the wider Greek world – a world battered by in-fighting – in a bid for harmony and better governance.

Stumbling about among the ruins at Assos, it's hard to see where the school would have been; nowhere, perhaps, other than in the minds and the teachings of its philosophers. Not a set of buildings so much as a school of thought. It's hard to picture what they would have been doing. Lecturing, presumably, to whoever would listen, probably not for money. I imagine them much like itinerant preachers, putting forward a carefully worked-out version of their understanding of life, its origins and how it should be lived; not as a static tradition, like a religion, but one that was constantly evolving. The school's understanding of the world around them was a matter of joint progress, joint thinking, all of which had to be explained and passed on to its younger members and acolytes. This was also, particularly, the case at Assos, because Aristotle and Theophrastus' position in relation to Plato's teaching was on the edge of a new, more empirical direction. Gathering sense-based evidence was the beginning of the natural sciences – and meant a huge increase in knowledge. Both Aristotle and Theophrastus thought this was best, quickest and most comprehensively done as the effort of a community. 'Each of us', Aristotle wrote in his *Metaphysics*, 'says *something* about nature, and although as individuals we advance the subject little if at all, from all of us taken together something of size results.'

It's difficult to see when exactly they made the shift towards a philosophy based on the findings of natural science: whether they arrived at Assos already intent on science, or whether it took longer to bring their joint aims into focus, whether what had been a vague unease in Athens only sharpened into precise aims through their work at Assos. In between my wanderings, I've been looking at Theophrastus' own book *On First Principles* (more commonly known as his *Metaphysics*). This was probably written at Assos, when he was in his mid to late twenties. It has a compressed, note-like quality to it. It is a comprehensive list of matters for enquiry. It looks like a template for the school's programme, both in terms of what it might address and in terms of how such enquiries might be conducted.

Its principal concern is the question of how it all began. Did some one thing, or things, come first, Theophrastus wonders, out of which everything else evolved or grew? If so, what might those first things have been – were they abstract like an idea, or concrete like a seed? Might they have been a law, or set of laws? And if everything grew out of and according to a law, would it just be one law, or many? Could just one law give rise to the whole of this world? Or is there a pyramid of things in ascending order and complexity, with something like God at the top?

Having established the questions, he moves on to the difficulties of method: how on earth might one go about looking for a first principle, or principles? Could it be done by analogy, he asks, since truth is so difficult to grasp? Are there comparisons by which these laws or principles might be more easily imagined or understood? Are there parallels elsewhere in the world that might be useful?

So much for method; next, he deals with the difficulties that the answers themselves tend to produce, and there are a great many of these. If you have a first law or power, for example, that is absolute and unchanging, why would it find its expression in life-forms that are subject to motion and change? Because every single thing that can be found in the world is subject to change. Everything either dies, or changes, or moves, or erodes, or dissolves, or burns, or melts, or lifts, or otherwise disappears. How could something absolute, that never changes, possibly give rise to a world that does? What is the relationship between things that change and things that are unchangeable? What is the difference between form and matter? Are they both a way of Being, or is only one? And, by the way, why are there so many more bad things than good?

All these and more are the questions that the twenty-five-year-old Theophrastus was energetically asking. Not that the thought is new – because this is all well-trodden ground – but it feels as though something else is at work behind the *Metaphysics*. As presumably they always do between master and pupil, differences are beginning to show in the tendency of their thought. Or perhaps it isn't anything so formal as a difference, more just a temperamental bias. Aristotle loved systems. Theophrastus just loved variety. His instinctive vision of things seems to be that they are more random, more varied and more unpredictable than systematization will allow. He admits, as Plato insisted, that the proper order of things would be to work from the first principle to its physical manifestation in the world – from tableness to table – but there is, for him, a problem with this. First principles, he says, would seem to have been devised by us as figures, shapes and proportions that we ascribe to things, while they in themselves have no nature at all. In other words, might it not be that we are looking at things and then abstracting from them some kind of principle or law, and not the other way around? Might it be that there is no such thing as tableness – just an accidental infinitude of tables? Might it not be that we just have a need for a metaphysical source – that we so much desire a cause and a reason for life that we end up imagining one? Perhaps, Theophrastus thinks, standing where I am standing, looking across a ruffled sea at the island of his birth, perhaps there aren't any causes or reasons. Maybe there is no connection between what we think of as laws and the things they are supposed to produce or govern. Maybe we have just made up the world of abstracts out of our need for such things. Perhaps the world simply is. Perhaps, he thinks, the world, the whole cosmos in fact, is one single, complete and coherent entity whose workings are the flexing of order and chaos held in an infinite balance. If so, all the observable patterns are nothing more than its minutely replicating, repeating and co-varying nature, adjusting and maintaining this balance. And us? We are just some of its integral, inseparable parts. I follow his gaze; look at Lesbos lying blue in the distance. Now that, in every sense of the word, is a radical thought.

Theophrastus is thinking far into the future, his mind reaching forwards through the uninvented centuries. It isn't until 1620, with Francis Bacon's answer to Aristotle, his *Novum Organum*, that our natural tendency to imagine metaphysical causes for things is properly acknowledged and taken into account and a new, strictly experimental method for science is devised.

I stand on the tipped-up pavement of ancient Assos, reaching back towards Theophrastus as he reaches forwards. He must have walked this way every day, this restless twenty-five year old, to lecture perhaps, or to listen to his seniors, stepping unnoticing across these stones, and he must have thought all the time, turning things round and round in his mind, this isn't really how the world is. It can't be accounted for, in all its whimsicality and diversity, with these man-sized, man-shaped systems of origination. Whatever Aristotle thinks, it just can't be. Because Aristotle had come up with the working principle that Nature, whatever it might be, does nothing in vain. Everything made has a purpose. Theophrastus puts his head on one side and debates with himself. He begins to draw up a list of things whose point is questionable. These, he suggests to Aristotle, are other things to consider, things without seeming coherency or purpose.

The ebb and flow of the sea
Dry and moist seasons
Male breasts
The female emission
Beards, and hair where it has no function
The size of the deer's horns and the trouble they cause
Certain forced and unnatural phenomena such as the heron's
method of copulation
And insects that only live for a day
Why do men have nipples?

Or maybe he just takes one thing. Maybe he just looks at the plants at his feet and sees how problematic it would be to decide which ones came from which law, which ones are related to which, and how exactly they might be different from the insects that live with them so closely. Where might the plant end and the insect begin?

However it was that it happened, it became clear to both men that the physical world, its actuality, was the logical thing to study and that, maybe, if you really gave yourself to the discipline, from that hard-won, thorough understanding of life in all its forms, a system or principle might emerge, against all the odds, in the end. Whether there would prove to be a system, or whether there wouldn't, Theophrastus and Aristotle were agreed that there was only one way to find out. They would turn Plato's direction, at least temporarily, on its head. They decided to stop everything else and make a study of living things, from the solid base of which to work upwards, literally from the ground, towards a system, supposing one could be found, a principle of beginning.

Where could they do this uninterrupted? Where could they dedicate themselves for a while to a discipline that hadn't yet been invented: the systematic study of natural history? Certainly not where they were expected to have a public function as teachers or lecturers. If they were going to come up with a new route for philosophy, they needed to stop with the old one – at least for a while. They could leave Xenocrates teaching at Assos and they could take a kind of sabbatical, perhaps somewhere nearby.

Assos is supposed to have been founded by colonizing settlers from Methymna, on Lesbos, and if you stand on the acropolis and look out you can see Lesbos lying with its back turned, its knees drawn up around its gulfs, like someone sleeping – dreaming, probably, of its own fertility. Lesbos was home for Theophrastus. It would have been an easy place to go to, not too far away from Hermias, and with no difficulty about finding accommodation. It had plenty of wildlife, if that was what they wanted to study; I've seen it in mosaic — the storks, the tiptoeing partridges, the green turtles and ducks and delicate doves. Looking out like this, every day, across the water at his homeland, did he point it out in passing to Aristotle?

Why could we not go there?

Because that, in 345 BCE, is where they went.

II

The Invention of Science

I am back on Lesbos, walking by the Gulf of Kalloni under a pale sky. The island has huddled itself around this great loop of sea, pulling it up into its centre, as if protecting the haul of fish and cuttlefish and birds it contains. No one is here. Just a small cat, sitting watching a blue boat cast up on its side in the reeds, as if resting. Further out, in the distance, long lines of bleached grass, blue mountains and a tumbled sky. And something like blossom has turned the salt flats pink. I have stopped to watch as this scattered pink rises up and twirls and settles again. Flamingos. They weren't here in Theophrastus' time. I look away. If I look down, things still look the same as they did in his day. Amaranth and tattered chicory. Thorny burnet rolled like balls of chicken wire. And every time I take a step, these dry mechanisms flick away: little traps set to snap with the sound of their own name. Cricket. Cricket. Cricket. Yet again: cricket.

Did he see what I'm looking at now?

No – or rather, yes, but it would have looked different to him. All my looking, however I try, is refracted by time and its changes. My looking is shot through with knowledge, like water is shot through with light. If I were to see the world that he saw I'd have to travel backwards through technological progress for two millennia. I'd have to unsee the clouds from the top, or unsee the ocean, reduced by distance, its surface wrinkled like the surface of my own shivering skin. I'd have to unsee the windings of rivers, or the forms of landmass – Aristotle's Chalkidiki, for instance, reaching forward like a swimming turtle, or Evia lying snug to the coast, or Kea with its serrated outline, like a leaf or a flint arrow. All the fractal repetition of the world's patterning.

I'd have to unstick men's feet from the surface of the moon and uncross that distance compassed by flying metal. I'd have to reel backwards from petrol-fuelled speeds – unimaginable to an ancient –

to something animal powered. I'd have to unknow knowledge that we've steadily accumulated over two millennia and passed hand to hand like a baton, progressing patiently away from a world thick with mythic intuition, through the rock crystal lenses used for magnification and for burning that were sold in the markets in Theophrastus' time, and through the invention of glass lenses – the microscope, the telescope, both Greek words nonetheless. I'd have to unsee photographs from both ends of the spectrum, from the Hubble's cold and terrifying extreme deep field, or from the world's hidden inwardness – the swarming communities of bacteria that inhabit our cells, the strange spirals of DNA, the complex variety of viruses, the ones like worms, the ones with round heads covered with protruding spikes like the head of the globe thistle, the neurons firing now, and again now, in the recesses of my brain. I'd have to un-think the atom, un-split it. Push down the mushroom cloud, unmix the genetic matter of plant or animal and go back to a place where matter was simple and closed to our gaze. And how could this ever be done?

Sometimes, reading the accounts of discoveries as they are made, it's just possible to see, as if through a door that is closing, a glimpse of the world before it is changed by the knowledge being recorded; the cells, for instance, that Robert Hooke with such amazed excitement found for the first time in a slither of cork-oak bark he'd put under his microscope. In his own description it is almost possible to see it, the unpenetrated thickness of wood – that mysterious, dead sprouter of leaf-fountains – before its mechanisms were understood. It is almost possible to go backwards just for a split second and see a different place.

Look. It is 1655. Hooke has been making his own microscopes and experimenting with them for several years. Through his lenses he has seen and recorded a flea, armoured like an ancient warrior, and a louse clinging to a hair the thickness of a ship's rope, and now he has turned his attention from insects to botany. He closes one eye and puts the other to the eyepiece and looks at the fragment of bark:

> I could exceeding plainly perceive it to be all perforated and porous, much like a Honey-comb, but that the pores of it were not regular; yet it was not unlike a Honey-comb in these particulars. First, in that it had a very little solid substance... for the interstitia, or walls... or partitions of those pores were never as thin in proportion to their pores, as those thin films of Wax in a Honey-comb... are to theirs. Next, in that these pores, or cells, were not very deep, but consisted of a great many little Boxes, separated out of one continued long pore, by certain Diaphragms. I no sooner discern'd these (which were indeed the first microscopical pores I ever saw, and perhaps, that were ever seen, for I had not met with any Writer or Person, that had made any mention of them before this) but me thought I had with the discovery of them, presently hinted to me the true and intelligible reason of all the Phaenomena of Cork; As, first, if I enquir'd why it was so exceeding light a body? my Microscope could presently inform me that here was the same reason evident that there is found for the lightness of froth, an empty Honey-comb, Wool, a Spunge, a Pumice-stone, or the like; namely, a very small quantity of a solid body, extended into exceeding large dimensions.

This extract about the cork-oak is the first sight of a whole new continent. No one has seen this before. It is a moment of major discovery. Before Hooke applies his eye to the apparatus the world is one way. And a moment later, it is another place altogether. And like an Adam or an Eve, Hooke is the first to wake up and find himself in it. There isn't even a designated word for the little boxes he has seen that make up this new structure in the bark. They are so new he is the first to need to name them in description. Are they like pores? They are squarish. More like monk's cells? He settles for 'cells'. He makes frantic calculations. The 'cells' are so minute:

> I... found that there were usually about three score of these small Cells placed end-ways in the eighteenth part of an Inch in length, where I concluded there must be near eleven hundred of them, or somewhat more than a thousand in the length of an Inch, and therefore in a square Inch above a Million, or 1166400, and in a Cubick Inch, above twelve hundred Millions, or 1259712000, a thing almost incredible, did not our Microscope assure us of it by ocular demonstration.

How much Aristotle and Theophrastus would have approved. 'Ocular demonstration' was the method they pioneered and preferred. What use they could have made of Hooke's microscope if I could only, in my imagined rush backwards, have got it to them before they died. Because the other thing Hooke's lenses change, although not immediately, is time. Telescopes and microscopes see right through it, so that now, from some angles, time can seem a flimsy invention, something that could, under the right circumstances and from the right place, be stepped behind like a stage-curtain, or simply, like a cobweb, be brushed aside.

Anytime I look up at night and see the stars in their apparently steady constellations I am looking backwards through time, even – in some cases and with a telescope – beyond human history. So, in theory, everything is visible if you're standing in the right place. And in these terms, you and I, Theophrastus, are almost neighbours. We are so near in time, relatively speaking, surely I should be able to see you quite clearly. If I looked back from the right place in light years. If I had the right telescope, I would be able to see you as you were, in your garden maybe, or at your desk on Lesbos, or lying at dinner, listening to Plato, in your youth. I would see how your hair grew, and its colour – the same for your eyes – and your shoulders, your height, what your mouth was like, your hands. I'm interested in hands. I think they reflect a person's character. I'm imagining yours as broad, practical hands, with honest joints and perhaps the veins corded in light relief, like gardeners have. The image would be fixed – I realize that. But it would be an image. And that's one of the reasons that it seems not impossible to reach you now, by following your footsteps, by looking for you here at Kalloni, or at Assos, or in Athens, because you must still be there, somewhere, waiting to be seen.

Out beyond the pinched neck of the gulf, in the channel between the Turkish mainland and Mytilene, someone has hung a little boat between the sea and sky. It's going so slowly, heavy with freight. People sitting on crates, catching the only ride there is from that place to this. Aristotle, his new wife Pythias, their household slave and a handmaiden, a small dog, Greeks from Asia Minor, sailors, merchants. And Theophrastus, who is still in his twenties and who is going home. He's a decade older than he was when he left for Athens. He is a man now, a philosopher, as he always wanted to be, and he is bringing with him the greatest thinker of the age – this mind around whom he revolved all his adult life, like a planet around a sun. And they have a high project in hand: the invention of what will become a whole new discipline.

When eventually they arrive at Mytilene they are perhaps met by Melantas, Theophrastus' father, perhaps by his old tutor Alcippus, perhaps by his friend and fellow horticulturist Phanias of Eresos; but, once the reunions are over and the introductions are made, they settle, not at Eresos where Theophrastus came from, but at Pyrrha, a town on the edge of the Gulf of Kalloni, just a little further round from the flamingos, where I too am now waiting, as if to greet them. Pyrrha is gone now, lying somewhere under this sheet of shining water. You can swim out, as I have done, and you can try to look down for its walls, or streets, for something to show which way they walked, or where they lived, but the water is thick and silty. It's impossible to make anything out in its fertile murk, just your own hands parting like pale fish ahead of you. It is now, as it was then, full of cuttlefish – descendants of the ones Aristotle would study here in such fine detail.

Here, on the shores of the gulf, they settled and began their joint effort in their new study, their work of looking. Even for men as famed for their industry as Aristotle and Theophrastus both were, it was a huge task: the effort of cataloguing everything living. Their focus was on what each thing is, in terms of its parts, its habits, its uses, its method of propagation. As far as possible, they started with the working parts that made up whatever it was they were looking at. For Aristotle, this meant arms, legs, heads, hands, feet. This was a deceptively simple approach, but as he pointed out, it was necessary to start with solid foundations, with the incontrovertible evidence; that way the structure that grew out of it would be sound.

For Theophrastus, looking at plants, this was more complex. What are the parts of a plant? Stem, leaves, branches, flowers. But what are fruit and seeds? Are they parts? Or things in their own right? Is a seed the same as a human baby? Or different? And what about galls and seaweed, petrified trees, moss and mushrooms? How might all these kinds of decisions be made?

Aristotle and Theophrastus started with sensory evidence, with the detail of how things looked. Then, as well as collecting, recording and dissecting specimens, they collected all the information possible concerning the habit, use and character of the object in question, as these things might change depending on climate or location. They spent time talking to those whose practical knowledge constituted a different kind of expertise: the farmers, fishermen, carpenters, shipbuilders, beekeepers, weavers, fullers, builders, painters and doctors. They corresponded widely, pooling information from all over the Greek-speaking world, from Rhodes, Sicily, Egypt, Asia Minor and so on. Other people's findings were always considered, so their respective works are full of references to how things are done elsewhere. *They say that the only dates that will keep are those which grow in the Valley of Syria, and They say that the palms in Crete, more often than not, have a double stem, and that some of them even have three stems. Mountain trees are of fair colour hard and smooth, as beech, elm and the rest; while those of the plain are more spreading, of less good colour and inferior, except for the pear apple and wild pear, according to the people of Mount Olympus.*

Although both men later wrote books on each, it seems that, for the time being, they split up their subject matter – Aristotle chose fish and animals, Theophrastus plants and stones. We have both sets of Theophrastus' works complete. They aren't formal writing. Like his *Metaphysics*, they are more like someone thinking out loud, jotting things down and collecting details – field notes almost – for something that would later be turned into the lectures for which he was so famous. Some of the subject matter is repeated. As if unhappy with the conclusion he arrived at the first time, he often returns to a question again and again, attempting to puzzle it out. Sometimes, in these repetitions, it's possible to watch him making up his mind about something; to watch his mind working. He is bothered by the question of seeds, for instance. Something as fine and small as this thistledown now sailing by on the wind, as I stand on the hillside, how exactly does it work? Where and when exactly are seeds like that first formed? This is a long-time conundrum; others before him have concluded that seeds must be somehow produced by the air. In the interests of proper inquiry, he lists the opinions of those who've gone before:

Anaxagoras says that the air contains the seeds of all things, and that these, carried down by the rain, produce the plants. Diogenes says that this happens when water decomposes and mixes in some way with earth… And there are other philosophers also who speak of spontaneous generation.

Theophrastus is not convinced. *This kind of generation is somehow beyond the ken of our senses.* In other words, it doesn't fit with what we've seen, with what seems likely. He goes on with what is 'accepted' and 'observable' in plant propagation. He talks about the ways that rivers flood and drop silt, which encourages seeds to sprout. At Abdera, in the north, where it's colder and it rains, a whole forest sprang up in a matter of three years. He talks about rain and the growth that results from it. His mind is turning between the lines. Where do the seeds come from? How did they get there?

His answer is thoughtful:

Now as the flooding of a river, it would seem, carries seeds of fruits of trees, and, as they say, irrigation channels carry the seeds of herbaceous plants, so heavy rain acts in the same way; for it brings down many of the seeds with it.

This, to him, seems to make sense – more sense than that seeds should simply be hanging around, produced by the air, waiting for rain to help them fall. He understands that rain is heavy enough to dislodge seeds from trees, for instance, and carry them down to the ground.

To modern understanding, this seems nonsensical, bafflingly trivial. But try and start again. Imagine a world where nothing yet has an explanation and where life is springing up everywhere and all the time, in dazzling variety and profusion, and through processes that are as yet undiscovered. It is so difficult to un-know our knowledge. Forget about bees and flying insects and the whole business of pollination and fertilization. Forget that plants come from seeds that come from plants. Think instead of how mysterious it still seems that plants should root from cuttings. Think of how vigorous and insistent the impulse to life must be if an oar left resting on earth in a wet season, as Theophrastus describes, can sprout into an olive tree, or the hinge of a door-socket suddenly produce shoots and leaves.

Always, in collecting his information, he must feel his way between observation, superstition and practical knowledge. *If they tell the truth*, he caveats when describing reports of an Indian drug that affects the blood, or an Ethiopian root used to tip arrows with poison. In answer to the cinnamon harvesters' tale, that the cinnamon bark left behind as an offering to the sun always and immediately catches fire, he is categoric. *Now this*, he says, *is sheer fable.*

But nothing is ignored, however fanciful. It is important to him to collect all the information available, to be fair to it, to give everything consideration. In the case of the herb-diggers and druggists, he picks his way through their observations, sowing disclaimers as he goes. These statements, he warns at the beginning of a section on root-digging and harvesting, *in some cases may be to the point, but in others contain exaggeration:*

> *In cutting some roots one should stand to windward – for instance in cutting thapsia among others, and one should first anoint oneself with oil, for one's body will swell up if one stands the other way. Also that the fruit of the wild rose must be gathered standing to windward, since otherwise there is danger to the eyes...*
>
> *These and similar remarks are not off the point, for the properties of these plants are hurtful. They take hold, it is said, like fire and burn...*

So far so good, the milky sap of thapsia is phototoxic. It will raise red weals on exposed skin in sunlight. Rosehips contain what children call 'itching powder'. The inside of the fruit is covered with tiny fine hairs that protect the seeds – painful and itchy if they get in the eyes.

*On the other hand the following ideas are far-fetched and
irrelevant. For instance they say that the peony... should be dug
up at night, for if a man does it in the day-time and is watched
by a woodpecker while he gathers the fruit, he risks the loss of
his eyesight. If he is cutting the root at the time then he will
suffer a prolapsed anus.*

Best of all is his description of the performance demanded of those
who dig up mandragora. This he dismisses as 'absurd' though he gives
it in detail all the same:

*It is said that one should draw three circles round mandrake
with a sword, and cut it with one's face towards the west; and at
the cutting of the second piece one should dance round the plant
and say as many things as possible about the mysteries of love.*

This is the world Aristotle and Theophrastus inhabited. I'm looking
out at the gulf, at the thin reeds ceremoniously bending at each other
in the shallows. I'm looking at the lines of blue hills lazing along the
horizon, and at the water, hiding its ruins, breeding its cuttlefish. I'm
unhooking from all of these the modern knowledge that veils my
sight, bundling it away like a dust-sheet, so I can see what's behind: the
old mythic world in all its wilful unpredictability, with all its majesty
and its horrifying power intact and unexplained. I'm trying to see
a place where it is commonplace to suspect the independent will of
everything because so little is yet understood. A place where people
digging up plants face carefully east or west depending on the root; a
place where they first draw circles round the plant and then pray out
loud, and all the while that they are digging they look anxiously to
their right and left in case of eagles, since an eagle approaching would
mean certain death. A place where, if you think this nonsensical or

superstitious, you are not in the majority because, although *these notions seem to be irrelevant, as has been said, there are, however, no methods of root-cutting besides those which we have mentioned.*

'Method' is apt in translation here. Theophrastus uses the word '*tropoi*', which more usually translates as 'ways', meaning also 'customs'; but 'method' offers something else. It is a scientific word after all, describing a process which in this case looks to be the very opposite of science, involving, as it does, nervous appeals to the gods and babbling about love's mysteries. But the mandrake is a plant that in Greek myth is sacred to Aphrodite – its apple-shaped seed-pods are used by her and by Circe, the *Odyssey's* great seductress, as an aphrodisiac. Digging it up demands an acknowledgement of the power behind its private mechanisms, an understanding of what nature both contains and implies.

In this newly old world, in which science has yet to take hold, this is the first thing to grasp: that the pantheon of Greek gods represents not just a religion but a kind of proto-science. It came into being, as Aristotle observed, as myth generated by wonder, in both senses, and as such it is an attempt both to identify and to explain. It is a very careful noticing and naming of all the forces at work in the world. It is interesting for two reasons. The first is the detail and precision of its observations, a discipline which the practice of science shares. Nothing is missed. Even something as particular as the push for growth in plants and seeds is recognized and given appropriate incarnation. Persephone may be the goddess of spring but it is another girl goddess, slender as a spring shoot, Chloris, who has responsibility for its pale growth. Her name comes from the Greek for 'yellow-green', later corrupted by the Romans into Flora. It is her power that drives the first springtime greening. It was her name the scientists chose when they first found the green in photosynthesizing plant cells and called it chlorophyll. Her power is linked to that of her lover, Zephyrus, the west wind, whose breath brings the rain, without which growth is impossible, and their son is Carpus, which means fruit. It is a very complete, very observant system; minute in its attention to detail.

The second interesting thing about the Greek pantheon is its tendency to equate the human with the non-human. In its drive to identify all the forces beyond our control, both in ourselves and in the world around us, love and war and jealousy and the thirst for knowledge are each accepted as potentially lethal powers which, in their wildness, are no different from the wildness of the sea or its storms, or the pull of the moon, or the raging of fire. Aphrodite and Ares, as incarnations of the frenzy that drives us to love or to war, are the equals of Poseidon and Apollo, who represent the force of the sea and the sun. More than equals, they are family, and in many cases their attributes spill across both abstract and concrete to govern both human and non-human aspects. Apollo, for instance, is not just the sun god but also the god of the power of music. In other words, we are emotionally absorbed into the chaotic forces that conflict or combine all around us so physically in the material world. We are among its mechanisms; less differentiated than we now see ourselves, less distinct. This is a place where the scientific impulse expresses itself as religion or myth, where things are in constant flux, where nothing is yet finally fixed either in its form or in its processes.

*

Sometimes I place myself behind Theophrastus as he writes. That way, I hope to see past the text, out beyond it to the world that he himself was looking at, the mythic world still laid out before him. It's the last glimpse of that ancient place that I'm after – that place of slippage, before taxonomy closed each thing inside the walls of its own species, or kind. Somewhere provisional, where everything is still up to its neck in everything else, where plants and humans are closer, more like each other, and where the boundaries between things are so fluid, so not-yet-delineated, that a boy looking at himself in a pool might look long enough, and be still enough, to turn into a flower; or a girl, escaping her pursuer, might turn into a bush.

I think they knew this, Aristotle and Theophrastus. When they set out from Assos to start a new discipline I think they knew that what they were doing would change the world. How could they not? They meant to disentangle everything, to pull everything free, so as to know what each thing was and how it differed from everything else, because only then would they know what the world was made of. The shift from the intuitive knowledge of mythic interpretation, to knowledge that is empirical and scientific, was nothing short of a sea-change. Looking back from here, Theophrastus, I see you and Aristotle standing on the threshold of my world, patiently, like a pair of safe-crackers trying the door.

Perhaps it was spring when they arrived on Lesbos. I hope it was spring. Such a spring as there is in Greece, when the new light strikes straight through the opened fingers of the fig trees, the colours so clear that everything seems incorporeal, a spirit world; the whole landscape a kaleidoscope of coloured light. Or green fire. Or water. Because in spring, on Lesbos, light-filled water seems to be everywhere. Rising up out of the ground, running through new grass, up through roots and stems, coursing through green veins. It is water that I'm looking at in the unfurling spring leaves, light-soaked, sap-green water.

Then, there are flowers. Greece, which at summer's end seems burned down to a brittle stub, is growing. Because spring is a verb, a vivid return. Not just winter's white, shiveringly expressed in snowdrops, heads huddled downwards against the wind, nor the bright endurance of the daffodil. Instead, a whole hillside of lollipop colours, a mix of anemones with their skirts out, crammed up against muscari, narcissi, bee orchids, vetches, small Star of Bethlehem, so many that you can't put a foot down without crushing some delicate, dancing beauty. Down in the valleys, black and green tuberose irises clump in fistfuls by new streams, and daisies drift as far as the eye can see, like snow. Even high up, even on the edges of starved plateaus, among wildernesses of grey shale, little reclaimed crescents of cultivation as thin as nail parings prickle green with corn, while on the rocks, all around on every side, tiny tulips with pale pink petals open their faces out flat, all the way to their yellow throats, as if thirsting for sun. That's what spring in Greece is like.

So, picture a breeze. Picture it animating the fig leaves, tossing the flowers' heads, sowing scent over small villages, so that people look up and sniff the air. Picture a man stepping as lightly as this wind, in garments that flutter; well dressed for the time – nothing ostentatious, but clean clothes in fine materials. His father was a fuller, after all, and they minded about dress, the philosophers. It was part of living well, to take care with one's appearance. Picture the energy and purpose in his movements, spring in his step, his bare legs and ankles, his inward rejoicing because this is the time that the world looks its most wonderful and he is here to wonder. He is here to take notice of it all, in all its parts, officially and for the first time.

How do you invent a new science? What rules should you make? Once, in pursuit of Theophrastus and his way of thinking, I did a day course on botanical classification. The instructor tipped out his son's Lego box. We had half an hour to taxonomize the whole – to put everything in front of us into families, types, species. 'Good luck,' was all the instructor said. There were all different types, sizes and shapes of brick. But that wasn't the worst of it. There were roofing parts, little windows and windscreens, wheels attached to bricks, sticks, bumped tops and flat tops, pieces with regular geometrical shapes and pieces that were round, many-sided pieces, pieces with wheels and tyres, pieces with wheels and no tyres, pieces that were part smooth and part bumped. Several precious minutes passed in hopeless inactivity. It was impossible. Should something square *and* wheeled be categorized as square or as a part of the wheel family? What about something round and wheeled? Were bumps more important than flatness? Were sticks a type of block, or something else in their own right? What on earth would be the best way to go about it?

For Theophrastus, looking at the incredible profusion at his feet, there is the even greater impossibility of deciding how to order what he sees. What is it about a daisy that makes it not a buttercup? Is it the shape of the flower, or the shape of the leaf? Is it to do with how big or small it is, or its growth habit, or its type of seed, or where it grows, or when it flowers? Is it numbers of petals that matter, or shape? And which difference is most significant? What makes it itself? Should he categorize, or list, all the plants in existence by name? Or should he order them into family or type, neither of which yet exist, setting down, in addition, all that is known about their appearance and uses?

Once he's made a decision, does he change his mind about what should go where? Because even modern botanists change their minds. Look at the Michaelmas daisy, for instance, which has recently been reclassified as a symphyotrichum just because of a difference in the invisible hairs on its invisible ovary.

Does he take notes as he goes, and if so, how? Is he carrying a bag or a basket with him? Does he collect specimens to study at home, or does he make mental lists? Here, just in this small patch alone, if he looks down at his feet, are anemone, grape hyacinth, tassel hyacinth, asphodel, narcissus, orchid, orchid, different orchid. How close does he look? Does he have a rock crystal magnifier with him, to turn the smallest plants up to the light and inspect their details? Does he count, for instance, the four spots in the throat of the tiny lilac orchis quadripunctata to differentiate it from its close family members that look otherwise so similar? And are markings significant? Is colour?

Most of what he is doing is broadly classifying. Among the wild plants as he walks about, among the fruit trees on the mountainside, for instance, there is so much variety. *There are differences in fruit and leaves, and in their forms and parts generally.* No one yet has noticed. No one else has thought to look. *Most of the wild kinds have no names and few know about them.* He muses on how to separate things out into different categories: should it be by their stems – woody and not woody? By their seeds – some are *small in body*, some are *naked* and some *in tunics*? By their flowers? What is the difference, I would like to ask him, between plants and people? *Plants are united to the ground and not free of it like animals*, is his answer, although when he describes his plants they sound like people. Some are *lazy*, some *greedy.* Some, like the almond, need their luxuriance *humbling* because they have too much sap.

Hurrying behind him as he thinks, I run my hand over the trunk of a bitter almond tree as I pass. It is bobbled with amber beads of sap, leaked through the thinness of its bark. Wait, I'd like to shout, what is this? Is this what you mean? Is this the almond's normal habit, or is this a special type of almond? Or is it just a disease? And how can you tell? But he's moved on. He is looking at other things. He is ahead of me, wondering about growth habits.

Some seeds are stubborn in sprouting and some, like the cumin, are so unpleasant that their seed needs cursing as you cast it on the ground. His plant world is more human than we've allowed. Or perhaps his human is more plant. The term he uses for spring is the *laughing of the seasons.* He refers to the earth being *in heat,* as though the planet were an animal, instead of saying, as gardeners do now, 'when the ground is warm'. Seeds have *pregnancies,* where we only allow them 'germination', a narrower word that we have created especially for that purpose out of the Latin for seed. Where Theophrastus refers to the *knees* or the *armpits* of the grass he is describing, we translate with 'axil'. This is another purpose-built botanical word. In the dictionary it has no other use. It is only used to describe 'the upper angle between a leaf or petiole and the stem' of a plant. All the same, we chose it because 'axilla' means armpit in Latin. Where Theophrastus calls seeds *small-bodied,* we just call them 'small'. Where he categorizes a seed as *naked,* we use the word 'gymnosperm', which means exactly the same thing but in Greek – literally, naked seed. Each time, we are careful to bury our old kinship in languages we no longer speak, as if the similarities between us and the plant kingdom, though descriptively unavoidable, were a source of shame.

What a strange hiding. In the gaps between these separate sets of words, the centuries of steadily accumulated distance between us, and the world we live in, open out their desert spaces. And why are we pushing the world away? Is it perhaps so as not to notice our connection? So as to allow ourselves to use it more freely? What would I say to Theophrastus now, if I met him on this hillside, full of the excitement of his project, wondering at the world around him? Would I tell him what we've done? The long-standing slavery that we've imposed on the rest of creation; how hard we've worked it, how we've broken it, burned it, traded it, cut it, spoiled and undermined it, all for the sake of human progress. Because we believe we are in control. Would I dare tell him that? He would fix me with the intensity of his disciplined gaze, no doubt. Tell me quietly but matter of factly that, whatever we'd done, we'd done to our own bodies, to ourselves. We are indivisible from the world. Then, he'd turn away and pass on, leaving me alone on the hillside, as if I were some unintelligent thing, some blind and parasite grub, moving its lips over the ground, slowed to a standstill by unnatural fattening.

Difficult as it is to systematize plants, Theophrastus follows the method of comparison he outlined in the *Metaphysics*: this is most like that, and this is different from that in the following ways. Always he uses analogy and parallel to help him in his categorization or description. He tells us what each plant looks like, how they reproduce, how to cultivate them, how to use them for food or for medicine, or for anything else. To read him is to lose yourself in a blizzard of observed detail. He is looking very close, turning the seeds over in his hand, comparing them one with another. The *starting point* of some seed is *plain to the eye. In some cases it actually looks like a penis, as in bean, chickpea and especially in lupins.* He tells us the character of the plant's growth; whether it is lazy, or forward, or hubristic, or sullen.

Wheat is better at *mastering its food* than barley. Barley is *weak and naked* whereas wheat *wears several coats and is generally stronger*.

He tells us the hundreds of precise different uses each plant is put to. We find that cobblers use wild pear to make their strops, that Athenian warships are made of silver fir, with oak keels to withstand hauling on pebbles, that their cut-waters and catheads are always of manna ash or mulberry. Elm wood is for doors and weasel traps. Bay, because of its lightness, is for old men's walking sticks. The bark of lime and bird-cherry is excellent for writing cases.

He tells us the medicinal properties of plants, which ones are healing and how, which ones in what quantities are poisonous. Of the thorn apple, for instance, *three twentieths of an ounce in weight is given, if the patient is to become merely sportive and to think himself a fine fellow; twice this dose if he is to go mad outright and have delusions; thrice the dose if he is to be permanently insane.*

He tells us the names of things. The celandine is called the swallow-flower (as it still is – 'chelidon' means swallow) because it flowers at the time the wind blows the swallows across the sea.

He tells us how to plant and prune and prepare ground. If you are in dry country, for instance, fill your planting hole with river stones to cool the roots and to hold in moisture through the summer. If you are on salt ground, lay a mat of stones that will act as a membrane to soak up the salt and hold it away from the plant. If you are planting the slip of a fig, push it first into a squill bulb and then bury it. That way it will stay damp. If you want your almond to be sweet instead of bitter, bleed it of some of its gum. If you are preparing ground, a mattock is a better tool than a plough. It cuts deeper.

*

For both Theophrastus and Aristotle, collecting information is important. Two of Theophrastus' studies on plants have survived, each one running to two volumes and each volume containing many books. They are separately titled *An Enquiry into Plants* and *The Causes of Plants*, but some of their matter overlaps. The *Enquiry* seems to have been written first but both have the feeling of a study continued, added to and developed over many years. Theophrastus recycles some subjects, returning to them again and again in an attempt to understand. The question of darnel (*Lolium temulentum*) – the unwanted, Biblical tares – and how to tell it apart from wheat, is a good example. The difference is important because darnel is a poisonous intoxicant. It is almost impossible to differentiate between the two at the seed stage, so a farmer looking at grain for sowing might naturally assume he was only sowing wheat. Similarly, when the crop is growing, the tares are tricky to tell apart. 'Shall we gather up the tares?', the Biblical servant asks their master and the master answers them, 'Nay, lest while ye gather up the tares, ye root up the wheat also with them.' Theophrastus addresses the problem repeatedly in both treatises, thinking it patiently through, puzzling over the question of its sudden appearance in the field. At what point did it change? At what point do two seemingly identical seeds become two different plants? Within the seed? Underground? In the first shoot? Or was the differentiation caused by weather conditions, or irrigation, or soil? All of Aristotle's carefully formatted logical process applied to this mystery that the existence of a microscope could solve. I can see Theophrastus, sitting at his writing, trying one connection and then another, listening for the hum of nature's invisible machinery. Would he be pleased or sad to know that darnel is now so identifiable that we've almost eliminated it altogether? It is red-listed, among endangered plants.

Wherever he goes, Theophrastus gathers information. Walking out among the cultivated plots at Megara, with Salamis like a bruise on the horizon, stopping, looking, asking the man bent over in the last buffeting of the summer winds why he is covering his fruit so assiduously. *At Megara they also hoe and cover with dust the cucumbers and gourds when the Etesian winds have passed, and by this means render them sweeter and tenderer without having to water them.* You have to grow things in accordance with local conditions. You have to pay attention. *A man returning to Syracuse from Corinth ruined his farm with imported practices.*

He likes talking to people. And it's also clear that people like talking to him. Something easy in his manner. Leaning lightly on the garden fence discussing cucumbers. *The harvest is the year's and not the field's.* At Megara, they double-dig every four to five years to make the soil new again, the cucumber-grower informs him.

Talking is the other way that Theophrastus amasses information. When he isn't travelling or collecting in his own right, Theophrastus writes letters. He writes to other philosophers, or growers, or gardeners. He writes to the meteorologists who watch the weather from Lykabettos or Mount Ida. And he talks to the small group they have gathered around them on Lesbos. He understands that plants are only one part of a wider whole, that all parts of the system must be considered.

At his side, he has the electric and focused example of Aristotle, working at his new discipline at a furious pace, his eye pressed to the keyhole of life. In the few years that the two men spent on Lesbos, Aristotle covered an enormous amount of ground. He was performing dissections on fish and animals and birds. He was recording his dissections in drawings. We know we have lost eight books of these. They are listed among his works in Diogenes Laertius' account of his life.

I am trying to imagine his tools. He must have had precise knives, scalpels, a clamp to hold the eggs he cut every day for ten days, to observe in minute detail the development of the chick inside. Did Theophrastus see, in those moments he stopped his own collecting to come to watch Aristotle's deft movements, the little embryo with its enlarged eyes, its heart beating and moving 'as though endowed with life'? Did he watch when Aristotle removed the ten-day-old embryonic chick's eyes from its head to assess their size and quality, holding his breath because they were so small, the size of vetch beans, because they were so difficult to hold and cut when it came to peeling off the outer skin? Did he marvel with Aristotle, once the surface of the eye was removed, at the sight of the 'white and cold liquid' inside, that was so 'glittering in the sunlight'? Did he see all that?

When it came to his own plant studies, did Theophrastus too draw what he found? He must have done, if only for identification records. But if he did, these, too, are lost, which has caused some confusion among botanists who came after him. I have seen in a medieval herbal in Winchester, for instance, a delicate watercolour drawing of a daffodil with 'asphodel' – instead of 'narcissus' – written in curly letters beside it. Even though we have since corrected the scientific name, our common name for this flower – daffodil – remains the corruption of a misattribution.

Chinese whispers down the centuries between us. It's a what? An asphodel. A what? A Naffodel. What? A daffodil. What does it look like? Leaves straight like blades growing out of a bulb, yellow flowers. So it must be this. I am struck by the fragile materiality of knowledge before printing, before photographs and the internet. Carefully drawn in ink that is soluble in water and fadeable in sunlight, on papyrus that moulders or degrades to dust, gone within three hundred years if it isn't copied. And if it is copied, how exact will it be? One copy, two copies. It takes such time, such effort of the arm, scratching away, such head-bending and neck-cramping and careful peering. Such not losing of place or concentration, such steadiness of hand and execution, such clear characters. It is a labour. Three copies. Three perishable physical copies.

Slowly, slowly, knowledge disseminated. Some people who didn't have access to the manuscript scrolls simply listened to the lectures and then remembered as best they could what had been said, incorporating it, out of context, in their own works. So that the knowledge flexed and changed over time, depending on which minds it passed through, or on how diligent the copyist was, how persistent and tenacious their focus. It was both more and less solid than it is now. Aristotle's dialogues have all been lost, but in Afghanistan, in the palace of a garrison town, Ai-Khanoum, some scrolls had lain for so long in the damp of a mud basement that the ink on the bottom-most one had bled into the clay brick. Neat black rows of letters reversed in mirror writing, stamped on to the floor. It is from a dialogue, possibly Aristotle's. The name of Xenocrates is visible, in conversation with another. They are discussing a theory of ideas. Aristotle's pupil Clearchus lived and taught at Ai-Khanoum. The scrolls were presumably his. The columns of letters look ordered, full of authority; such a confident progression of thought come suddenly into view, solid, like some sharp mountain-top riding clear of mist. It is the peak of some polished and formal treatment of one of philosophy's major metaphysical matters. It is a small part of one of the finished products of Aristotle's thought. But the papyrus that contained it, carried carefully to one of the outposts of Alexander's empire, so that thought could progress there too, is gone, vanished as if it had been a living thing, just leaving behind in the mud the footprint of its passing.

*

But they don't think about that – about the fragility of knowledge – Aristotle and Theophrastus. They just work. They just collect and dissect and draw and collate and arrange and define and categorize. There is, as I said, so very much to do. Everyone on the island would have known of the project, the great project afoot at Pyrrha. All of the Greek-speaking world knew. It was an event, that one of the world's leading philosophers, Plato's favourite pupil, should abandon his teaching for something of this kind. Something that had not been necessary before. So why should it be now? Not everyone could see the importance of what Theophrastus and Aristotle were doing. The Sophist Theopompus, and his tutor Isocrates the rhetorician, for instance, were dismissive. They thought philosophers had a moral duty to society, to the education of the young. Aristotle was wasting time, neglecting his position, frittering his powers. Philodemus asks:

> Why did he turn away from exhorting the young and incur the terrible wrath and enmity both of the followers of Isocrates and of some other sophists? He must surely have implanted a great admiration for his own powers, from the moment he abandoned his proper business and was found, together with his pupil, collecting laws and innumerable constitutions.

So it was controversial, Aristotle's instinct to collect, whether he was collecting living creatures or abstract things like customs. But there were plenty who found the project exciting. On the island, many would have been attracted, to see, to listen to the philosophers' findings, or to help. Theophrastus had his friend and fellow townsman, Phanias, who knew about plants and who loved and collected music. There was his tutor Alcippus. There was another philosopher from Mytilene, Praxiphanes, who later would follow them back to Athens. And there was Pythias, Aristotle's wife, who is said to have helped with specimen gathering of all kinds, and even to have made studies of her own.

An atmosphere of work has gathered itself around the house at Pyrrha, an intensification of something, concentration perhaps, made solid, like a cloud hanging above the waters. From dawn every day now, there is quiet activity. People passing back and forth. Greeks gather, as they will wherever something interesting might be happening, sitting talking on the low wall outside. What are you collecting today? Still woody plants, the same as yesterday. And we're digging up some of the bulbs for examination while the soil is damp enough. Pythias leaves in the cool of morning with a basket and various tools. She walks out, up the narrow track away from the shore. Mastic bushes and myrtle trying to reach across on either side. Does she pick a juniper berry, as I do, squeezing it between finger and thumb so she can inhale its resiny smell – for me the smell of gin? I would like to have gone with her, just to see what it was like; how she thought of herself in relation to her husband, in relation to the project as a whole. I would like to know whether she was happy and fulfilled, gathering flowers and beetles in the Greek morning, with the dew still on the ground and the lagoon full of fishing boats setting their nets, and Assos, where she came from, out of sight behind the mountains at her back.

What did you think of women, Theophrastus?

I've read his thoughts on 'piety', on how to be a good and dutiful person – more specifically, how to be a good and dutiful man. I know he thought a man should care for his mother and father, adapting his life to suit their wishes. I know he thought a man should care for his wife and children *in a fine and loving way*. But of women, as individuals, what did you think of them, of their minds, Theophrastus?

The waters of the lagoon darken and then silver again as a breeze passes over it, but nothing answers my question. Around my feet the crickets spring their traps.

As far as Theophrastus' masters were concerned, Plato and Aristotle differed slightly in their approach to women. Plato seems to have treated the sexes as more equal. He denies love in favour of eugenics, at least until women are safely beyond the breeding stage, and he rejects the family as a unit. In his ideal state children are brought up away from their biological parents. The *Republic* sees women as a huge untapped state resource, wasted in their sacrifice to the ideas of family and domesticity. Its women are educated, as its men are, both intellectually and physically. They exercise naked with men in the gymnasium and learn the arts of war. The only difference is that because of their lesser strength, the tasks they are given are lighter. In all other respects they are treated the same.

Aristotle, it seems, thought differently. He did believe in love and its importance to human wellbeing. He believed in the family. But he thought that women were less equipped than men when it came to intellect and authority. It is known that Plato had women among his students. Two are even named: Lastheneia of Mantinea and Axiothea of Phlius, who dressed as a man. Aristotle is supposed not to have had any female pupils but then, how could this rumour of Pythias' contribution to his studies have arisen, why would she be remembered by some as a 'biologist' unless he thought she was capable of education, unless there was a grain of truth in it somewhere?

Scattered through the writings that have come down to us there are these little fragments of evidence, all these tiny details, like chippings off a giant mirror, whose brightness flashes up in the texts I read. Things like the names of female poets. So there were female poets. How many were there? These are so casually mentioned, as if they are nothing at all out of the ordinary, but we aren't always told. With the exception of Sappho, I didn't know any of these existed. I found them in an epigram written by Antipater of Thessalonica. He lists them:

> Praxilla, Moiro, the mouth of Anyte, Sappho,
> The female Homer, the jewel among the lovely-haired
> Lesbian women,
> And Erinna, far-famed Telesilla, and you, Corina,
> Who sing of Athene's battle-storming shield,
>
> Nossis with her ladylike verse and sweet sounding Myrtis,
> All working at writing their everlasting pages.

If there were female poets and female philosophers, then the classical world should look different from what we've been taught. But the past is so hard to see. Each time I pick up a detail, each time I scan its surface, hungry for the wider picture it implies, I am aware that what it shines back at me is only the crooked reflection of my own inescapable time.

I'm at Eresos now, where you were born, Theophrastus, both you and Phanias. I'm watching the bare backs of these brindled hills, sleeping like animals. The wind is warm and the cloud shadows that sweep down the flanks of the hills make them fleetingly spotted and mottled. I'm still trying to find you, still looking for things as you would have seen them; the remains of the old harbour wall here with its close-joined polygonal masonry. This burnt-gold, barren landscape. Rocks. Scrub. Dust. Little piles of fallen stones that might be cairns, or might once have been buildings. Dusty, stone-coloured sheep. Dusty stone-coloured hawks overhead; circling, picking up pieces of stone-coloured straw.

Under the surface of the water, I've seen the ancient harbour wall stretch out where it used to be land. Dressed stone with the small fish finning and mouthing at its narrow joins.

Down in the square I've seen your statue. It looks restrained, conventional, just your head and square shoulders rising out of a pillar – a little inscription. It doesn't feel very like you. None of your energy or intensity. None of your softness or your interest in the world. And it's dwarfed by Sappho in bronze next to it, open-winged and open-throated, dominating the coastline behind her, vibrating with confident song like some great bird.

When I get back to the hotel the patron is doing his books. He has a superior and disconsolate air. This house was once his family's. He has many others. Grand townhouses, so he tells me. Many of them are hotels. 'That one there.' He points diagonally across the street. 'That one is also mine.' He has dyed hair and heavy Levantine looks. As we talk, an orange drops noisily to the ground outside. We both look round. 'The summer went on too long,' he explains. 'They ripened too early and then the flies got into them and made them drop while they were still green.' His explanation makes no sense to me. I don't know what to say. It seems to be the science of another time. I think of Theophrastus. *Horned worms*, for instance, *have their origins in fig-trees.* In the stillness of the courtyard, time telescopes to a pinprick.

What happened next? Well, the work continued. For three years, Aristotle and his entourage wrote books of natural history. Theophrastus and Phanias both began works on plants, as did Aristotle himself. Only Theophrastus' books (which he went on adding to for the rest of his life) have survived, which some have taken as evidence that they were either the best or the most comprehensive – at any rate, that they superseded Aristotle's contribution in this field, surviving pre-eminent into the late Middle Ages and even beyond. By the time of his death, Theophrastus had covered as many as 550 plants, numbering their appearance, habits, origins, uses, propagation and cultivation, and including plants from as far afield as Asia, the Sudan (then Ethiopia) and even India. So wide-ranging and so meticulous was his study that Linnaeus, when he came to formulate his own system of plant taxonomy, in 1753, used Theophrastus as his starting point.

Then something else. A change came, as so often in the ancient world, in the shape of a ship, bearing down on them as they worked. A ship, sent out over the sea from the mainland, tipped forward with concentration like a runner, coming steadily on towards Lesbos. See it break out of the horizon, eating up the watery miles, growing as it nears. Insisting onwards until at last it rounds the point, suddenly life-size, manoeuvring into a spare anchorage, to unload its varied cargo in Mytilene's lovely harbour. And who is this stepping ashore among the crates, minding his feet where the sailors throw things down, picking his way quickly with the look of someone who has business in hand and a reasonable distance still to go? A messenger.

It was late in 343 BCE when this sprightly messenger arrived, in his short tunic for ease of movement and carrying his little packet of folded papyrus tied around with string, sealed so that none but its recipient could see.

A letter from King Philip of Macedon to the philosopher Aristotle.

The messenger finds himself a stall on the quayside, where he can buy something sustaining to eat before he sets out. Here he is, standing up and eating it fast, the way a bird eats, alert and watching. Then he takes a drink and makes his way through the streets and out along the uneven stones of the road from Mytilene to Pyrrha. He walks all day, arriving late in the afternoon, at the first houses of the town. Here he looks around for help; his instructions are not specific, stopping a passer-by bent under a basket full of something heavy, so that the man puts the basket down and eases his back and hopes to be asked something that will take a long time to answer. Which is the house of Aristotle the philosopher? The messenger has to ask it more than once because Macedonians have a different way of speaking. It takes time for the man to hear the words when the consonants are pronounced so differently, their softnesses hardened, all the 'th' sounds become 'd'; all the aspirated 'ch' sounds spat forward into the mouth to become 'g'. What did you say, Stranger? I asked for Aristotle. I am looking for the house of the philosopher. Which one is it? Aristotle the philosopher's house – which way?

And then, at last, the messenger is here, knocking at the gate and entering, to find Aristotle himself, at his desk perhaps, or in conversation with his fellows; he sees him look up and meets those thought-filled blue eyes with his own. He hands the letter over, and takes the refreshments he is offered and the whole task slips from his mind like a garment dropping to the floor. Aristotle reaches across for his knife, cutting and letting fall the binding strings, and breaking the seal, and unfolding. Lines of small writing open across the page, long lines unbroken either by punctuation or by word endings, scratched over the papyrus in some kind of sooty ink. From Philip the King to Aristotle, Greetings. Aristotle's lightning attention scanning the text.

It is an invitation. Or, since it comes from a king, a command, to move again, to come to Pella, where the Macedonian court is, to work, or to teach, so that Alexander, Philip's son, might benefit from philosophy. Plato's project, once again: the education of a king.

The messenger is given a bed for the night. Perhaps he sits in the kitchen for a while, talking before he falls asleep. Or just listening, in the fug of his tiredness, to the rise and fall of the philosophers' voices. Because elsewhere, in some inner room, Aristotle and Theophrastus must have sat for a long time, discussing the answer they would give in the morning. Was it an easy decision? Breaking the quiet of retirement, changing scholarship and simplicity for the world of court and politics. Were they in agreement?

It is patronage after all. Philip is the power. There's no denying that – Stagira and the siege of Olynthus are proof, if proof were needed. He is the coming power. They would be able, no doubt, to continue their natural history studies. It would be money and protection – what we would now call funding. They would likely be at the centre of their world, if things go as they look like they are going. And what is philosophy for except for educating and guiding the ruling power, whoever it or they might be? Think of Plato's efforts in Syracuse. Yes, he failed, but think of his letter – remember what he said, when he set out to advise Dionysius. 'I sailed from home… through a feeling of shame with regard to myself, lest I might someday appear to myself wholly and solely a mere man of words, one who would never of his own will lay his hand to any act.'

And then, where was Pythias while they sat there discussing Philip's invitation? – somewhere inside, turning over her specimens by the light of an oil lamp, or making lists for tomorrow. I must bring the pot herbs, for instance. Tomorrow, I must collect sage apples for dissection, to find out whether they are a fruit, or a gall. Maybe she was happy, in her room, making her plans, unaware that elsewhere in the house a decision was being made that would change things, take her away from this work, reduce her to whatever a woman at a foreign court might be, remove her even further from what family she had at Assos. Bundled along with the household items, the blankets and books and pots and pans, to face the various trials of her life – childbirth, for instance, in an alien place, with only slaves to attend her – or bereavement.

Or would she be happy to go because there were shadows over her already? Sitting in a chair, waiting for Aristotle, so lost in anxiety that she doesn't notice her fingers picking and pulling at the thread of her robe. Why am I not yet pregnant? Am I a barren woman? A woman of no biological purpose. Am I defective? Because Theophrastus, in a lost treatise on water, mentions in passing that there was a stream at Pyrrha whose waters made women infertile. If only we could move away from here, I'm sure things would change.

Whatever her feelings were, they went. They packed up their scrolls of papyrus, their notes, their drawings, their instruments for dissecting or magnifying, such as they were. They loaded them onto carts, together with Pythias and what maidservants she must have had. And they made their slow and jolting way back to Mytilene and down to the harbour to board a ship.

*

At this point, the picture widens. To begin with, on deck, as well as Aristotle and Theophrastus, settling themselves in for the crossing, there is one other; someone who has been forgotten from the account so far, someone important, who has been overlooked but who has probably been here all along. A seventeen-year-old boy, wrapped in his cloak against the coming sea-cold; Aristotle's beloved nephew Callisthenes.

Callisthenes was born c.360 BCE, making him about ten years younger than Theophrastus. He came from Olynthus, the town that Philip besieged and then razed to the ground. So it's likely that Callisthenes had been in Aristotle's household since then, working and being taught alongside Theophrastus. Plato's aphorism about Aristotle's quickness of mind when compared with Xenocrates was also something Aristotle said of Theophrastus and Callisthenes: 'that one needed a bridle and the other a spur; for Theophrastus interpreted all his meaning with an excess of cleverness, whereas the other was naturally backward.' Theophrastus was kind. Probably he helped the boy understand. Probably he spent time teaching him. He was very fond of Callisthenes.

If Callisthenes was in Aristotle's household, then he would have been present in that other small boat, the one which put to sea in that forward-looking grey dawn, after Plato's death, to establish a school at Assos. It isn't exactly proof but when Hermias the tyrant died, years later, Callisthenes would write an effusive encomium, so the likelihood is that he must have known him, probably from Aristotle and Theophrastus' time at Assos. In which case, when they left for Lesbos, Callisthenes would have gone too, and would have stayed and perhaps helped in some way, watching his uncle making his collections and trying to find where it might be that his own contribution could one day be made. And now here he is, setting out again, bound for the Macedonian court, where in the dreams of a seventeen year old, anything might happen.

One of the things the letter from Philip to Aristotle may have offered, along with its invitation, was to put right the wrongs he had committed against Aristotle's home town, Stagira. This, like

Olynthus, had been razed to the ground, its people either exiled or sold into slavery. Whether it was part of the initial offer or not, once Aristotle had agreed and accepted, Philip rebuilt Stagira and returned its population. Perhaps something similar might be achieved for Olynthus. Callisthenes, watching the wake of the boat and dreaming himself a glorious future, tried to picture the king he'd never met. This warmongering bogeyman from the highlands. Do something great and gain his favour... My chief philosopher. How the king would turn and smile. This is the most brilliant of the men at my court. This is the man I can't do without. And then his town would be so proud of him. The people move aside, folding and widening like this wake. Bowing at the waist, although the good man is modest. Build back his father's house. Buy back the fat cattle and all the old life: the slaves, the artisans, all the people he remembered. Perhaps those were the stories he told himself, watching the sea pleat itself away behind the boat's stern, because he could feel the strength thickening in his boy-to-man muscles. And because the boat was going somewhere new and the wind in its freshness suggested possibility – possibility with Callisthenes in the middle of it.

So the journey wears on, until Lesbos is just a thumbprint that someone has left on the far horizon, and the boat drives onwards, endlessly north, until it comes round the last prong of Chalkidiki and into the Thermaic Gulf. And at this point, it is Aristotle I see most clearly, drawn out of his retirement and into the history books, as he stands on deck and watches the familiar coastline pass. Meanwhile, somewhere inland, Alexander the Great, aged thirteen, who knows little and cares less about the man coming to teach him, cocks around the gymnasium, boasting like any other boy his age – I can throw further, run faster, ride harder. I will be the greatest the world has ever seen, and the older boys raise their eyebrows at each other – ignore him, he's an annoying little prick. Because none of them yet knows that he really does mean it.

In the storybook dazzle of this – the great philosopher arriving to teach the great hero-in-waiting – it's hard to see anything but these two. It's hard to see, behind him, Aristotle's constant shadow, Theophrastus. But his shadow is there, on the deck of the boat, watching and wondering no doubt what this new chapter will hold – a different flora at the very least. And behind him too is Pythias, Aristotle's young wife, and his ambitious nephew Callisthenes, all thinking their different thoughts and watching the coast slip by as the boat noses its way up the Loudias river and into the silty waters of the lagoon that opens itself out at Pella's feet.

For Theophrastus, this place is all the more alien for its similarity; another lagoon, like Pyrrha, but yet so unlike. Because this is a country of snow and marsh and military muscle, of heavy, provincial grandeur and constant manoeuvres, of swamp grass and mosquitoes.

Did they feel it, I wonder, the sick pull of the returning world, as they entered the harbour? Because that is what they were doing: coming out of the trance-like focus of their life on Lesbos right into the eye of power and the push for precedence. It must have been like waking up.

III

The Backdrop

Pick a side. Any side. Quick, because ideas don't matter any more. Only events. Everything is different in Macedonia. Life here is faster, shallower, more showy. Everything is power and politics, and everyone is trying to be noticed. I can't help worrying about Theophrastus. You won't like it, I can't help telling him. It is everything you don't believe in.

Pella is incubating history, as if it were an organism, accumulating momentum and focusing intent. Things haven't stood still since the fall of Olynthus. Over the intervening years Macedonia has been steadily strengthening itself, extending its control, sometimes openly in battle, sometimes in more roundabout ways, through treaties or alliances, or by bribery or influence, and a new and terrible force is about to be unleashed on the world. As the philosophers pull safely into the harbour, they are sailing right into the eye of it.

Do they feel it? This is a strange place, both the same and different. These men in the harbour, like something from a heroic past, in heavy woollen cloaks that swing as they walk, all these people in hats that are round and white like cakes, all these horses. Great piles of timber for export. This colder air. These herdsmen and huntsmen. This feeling – what is it? – of watchfulness, as if nothing was sure, as if power and possibility were always present, but a single wrong foot could cost you your place. And there's one family here that counts. There is Philip, this canny and restless conqueror, and there are his wives, or one in particular – Alexander's mother, Olympias, who comes from Northern Greece, from Epirus, and who is calculating and tempestuous and power-hungry and very, very frightening. There is an aristocracy whose loyalty must be coerced or manipulated, and on all the borders there are tribes that are waiting for the chance that something in the great Macedonian machine might falter. Much has been happening since the philosophers left Athens, since they've been away at Assos, or on Lesbos, at their study of natural history.

When Philip came to the throne, in 359 BCE, Macedonia was a small and threatened state, a territory needing to be made secure. He has done this with extraordinary speed and effectiveness. He has juggled the different players, both the wild tribes and the greater Greek powers – Thebes and its spreading territories, and Athens with its navy and its high historical opinion of itself. He has extended his borders by force and he's held off Athens with cunning and diplomacy, all the time steadily depriving it of outposts it thought of as its own: Amphipolis, Methone, Pydna. So, as the philosophers arrive and find their feet among the grand buildings in these chilly new streets, they must notice that what matters here is speed and decisiveness and physical prowess. What matters is information and quick thinking and money – or influence – to bribe the diplomats that arrive, one after another, to negotiate this or that treaty. And drink, to fuddle them, and sometimes fear. Because each time they leave, whatever they think they've agreed, their own borders mysteriously contract a little more. Whatever they think they've negotiated evaporates, or lifts, or changes as if it were smoke, or mist.

Has no one noticed that the Greek-speaking world is spinning increasingly off-kilter, as if its axis has changed?

From Athens it's obvious, or it's obvious to Demosthenes, its leading orator. Athens is sinking. It's losing its old pre-eminence. For almost a decade now, this has been his fear – his obsession. Although no one, despite all his efforts, seems to see it as clearly as he does, and he can't understand it. He has been among several of the Athenian embassies to Macedonia and he has seen enough to know. He keeps telling the Athenians, warning them of what he's like, Philip of Macedon. Why can't they feel this, as he does, like a kind of sea-sickness? Everything is tipping. Athens will be swallowed. Philip will stop at nothing. His greed is to overtake all – the Chersonese, Thessaly, Athens, Sparta.

Late into the night, Demosthenes sits up by lamplight, shivering into the future it seems that only he can see. He does nothing unprepared. He is too nervous to extemporize so all his speeches are worked up in advance and memorized. But sometimes it's hard. In the dark, being the only one – picturing the army that will bulk against them, its spears, its sarissas, bristling against Athens' free sky – when no one at all will listen. Meanwhile, the Athenian world that he knows continues to wander around the Agora, self-satisfied and ornate, chinking its gold and gossiping, lazy-eyed, under the same old sun. He feels jittery. All the time. Febrile. Maybe he's ill. Maybe it's the lack of sleep.

Night after night, he drives his rhetoric to new heights. 'You who see Philip, showering out gifts and promises', like Persephone scattering flowers. 'Pray, if you are wise, that you may never know him for a cheat and a deceiver.' 'Mistrust', he mouths into the darkness. 'Mistrust.' Like a mantra. This one-eyed, whoring, brawling king from the backwoods, whose hot and wine-soaked breath he can feel breathing at him from the corners of this room. But that's not even it, because he isn't a savage. He's clever. He's wily. He's almost demonic. Demosthenes has seen him. He has stood among the other ambassadors, in the palace at Pella, and felt the hunger – it doesn't matter for what – for land, for the gold mines of Thrace, or the Black Sea ports, or for drink, or recognition; or for small and personal things like humbling haughty Athens, or smashing Thebes which took him prisoner in his youth, or just for more and younger women. He's seen it and it's cavernous. It has no end, Philip's hunger; it's insatiable.

Philip is a formidable adversary, devastating in his ability to remember and retain diplomatic detail, eloquent in reply. You don't know what he's said to your colleagues. You don't know what he's tempted them with, who's trustworthy, who's not. He gets in amongst you and he separates you out like a wolf will separate sheep. And then, afterwards, the drinking – the drinking is on an epic scale. He stares into the dark, remembering.

There had been ten of them, ten ambassadors, sent to negotiate peace and the return of Athens' colony, the port of Amphipolis. All the way there, although he was the youngest, Demosthenes had boasted of the fountains of oratory he would unleash when they arrived. They'd see. He would make such a speech about Amphipolis that he would sew up Philip's mouth with an unsoaked rush. But that wasn't altogether how it went. Something got in the way – fear of Philip in the flesh maybe, or disorientation at the intent, the brutality of his court, or (as he chose to argue later) fury at Aeschines, the second last ambassador to speak, for making a speech that was crass in its lack of diplomacy. Whatever it was, when it came to his turn, Demosthenes found himself dumb. He just stood, opening and shutting his mouth like a netted fish, and not a sound came out.

'Philip', as Aeschines will later publicly recall, 'saw Demosthenes' plight and bade him take courage, and not to think, as though he were an actor on the stage, that his collapse was an irreparable calamity, but to keep cool and try gradually to recall his speech and speak it off as he had prepared it.' But Demosthenes, having once been upset, and having forgotten what he had written, was unable to recover himself. 'Nay', Aeschines remembers, 'on making a second attempt he broke down again. Silence followed; then the herald bade us withdraw.'

Demosthenes shifts in his chair. The memory burns. Is it for this reason that he hates Aeschines and Philocrates so much – that they witnessed his shame? But these men lack his ability, his imagination. They see nothing. If Philip takes the Black Sea ports, for instance, Athens' wheat imports will be blocked and the city will starve. Attica produces no corn of its own. It will absolutely and for certain starve to death. Meanwhile, Philocrates and Aeschines go on telling the city what it wants to hear: that all is well. They are pocketing Philip's bribes like pimps. They must be. I bet they are. He's suddenly sure of it.

How to shake Athens from its complacency before it's too late? How could it be so slow to rouse? Because its attentions are focused elsewhere, that's why – its embassies too easily bought or cajoled. For eight or nine years now – almost a decade – it has preferred to placate, to make agreements. The craven bargaining makes him sick: even if you have taken what wasn't yours, O great one, Amphipolis for instance, Potidea, Pydna, Methone, all these critical trading ports, these life-lines – that's what the embassy caved in over – even if you took it unlawfully, O king, by force, let's not argue. Let's each keep the territories we hold at the signing of the treaty. Let's agree on no more land grabs. As if Philip cared. And Athens continued to rest on remembered laurels. We, the older power, condescend to call you equal. Together we will police the Mediterranean, keep it free of pirates. We two major players, together. But it doesn't work, as it never could have. Somehow Philip's armies are still marching, unstoppable. Look at them. They're in the Peloponnese, in Thessaly, in Phocis.

By the summer of 343 BCE, just as Philip starts looking for a tutor for his son, even the slowest or most corrupt of the status quo supporters in Athens are beginning to feel uneasy. As Philip hears of Aristotle's work on Lesbos and decides to write and invite him to Pella, the Athenians, like people waking from a long sleep, start anxiously asking each other what Philip's soldiers are doing, for instance, at Porthmus on Euboea. Is he planning an attack on Attica? And what are the implications for democracy here, or at Elis, or at Megara where he seems to be meddling in something that is none of his business?

Meanwhile, in the background, Athens' old enemy Persia is shifting its ground. Artaxerxes has conquered Egypt and now what? Have you heard? Philip has made an alliance with him, with the king of Persia. Macedonia and Persia together. This is what fuels Demosthenes' late-night fears, as he tries out his sentences, mouthing and gesturing into the dark. He had hoped to persuade Athens to ally with Persia. That would have given them some weight. That might have been a counterbalance to Macedonia's growing might. Now the scales have truly tipped. It's coming. Disaster is coming.

'I see the plot thickening. I hope I may prove a false prophet, but I fear now the disaster is all too near.'

He widens his eyes, peering into the lamp like a moth. He can feel it. The ruin of Athens like something breathing at the bare skin of his nape. It's nonsense but he puts a hand up all the same. He can't help it. One quick, nervous brushing gesture at his neck.

'You want freedom,' he will tell them tomorrow, 'but can't you see, Philip's titles are utterly at odds with that? Every king, every despot is the sworn enemy of freedom and also of law. Beware lest seeking deliverance from war you find yourselves a master.'

Never mind Demosthenes – he is unnecessarily highly strung. He's not manly, some would say. Because even now, some still don't see it his way. Not everyone agrees. Some look to Philip to take charge, a necessary strong man. Some don't see him as an enemy at all. He's a Greek. Look at the sophistication of his court, its cosmopolitanism. And it has long been the case that Macedonia has made a home for talent from elsewhere – like Zeuxis, for example, the famous painter from Heraclea in Italy's instep, commissioned to decorate the palace at Pella. Or Agathon the playwright or, more famously, Euripides who composed *The Bacchae* at Pella, during his Macedonian exile. So, while Demosthenes makes his speeches of alarm, many of the Athenian intellectuals, bowing to Philip's rising star and his plentiful Thracian gold, now look to him for patronage. Among these are the heads of the philosophy schools, Speusippus, who took over the Academy after Plato, and Isocrates the rhetorician, who has suffered financial misfortune and never got over it.

Naturally both of these men hear, when the time comes, that Philip is looking for a tutor for his son. Isocrates is a very old man. He doesn't have much time. He is in his nineties now. He doesn't speak in public like Demosthenes. He sits at home writing letters to tyrants, pursuing his own pet project – an avant-garde and long-held view of Greek political union: Panhellenism. For many years now, he has flown the kite of this one idea through his endless windy prose. For many years, he has tried to persuade this person or that. But there is something in his mode of address that irritates, or at any rate always fails. His argument is sometimes ornate and sometimes manipulative but always there is something shrill and insistent in its expression. I will be listened to, he seems to be saying, behind his important idea. I am a person of influence. Still.

'I so impressed my audience with the stating of my case,' he says after making a particularly sophistic point about Amphipolis, 'that when I finished they remained open mouthed and silent. None of the customary compliments about style and purity of expression – No. None of the customary applause, because they were simply too astonished by the truth of my argument to clap.'

An old man wheeling out his battered vanities. In the beginning, Isocrates had come from a privileged family. He was born in 436 BCE, a little older than Plato and four years before the start of the Peloponnesian War. His youth, despite the war, was the same as that of any of the well-bred, moneyed young men of Athens. He was well educated, knew Socrates, and Socrates thought highly of him. He would make a great speaker, a great philosopher for sure, one of these days.

Then came the peace, and with it Isocrates' dreams fell toppling down. Somehow, through the long and weary years of war, everything had been lost so that, when it ended, his family found themselves financially ruined. He was young and his future was bright. It was so hard to believe. His mind kept resisting. How could it be? It was so unfair. While Plato continued, rich, noble, high-minded, Isocrates was forced to scrub about for his living among the Sophists, or writing legal speeches for money, before setting up his own school, teaching rhetoric. Even today this remains a humiliation. Plato doesn't mention Isocrates specifically – he is kind enough not to do that – but he excoriates the Sophists, those who trade in philosophy as if it were a commodity.

For the rest of his life, Isocrates' cause is Panhellenism. He wants never to experience war between the Greek states again. As the years go on, he tries to persuade first one power, then another to see the sense in uniting. First, he tries the old enemies Athens and Sparta, but nothing comes of it. Then, he tries individuals: the tyrants Jason of Pherae in the late 370s, Dionysus of Syracuse in the late 360s, Archidamas III of Sparta in 356, suggesting they band themselves together against the Persians. In 346, he turns his attention to Philip of Macedon, arguing against the likes of Demosthenes, in favour of alliance. But he doesn't go into the Assembly to speak up in opposition. His voice is weak. He is unpopular. He gets too nervous and he's afraid of being mocked. He writes Philip long public letters instead, winding himself around his arguments, flattering both sides at the same time. But the masses resent his haughtiness, the impression that he gives of being above public service, so how will he ever persuade them?

Solve the problem of Amphipolis – that's how. Get Philip to give it back to Athens.

'You must realise that by formally surrendering this territory to us, you would in fact still have it in your power. Added to which you would gain our great good will and as many hostages to our friendship as we sent out settlers.' Don't imagine we do this for our own gain, he argues; it is nothing to us. We don't want it. It is almost an inconvenience.

But he's behind the curve. Before he has finished his letter, peace is negotiated by Demosthenes' co-ambassador Philocrates and it is decided that Philip should keep Amphipolis after all, just as he'd always intended. Never mind. Its inclusion in his letter will be a useful tool, an indication to Athens that Isocrates has her interests at heart. He doesn't believe in the peace anyway. The only hope for permanent peace, in his eyes, is for Philip to unite the Greek states under his own rule, by force if necessary, and lead them against Asia. That is the real matter of this letter – but again, nothing comes of it.

Two years later, in 344, while Aristotle and Theophrastus are still in their seclusion on Lesbos, Isocrates writes again. This time his excuse is a letter of nannying concern about an injury Philip has sustained in battle. Philip is too great a king to run the risks of a common soldier, so Isocrates' argument goes. Only two-thirds of the way through the letter does he get to his real matter: Philip should take no notice of the growing anti-Macedonian feeling in Athens. Because Athens is at last waking up. If necessary, Isocrates suggests, Philip should enforce the city's allegiance, strong-arm it for its own good, as he has just so successfully done in Thessaly. He closes, drawing a parallel between himself and Philip.

'Like yourself, I am misunderstood and disliked by the Athenian masses; you they dislike for your great power and prosperity but me for my great wisdom.' Did Isocrates have more than Panhellenism in mind when he was writing, or when he painted himself as Philip's equal in unpopularity in Athens? It seems preposterous, these unasked-for letters, the barefaced boasting, the auto-flattery, twinning a ninety-year-old man, a word-chopper, with a brutal and charismatic king, to his face. What did Philip think when the messenger handed him another letter?

> You should not honour the kind of courage that accompanies heedless folly and unseasonable ambition, nor, when so many hazards which are inherent in monarchy are at hand, should you devise for yourself still others that bring no glory and belong to the common soldier.

Inexplicably, for the moment at least, Philip seems indulgent. Isocrates told himself that at last his star was in the ascendant. His pupil, the historian Theopompus, was invited to stay at Pella at around this time, perhaps in the hopes that he would be chosen for the job of Alexander's tutor. Then, as if further proof were needed, when Philip sends an embassy to Athens, early in the summer of 343 BCE, he chooses Isocrates' pupil, Pytho of Byzantium, to be at its head.

The embassy's purported aim is to repair the damage his Thessalian campaign has done to the peace of Philocrates but it goes very badly. The atmosphere in Athens has turned sullen. Demosthenes has never lacked an audience but at last his speeches seem to have gained some kind of traction. Athens sends Pytho back with a return embassy and this time the envoys are openly obstructive and insulting. They demand two modifications to the treaty that Philip has so disregarded. They want Amphipolis and the other strategic places – Pydna, Potidea and Methone – to be returned, and they want the alliance extended so that it includes all Greek states. Philip refuses the first of their requests. He is more receptive to the idea of the inclusion of all Greek states but then he has a slightly different model in mind.

*

And while all this is happening, Theophrastus and Aristotle continue to collect plants and open up animals on Lesbos. Maybe they hear the news. Maybe, in their absorption, the squabbles of the world don't matter. Either way, back in Athens, after the embassy, things start happening very fast. In the envoys' absence feelings harden against Philip. Demosthenes and his fellow anti-Macedonians bring a case of impeachment against Philocrates. He is guilty, they say, of taking bribes. He is a traitor. This time, the Assembly listens. Philocrates flees the country by night and is condemned to death *in absentia*. One down. Demosthenes gathers himself and turns his searchlight on Aeschines. Aeschines stands his ground. He doesn't flee.

The trial, which is huge, takes place in the Agora. Almost the entire male populace is present and the jury runs into the thousands. There is noise. A crush of bodies. People craning their heads to see. Is that him? Is that the man? He doesn't look like a traitor. But then you can never tell. The defendant, who stands to lose his life, looks calm, although he is just one man in all this great mass. All these eyes turned on him, the hum of all these voices talking about him. He must have great faith in the process of democracy. His little life to be weighed so publicly; so precious a thing to be decided by these many, workaday, careless heads and hands. There is hush. The klepsydra, the water clock, which measures the time allotted for each speech, is started. Demosthenes, as accuser, speaks first.

His main claim is that Aeschines too took bribes. This is the accusation, although he can provide no solid proof. Aeschines has betrayed the trust of the city, his interests were always his own. When they travelled to Pella he purposefully delayed. If only he 'had chosen to travel by sea and to do his duty', Demosthenes says. 'What might have been saved by sailing, he lost by insisting on travel by land; and, what might have been saved by telling the truth, he has lost by telling lies.'

Repeatedly Demosthenes hammers it home: if Aeschines bungled and spoke crassly, let him off, but if he lied for money let him die. If his words were simply clumsy, if his speeches were inadequate, no matter; if his words were 'false, venal and noxious, let him be convicted'. If in the service of the state a man takes bribes and speaks in the interests of their enemy, is the danger not untold? And, after all, they all of them had to resist bribery.

'You must know', Demosthenes says, 'that Philip was already sounding us all in this way: he sent private messages to each of us in turn, with the offer, men of Athens, of a really large sum in gold.'

Demosthenes' speech is long. When his criticisms of Aeschines' diplomatic integrity are exhausted his attack becomes personal. Aeschines is a man of no character and questionable background. When Demosthenes was being educated with the best, Aeschines was nothing but a miserable ink-grinding bench-wiping classroom assistant, the grimy servant of his mother's Mystery cult, who grew up to be a common actor. Is it any surprise that he behaved so badly on the embassy? Because he did. After the audience with Philip, the Greek envoys were bidden to dinner, by someone despicable, so goes Demosthenes' account. They were bidden to dinner by the son of one of the Thirty Tyrants – those oppressive, extremist, pro-Spartan rulers who ran Athens after the Peloponnesian War, the fathers of a purge in which over 1,000 people were killed. So, when they were invited by this man, Xenophron he was called, Demosthenes, who had a conscience, was busy trying to buy the freedom of Philip's captives, so he refused – but Aeschines? Aeschines went. Men of Athens, let me tell you a story.

> When the drinking began, Xenophron introduced an Olynthian woman, a handsome, freeborn and, as the event proved, modest girl. At first, I believe, they only tried to make her drink quietly and eat dessert; so Iatrocles told me the following day. But as the carouse went on, and they became heated, they ordered her to sit down and give them a song. The poor girl was bewildered, for she did not wish, and she did not know how, to sing. Then Aeschines and Phryno declared that it was intolerable impertinence for a captive, and one of those ungodly, pernicious Olynthians too, to give herself such airs. 'Call a servant,' they cried; 'bring a whip, somebody.' In came a flunkey with a horsewhip, and I suppose they were tipsy, and it did not take much to irritate them. When she said something and began to cry, Aeschines tore off her dress and gave her a number of lashes on the back. Maddened by these indignities, she jumped to her feet,

upset the table, and fell at the knees of Iatrocles. If he had not rescued her, she would have perished, the victim of a drunken orgy, for the drunkenness of this blackguard is something terrible.

But at this point there is a stir in the Agora. The story is too much. Demosthenes is interrupted because Aeschines has his supporters and no one wants to listen to such filth. Demosthenes should stick to his proper matter. Move on.

When the clock runs out on the allotted time, it is Aeschines' turn to speak. How to come back from such accusations? Right or wrong, Demosthenes' pictures are so vivid they must be lodged in every single man's head. When Aeschines stands up, he knows he is speaking for his life. He is speaking to the city of his birth, in front of his own family, and in the face of such vivid slander. He has to remember all the points made against him and answer them effectively. He has somehow to dispel the idea of him as corrupt and, looking out over the crowd of faces, how to know whether this idea has taken root, or where, or how deeply? If he fails, he will be put to death.

The first thing to be dealt with is the horrible accusation of his drunken abuse of a high-born captive:

> I would not shrink from defending myself against this charge. For if there is any man among those who are standing outside the bar—and almost the whole city is in the court—or if there is any man of you, the jurors, who is convinced that I have ever perpetrated such an act, not to say towards a free person, but towards any creature, I hold my life as no longer worth the living. And if as my defence proceeds I fail to prove that the accusation is false, and that the man who dared to utter it is an impious slanderer, then, even though it be clear that I

am innocent of all the other charges, I declare myself worthy
of death.

His defence is open and direct. He has a good, strong voice. Once he's
started he feels better. The audience is quiet. He gathers his strength,
his manliness and all his powers of persuasion:

> Now, fellow citizens, as regards the rest of his accusations, if
> I pass over any point and fail to mention it, I beg of you to
> question me and let me know what it is that you wish to hear
> about, and to refrain from forming any judgment in advance,
> but to listen with impartial goodwill... When now a man
> has shown such trickery and effrontery, it is difficult even
> to remember every single thing, and in the face of danger it
> is not easy to answer unexpected slanders. But I will begin
> with those events which I think will enable me to make my
> presentation most clear and intelligible to you, and fair... In
> this way I shall best remember his charges and best be able to
> speak effectively, and you will be best instructed.

He answers each of Demosthenes' charges, item by item, making use
of the official records, having decrees, letters and the testimonies of
witnesses read out to the court. Keeping calm. We have time. Eleven
jars of water have been allotted to my defence. When the defence of
his own diplomacy is complete he turns to the matter of his character.
He gestures into the crowd. 'Yonder is my father, Atrometus.' Heads
turn to look, and an old man – another one beggared in youth by
years of war (he is ninety-four) – lifts his head and looks back at the
city for whom, in his time, he has fought, and which is now sitting
in judgement on his son. Hard to see anything more than weariness
and puzzlement and pain in the ancient eyes. Although he must be

thinking bitter thoughts of his city. Acquit him. Look at him. How dare you? For what did I risk my own life in your endless wars? Aeschines is still speaking. He points to his brothers, also present, also servants of the state. Finally he points to his children, a girl and two little boys who have been brought into court to serve his peroration.

> I ask, fellow citizens, whether you believe that I would
> have betrayed to Philip, not only my country, my personal
> friendships, and my rights in the shrines and tombs of my
> fathers, but also these children, the dearest of mankind to me.
> Do you believe that I would have held his friendship more
> precious than the safety of these children? By what lust have
> you seen me conquered? What unworthy act have I ever done
> for money?

In closing, he turns to Demosthenes and addresses him directly. Unlike you, I did my two years' national service, guarding the frontiers. I fought and well enough to win the praise of my superiors, to be crowned with the wreath of honour. None of which Demosthenes has done. If you've known battle, then you know that peace is preferable. It is no bad thing to be an ambassador for peace. Once again he indicates his father, his brothers, his little children. Let them plead for him, as father, brother, son, as an upright citizen. How terrible it is to be publicly defamed:

> Is he not indeed to be pitied who must look into the sneering
> face of an enemy, and hear with his ears his insults? But
> nevertheless I have taken the risk, I have exposed my body
> to the peril. Among you I grew up, your ways have been my
> ways. No home of yours is the worse for my pleasures; no
> man has been deprived of his fatherland by accusation of

mine at any revision of the citizen-lists, nor has come into
danger when giving account of his administration of an office.

He calls his final witness. The clock runs dry.

'My speech is finished. This my body I, and the law, now commit
to your hands.'

Aeschines stops speaking.

Silence.

He is acquitted by thirty votes.

Meanwhile, Philip absorbs the anti-Macedonian mood in Athens. Pytho's embassy failed. Whose fault could it be? In the autumn of 343, sensing the change, Speusippus now writes to Philip putting the virtues of the Academy to him in the hope of patronage, in the hope that an Academician might be chosen instead as Alexander's tutor. His letter is mostly a long and detailed shredding of the arguments in Isocrates' last public letter. What could Philip expect? Isocrates was an old fool. As far as Speusippus is concerned, Isocrates is guilty of many things, starting with diplomatic under-flattery. He had not praised Philip nearly enough. He had not enough extolled Philip's acts of friendship to Athens. His rhetoric is unbecoming. He should have kept silent. Added to which, in case Philip thought Isocrates was paying him any kind of special attention with these letters, he is not. He is simply recycling old arguments, hobby-horsing on Panhellenism, which he has already tried, many times, on others and failed:

> [H]e has sent you a discourse that he was writing at first to
> Agesilaus, and then, fixing up some small points, hawked to
> Dionysius, the tyrant of Sicily, and in the third place, deleting
> some things and adding others, tried to pass off on Alexander
> of Thessaly, and finally now he has shot it off in his miserly
> way to you.

Speusippus ends abruptly, in the middle of all his irritations. His letter must have been written sometime in the autumn of 343 BCE, after Artaxerxes III's defeat of Egypt. He would like to write more. There is much more to be said on the subject of Isocrates' inadequacies but he can't. He is out of space and there is no papyrus to be had in Athens since the subjugation of Egypt. Speusippus may have had some particular philosopher in mind but he doesn't say. Nevertheless, his rant is broadly successful, as far as the Academy is concerned – or perhaps it's just that Philip remembers Aristotle from before, from the days when his father was court physician. Either way, the Academy wins out over the rhetorical tradition of Isocrates. Aristotle is chosen as the tutor.

*

So this is the background. This is the world that, as their boat edges up the chilly reaches of the Loudias river in the late autumn of 343 BCE, Aristotle and Theophrastus re-enter. It is a world of growing political tension. Athens, although still officially bound to Macedonia by treaty, is growing discontented and restless. Word arrives that they have sent embassies into the Peloponnese to agitate against Philip. Philip doesn't care. He's secure in his power and the scope of his plans.

Life in Pella has a new rhythm. A city. A capital. Foreign enough in feel, and cosmopolitan, like a hive in its comings and goings. Could any work be done among this constant buzz? News. News arrives all the time. Corinth is wavering in its allegiance. Corinth and Messenia and they say also Achaea have changed sides in favour of Athens. Messengers, letters, envoys, rumour-mongers. Whisper and counter-whisper. Then there is the scrabbling and sliding and head-treading that always happens around power. Who's in, who's out. Who's told what, or invited where, in the slippery pit that is the constant condition for living that power creates.

You must adjust, Theophrastus. You must adjust fast, or be trodden underfoot. You mustn't mind not knowing who your friends are because everyone now is caught up in this tide of self-interest and advancement. Those who flattered you last night will be cold by morning. The sudden withdrawal of favour. Then there are the dinners, the drinking. Macedonian manners seem different. Here excess is manly. The wine goes round the dining room unmixed with water and Philip's appetites are in scale with his ambitions. So it's hard to keep your head, hard to practise industry or moderation, or to keep a sightline on the truth, or the notion of the good life. Is it relevant, the good life – even just as an idea; could it have any purchase here at all?

After a while, perhaps for these reasons, Aristotle and Theophrastus move from Pella to a quieter place, on the edge of the mountains and among woods and streams. It is called Mieza, and it's here, in a complex of caves and buildings around a temple to the Nymphs, that Aristotle is supposed to have taught Alexander and the group of Macedonian nobles who would grow up to be Alexander's companions. I wonder what Theophrastus made of them, these hardy highland boys, down from the mountains, in their russet and cobalt cloaks, with their physical toughness and their terrible table manners and their horsemanship. As well as Alexander there would have been the sons of Philip's Viceroy, Antipater; perhaps also Ptolemy, who was later to govern Egypt, and Harpalus, who was lame, and Hephaestion, Alexander's lifelong lover and soulmate. We have it from Curtius Rufus, a first-century Roman who wrote a history of Alexander the Great, that:

> It was customary for the Macedonian nobility to deliver their grown up sons to their kings for the performance of duties that differed little from the tasks of slaves. They would take turns spending the night on guard at the door of the king's bedchamber, and it was they who brought in his women by an entrance other than that watched by the armed guards. They would also take his horses from the grooms and bring them for him to mount; they were his attendants both on the hunt and in battle, and were highly educated in all the liberal

arts. It was thought a special honour that they were allowed to sit and eat with the king. No one apart from the king himself had the authority to flog them.

This was partly tradition, partly political expediency. It kept the old highland families sweet and it meant that Philip's kingdom kept pace culturally as it expanded territorially.

At first this went very well. Alexander's guard grew up to be, as Curtius Rufus says, 'highly educated in all the liberal arts', so the boys, sitting wrapped in their coloured cloaks, must have been quick and responsive. They were taught philosophy, logic, mathematics. They were taught how to speak and how to formulate argument. Tuition would have been communal, by lecture as well as by formal discussion; that is, by the argument and counter-argument of the tradition that Plato had established – what was known as the 'eristic' tradition, derived from the Greek word 'eris' meaning strife or quarrel. If, as well as all this, Aristotle and Theophrastus spoke about their recent findings, if they discoursed on the anatomy of cuttlefish and the growth of the chicken embryo, if they unrolled their drawings of plants and animals, while the boys leant forward to see the world newly ordered, then this was the first time science was taught as a discipline and Alexander and his guard were the discipline's first ever pupils.

Rumours about the philosophers' school had reached Isocrates as he sat writing his letters. Sitting on Chios, staring irritably in the direction of the mainland, he fidgeted and was dismissive with his servants. Why hadn't he been chosen? What news was there from Pella? How was it going? He kept hearing things that were not at all to his liking. What could he do to undermine the project, to reinstate rhetoric as the prime discipline? In his next unbidden communication to Philip, he included a sycophantic letter to Alexander.

'Since I am writing to your father I thought I should be acting in a strange manner if, when you are in the same region as he, I should fail either to address you or to send you a greeting, or to write you something calculated to convince any reader that I am now not out of my mind through old age and that I do not babble like a fool.' He paid Alexander compliments. 'I hear everyone say of you that you are a friend of mankind, a friend of Athens, and a friend of learning, not foolishly, but in sensible fashion.' And he tried to undermine Aristotle's method of teaching. He put thoughts into his head with invented hearsay. 'As regards systems of philosophy,' Isocrates observed untruthfully, 'they say that while you do not indeed reject eristic, but hold that it is valuable in private discussions, you regard it nevertheless as unsuitable for either those who are leaders of the people or for monarchs; for it is not expedient or becoming that those who regard themselves as superior to all others should themselves dispute with their fellow-citizens or suffer anyone else to contradict them.' In other words, a king must be a king. He mustn't engage in logic-chopping with those born beneath him. No matter, Isocrates closes disingenuously, that Plato's tradition is something, 'I am told, you are not content with, but you choose rather the training which rhetoric gives, which is of use in the practical affairs of everyday life and aids us when we deliberate concerning public affairs.'

Isocrates' plan, if that's what it was, didn't work. According to Plutarch, 'Aristotle was the man Alexander admired in his younger years, and as he said himself, he had no less affection for him than for his own father. From the one he derived the blessing of life, from the other the blessing of a good life.' To Aristotle and Theophrastus, this must have seemed the ideal in practice at last: to shape a future ruler in heroic mould, to train him into a love of truth and justice.

'What makes a king's rule good?' Alexander asked Theophrastus. *When the subjects are obedient to their king and their king acts in accordance with tradition and justice,* Theophrastus answered. And then, elsewhere, he repeated, *You shall feel no self-satisfaction in rule without justice, wealth without prudent management, eloquence without truth in speech, misplaced generosity, education without sound judgement, and beneficence without proper consideration.* These were his absolutes. Both he and Aristotle, perhaps even at this time, wrote books on the education of kings and on kingship in general.

Besides this, it seems that they were still amassing information, still collecting, but now the collecting was of a different kind, no longer plants and living things but laws. They were thinking about government and how it might be done. In the list of Theophrastus' works there are, 'Twenty-four books of Laws distinguished by the letters of the alphabet', 'Ten books of an Epitome of Laws', one treatise on laws, four books of social customs, one book on the best kind of constitution, and one treatise, 'On How States May Best be Governed'. There are also six books on politics, a 'political treatise dealing with important crises' which ran to four books, three books on legislators, and a further two-book treatise called 'Concerning Politics'.

In the list of Aristotle's works, by comparison, there are four books on justice, two on statesmanship, and seven books of laws, three of which are extracts from Plato. There is a book 'on the Constitutions of 158 cities, in general and in particular, democratic, oligarchic, aristocratic and tyrannical'. There are two books of politics, and 'Eight books of a course of Lectures on Politics, like that of Theophrastus'.

By now Callisthenes too was working. He started helping Aristotle to research and compile a catalogue of the victors at the Pythian games. And he was beginning to strike out on his own. Perhaps he would be a historian. He began experimenting with writing a history of Greece.

So it must have been a good balance, life at Mieza – quiet compared with Pella, or quiet enough for concentration, but still at the centre of an emergent power. The philosophers were busy, not just with their teaching and writing and researching, but also absorbing a different set of conditions; life under an active and expansionist tyranny. Both men were pragmatic and sociable. Both believed in experience as a foundation for knowledge – both in its broadest sense and its narrow scientific sense. 'A wise man', Aristotle said, 'would fall in love and take part in politics; furthermore he would marry and reside at a king's court.' Although later on, when he came to divide life into three possible categories – the contemplative, the active, and the pleasure-loving – he was clear that the contemplative life was the one he preferred; the contemplative was the ideal.

Part of the reason things went so well at the outset must have been that, almost as soon as they'd arrived in Macedonia, Philip had left to continue his conquest of Thrace. He would be away for two years, during which Antipater, a hardened soldier and canny diplomat, was left in charge. Antipater was steady. He had authority. He was loyal. He could always be relied on to take the reins. When Philip wanted to get drunk, for instance, according to Athenaeus, he would say, 'Now we may drink, for it is quite sufficient if Antipater is sober.' And once, like a naughty child, 'when he was playing at dice and someone told him Antipater was coming he hesitated a moment and then thrust the board under the couch'. Antipater was a person of substance. He was someone you could talk to, someone who listened and didn't pull weight. He was wise and experienced and discreet. It would have been interesting to talk politics and diplomacy with him. It might even have been possible to exert some kind of influence. He and Aristotle began what was to become a close and lifelong friendship.

Theophrastus, too, was making friends. Harpalus, the lame boy who would grow into a rogue, had an interest in plants. Perhaps Theophrastus took him, halting, up into the mountains to look for specimens. Perhaps he taught him what he knew about their natures, or their cultivation, or their uses in medicine. In time, when he was made satrap of Babylon, Harpalus would remember Theophrastus' teaching. He would try out Mediterranean plants in the Hanging Gardens, and worry about the ivies that didn't like the climate and send strange, unnamed specimens back to Theophrastus with his correspondence.

*

At the centre of all of this, for Aristotle and Theophrastus and Callisthenes, was of course Alexander, the teenager who got up in the mornings with sleep-squashed hair, and who sat listening with the others while the philosophers talked, whose attention sometimes wandered and who nursed his fierce dreams and felt frustration and denied himself small things so as to eliminate weakness. Is there a real boy visible there? Could a person be visible in the blaze and the din of a myth like his?

What did you think of him, Theophrastus? Did you see through the myth? Because even in childhood the myths were already proliferating, like the one about his horse, for instance. For a year or so now, Alexander had been riding the black stallion no one else could approach. The story has been told so often but then it's such a good one – how the horse was first led out, snorting and rearing, onto the Macedonian plains as a present for Philip. How, with the crowds of strangers standing around, it wheeled and kicked its handlers, whirling up dust like a dervish. How everything seemed to sweat anxiety, the horse, the handlers, the watching crowd, while the time passed and the dust rose. Now the handlers, slipping in the sweat, cut it with whips although nothing would subdue the horse, so that Philip had repeatedly to back away. How the crowd held its breath, as the scene turned from tribute to public humiliation. How long before he lost his temper? Someone, do something, quick. Because everyone could feel it, the king's mounting impatience, slighted by a wild animal. What is this you've brought me, you fools? Send it away. Cut its throat. Stop wasting our time.

And how, suddenly, a shadow seemed to flicker on the edge of the picture. Alexander's cloak fluttering silently to the ground as the boy darted out of the crowd, like a blackbird flies with sudden intent, low out of a hedge. Because only the twelve-year-old Alexander, watching the whole thing unravel, was sharp enough to see that the horse was afraid, spooked by its own shadow – Wait! So that Philip in surprise and irritation looked round. What now? Only Alexander was swift enough, slim enough, to get close, cool enough to turn the horse's head into the sun and coax it softly and, then, when it had come to a shivering stand, to leap onto its back and master it in a triumphal canter. That's the story. The horse was Bucephalus, Ox Head in English, which Alexander rode all the way to India, although now, in 342 BCE, it was just a terrifying black stallion that recognized him with a whinny and that he rode daily in the woods around Mieza, out hunting.

I'm trying to see what Theophrastus saw; that little kernel of truths out of which the myth kept growing. The last traces of innocence in Alexander that were just beginning to mix with a consciousness of his position. The poignancy of will, of determination, in a body that is still boyish. His quickness of mind. The smallness of him, and his tendency to walk and talk fast, as if tipping himself onwards into the rush of his own destiny. How fair he was:

> He was of a fair colour, as they say, and his fairness passed
> into ruddiness on his breast particularly, and in his face.
> Moreover, that a very pleasant odour exhaled from his skin
> and that there was a fragrance about his mouth and all his
> flesh, so that his garments were filled with it, this we have
> read in the Memoirs of Aristoxenus.

Plutarch, who wrote that description of Alexander in his *Lives*, could be dismissed – he was writing several centuries after Alexander – if it weren't for the fact that Aristoxenus, his source, was Aristotle's pupil.

What else? His love of glory, not unusual in this modern version of ancient heroic culture, but which was daily evident in his cool risk-taking, his high-strung pride out hunting; how he pushed his body beyond reasonable limit, how he scorned pain. Anyone could see it: his longing for trial, for war, his susceptibility to Homer, to whom Aristotle is supposed to have introduced him. He had a special copy of the *Iliad*, so they say, which Aristotle had made for him. He kept it with him through all his campaigns and, like a schoolchild before a test, he put it under his pillow, in a Persian casket, and slept on it, as if that way Achilles' example might seep into him by night.

And what else? His temper, inherited from his father – Alexander's rage, as an adult, was legendary, as was his cruelty. So those things too must have been part of his unformed, teenage self. *Nothing that is good is easy*, Theophrastus said when someone complained that anger was too difficult to control. *Control of desire is also difficult.* Alexander must have been mesmerizing, as he havered on the edge of manhood, unfinished, and with so much possibility. There was the drama of the choices yet to be taken, of the childish reliance on the teacher, and there was the hope, always the hope, unfolding itself day by day like a flower, that this time, now at last, power will be changed by an idea – the idea of the good life, the life in balance, whose result is wisdom and justice and whose effect radiates from the ruler outwards into the individual lives he governs. The hope that this time Good would root itself so deep that there wouldn't be room for anything else.

In the meantime, these conflicting impulses, in a boy, are attractive, the unruly mix of it: his charismatic, passionate temperament, his struggle for mastery of himself in his yet unrealized manhood, his drive and his interest, and his ability. All of this, and his open admiration for Aristotle, made for a charmed atmosphere at Mieza.

Did you fall under his spell, Theophrastus, I wonder? You were so soft and you had an evident fondness for your students: Callisthenes and, in time to come, Arcesilaus and Nicomachus.

Sitting in English libraries, with the rain sliding down the windows, sifting through book after book for the little fragments left behind, I found a collection of definitions characterizing beauty: Socrates said that beauty is a short-lived reign, Plato that it is a natural superiority, Aristotle that it is a gift of god, and Diogenes that it is a better recommendation than any letter of introduction. What Theophrastus said is, *beauty is a silent deception.* What a weight of disappointment is in that line. It is the most human, the only one to contain emotional experience. He didn't necessarily say it about Alexander. It's just an indication of his susceptibility, of his ability to be disappointed if not hurt.

Inevitably, the atmosphere at Mieza was misleading; the hope and the illusion that they were fashioning a future king, not realizing how easily, in the end, power and drink and evil temper would topple their teachings.

*

Isocrates, although he hadn't been chosen as tutor, had planted a seed in Philip's mind with his harping on about Panhellenism, and by 341, despite the small technicality of the peace treaty, Philip was already thinking of how he could wage national war against his ally, Persia. All of Greece, with him at its head, subjugating the old enemy, that was the plan. And the plan was increasingly apparent. Somehow this found its way to the ears of Hermias, at his little court of Atarneus, near Assos. Someone told him how things stood in Macedonia. He weighed it in his mind. Philip was unstoppable, any fool could see that. His protection would be invaluable if Hermias wanted to hold on to his hard-won territories in Asia Minor, his little kingship. What to do? Perhaps he asked Aristotle's advice. Aristotle was family after all, and Aristotle was at Pella. He had Antipater's ear. He would know. Either way, Hermias decided to go back on his former treaty with the Persians and realign himself. He made a new alliance with Philip, offering his own kingdom as a valuable bridgehead into the east.

News travels fast. Hermias, unthinking in his new security, is invited to parley by Mentor of Rhodes, the Persian satrap. Come, let's talk. We, the controllers of Asia Minor – you with your western territories and I, representing Persia, on the eastern coast – we should work together. We'll meet at Atarneus, on your own ground. Mentor is a terrifying man, a Greek mercenary, a trickster whose methods of bribery and division worked so well in Egypt that Artaxerxes put him in charge of all Persia's holdings in Asia Minor. Hermias trusts Philip, or else he doesn't think. He isn't concentrating. He takes the message at face value; it is in his own territory after all, and he walks right into the trap.

Mentor, even as a guest, threatens him in his own palace, demanding to know about Philip's plans. When Hermias refuses to talk, he is taken prisoner, smuggled out in chains and bundled unceremoniously into a cart, day after day, night after night, rattled to his bones. Where are we? I'm thirsty. For god's sake, give me something to drink. Anything. But by now, he thinks, the news of his abduction must be out and Philip will hear. He will help. Any day now, he hopes, they will be outpaced. The Macedonian army will come tearing down the coast, slashing itself a passage with its famous sarissas, and set him free. In the back of the cart, he listens to the silence of the road. Nothing. Surely Philip is on his way. He is probably nearer than I think. I just have to hold out another day. Another two days.

He is taken deep into Persian territory, to Suza, in the foothills of the Zagros Mountains, among the foreign rocks and the dust and the vultures that wheel over the alien fortifications. Now, he is told, now you will talk. There is no one to protect him. Help hasn't come. He doesn't talk, and he doesn't talk, and still, he doesn't talk. The Persians torture him. Everyone knows it's happening. In Athens, Demosthenes hopes very much he will weaken. He hopes very much that Hermias will crack, that he will spill all the details of Philip's planned campaign and then Athens will be able to step in. The alliance with Persia that Demosthenes so desperately wants for Athens will at last become a reality.

But Hermias doesn't give in. He is crucified, but before he dies he is given the grace of one last request. 'Tell my friends and companions that I have done nothing weak or unworthy of philosophy.' The teachings of Plato and Aristotle, the notion of the good life, have taken a deep and tragic hold.

When the news reaches him, at Mieza, Aristotle is devastated. Is it partly his fault? Or not? He can't dismiss the horror that he might in some way be implicated. Philip's complete uninterest is hard to forgive. He just shrugged Hermias off. Not worth the effort of saving. Aristotle writes a hymn to virtue, to that lovely goddess, whose cult he paints as too wearisome for most, too demanding for any but the most heroic to follow. Achilles and Ajax and Hermias of Atarneus – they, alone, are brave enough. Follow her if you can, he enjoins the reader, with eyes full of tears. Your reward will be courage, 'imperishable courage, better than gold, more dear than parents or soft-eyed sleep'. Hermias' fame will live forever, or so his hymn maintains. It is published wide among the Greek-speaking world. A passionate cry of mourning for his friend and kinsman. Then he writes an epigram to be carved on a dedicatory tomb at Delphi: 'This man in violation of the hallowed law of the immortals was unrighteously slain by the king of the bow-bearing Persians, who overcame him, not openly with a spear in murderous combat, but by treachery with the aid of one in whom he trusted.'

In Athens, Hermias' death was greeted as good news. He was a nothing. Demosthenes and those of Isocrates' school, Theopompus and Theocritus of Chios, for instance – perhaps still smarting over Philip's choice of Aristotle as tutor – publicly blacken Hermias' character and criticize Aristotle. What was Aristotle even thinking of, choosing the court of Philip and his allies over Athens and its Academy?

'To Hermias the Eunuch, slave of Eubulus, this empty tomb was raised by the empty-minded Aristotle, who respecting the lawless nature of his belly chose to dwell at the mouth of the muddy Borborus instead of in the Academy,' so Theocritus wrote.

*

Now what? Athens, which has become increasingly and openly hostile, has been raiding Macedonian-held cities on the disputed Thracian coast and extorting duty from the merchant ships up and down the Hellespont. Someone has caught and tortured a Macedonian envoy. When they've finished, as a final insult, they ransom him back to Philip for the sum of nine talents. In the autumn of 341 BCE, in retaliation, Philip seizes a convoy of 230 merchant ships carrying grain from the Black Sea, which have gathered in the Bosphorus under the armed guard of Athenian triremes. Those ships that belong to neutral states, fifty in all, are released. The rest are taken to the Macedonian shipyards. The grain is sequestered. Some say the ships are broken up to make siege engines for Philip's campaign against the city of Perinthos. Philip sends a moderate letter to the Athenian council justifying himself and saying he will send the triremes back.

> Philip, King of Macedonia, to the Council and People of Athens, greetings.
>
> —Your ambassadors, Cephisophon and Democritus and Polycritus, visited me and discussed the release of the vessels commanded by Leodamas. Now, speaking generally, it seems to me that you will be very simple people if you imagine that I do not know that the vessels were sent ostensibly to convey corn from the Hellespont to Lemnos, but really to help the Selymbrians, who are being besieged by me and are not included in the articles of friendship mutually agreed upon between us.
>
> These instructions were given to the admiral, without the knowledge or agreement of the Athenian People, by certain officials… who were anxious by every means in their power

> to change the present friendly attitude of the people towards
> me to one of open hostility… They think that such a policy
> will be a source of income to themselves; it does not, however,
> strike me as profitable either for you or for me. Therefore the
> vessels now in my harbours I hereby release to you; and for
> the future, if, instead of permitting your statesmen to pursue
> this malicious policy, you will be good enough to censure
> them, I too will endeavour to preserve the peace. Farewell.

But whether he means it or not, Athens is too far gone. By the end of the year, the Athenians are drumming up support from their allies and openly gearing themselves for war with Macedonia. Now, if Aristotle and Theophrastus feel unhappy, no longer comfortable at Pella after Philip's betrayal of Hermias, it is too late. They fear they'll be unwelcome in Athens. This is particularly sad for Theophrastus. He loves Athens, the city of his ambitious teenage choice, the place that gave him Aristotle. How have they found themselves here, at the court of a coarse and brutal tyrant? *Sometimes,* Theophrastus says, trying to comfort himself, *sometimes it is necessary to resort to evil people for mutual benefit, just as the sandalwood tree and snakes benefit each other. The snakes profit from the fragrance and coolness of the tree which, in turn, protects the tree from being felled.*

There is a pragmatism about Aristotle and Theophrastus' thinking. Philosophy if it is to do good must operate in the world. Ethics are only really revealed in action, and action necessarily belongs in the world. So ethics must be contextualized; there is always the particularity of circumstance to consider. Statements about behaviour that are particularized are truer than statements that are general, Aristotle insists, 'since conduct has to do with individual cases… our statements must harmonise with the facts in these cases'. Yes, you can separate ends and means, they say to each other, but the important thing here, the thing as far as education is concerned, is that 'the character which a man acquires by acting is formed by the kind of ends which he habitually proposes to himself as desirable'. That's the task; to make sure of the attractiveness of good as an end. With time, that ought to bleed back into the means.

Maybe this was harder for Theophrastus to hold as a principle. His world is more conflicted, more fickle and more compromised than Aristotle allows, and the means, after all, are the things that constantly pertain, the immediate, human conditions. The means are all around him all the time and the ends are just some as yet unrealized, improbable, ideal future.

In fact, if he puts his mind to it, there is much for Theophrastus to dislike about Macedonian court life. The atmosphere under the sophisticated Hellenic veneer is brutal, a culture of hunting and drinking – and with the drinking comes the loosening of whatever controls there might be, the only half-remembered grabbing of pleasure, the shock-eyed serving girls scrabbling themselves back together in the palace passages. Keep your mouth shut if you want to keep your position. Because any foothold you have in court life is bound to be slippery. Those who are excluded, like the pupils of Isocrates, are bitter. They take a truth and spin it into slander and that can be tainting even if inaccurate. Philip, so Theopompus says, doesn't care if he's seen drunk in the daytime. His appetites are those of a beast. Anything goes. There's no constancy. His attendants and companions partner each other without preference, fornicating like whores. The partial truths rub like pieces of grit.

Then there's Alexander's mother, Olympias, a woman who looks capable of murder. Wild, power-hungry, suspicious, manipulative, and dedicated to the mystery cult of Dionysus. She's a snake charmer, so they say, liable to extravagant displays of possession by the god. By Plutarch's account:

> [She] affected these divine possessions more zealously than other women and carried out these divine inspirations in wilder fashion. She used to provide the revelling companies with great tame serpents, which would often lift their heads from out of the ivy and the mystic winnowing-baskets, or coil themselves about the wands and garlands of the women to the terror of the men.

The great pyres of animals that these orgiastic ceremonies involved. The blood of these endless sacrifices. And the women out of their minds. And the partial secrecy and the wild music. And the terrified animals dragged along. And the blood. The blood. *Whereas others sacrifice tens and hundreds of animals, Olympias sacrifices them by the thousand or ten thousand.* This, ever since his researches into animal life on Lesbos, is offensive to Theophrastus. He doesn't even eat meat.

> *Animals are akin and related to men in physical makeup but more importantly in the makeup of their souls... there is no natural basis for making distinctions among the souls of humans and animals. I have in mind that animals are subject to desire and anger, and further, in the ways in which they reason, and most of all in the ways in which they all perceive things... the kinship of their passions.*

Animals are too like humans. Even if they weren't, killing them is unjust. Most of the animals we sacrifice, or eat, Theophrastus thinks, are beneficial to humankind. Killing them shows ingratitude and gives back to the gods the gift of lives which are not, in the first place, ours to give. He must have looked on Olympias with something like revulsion; a cruel and superstitious woman, neither of which were qualities he found easy to forgive.

In the end, he didn't have long to wait. At sixteen, Alexander's education was over. When Philip set off again, this time to lay siege to Byzantium, he left Alexander in charge. No sooner was Philip's back turned than there was a rebellion in Thrace and the tribal lords looked like breaking free of Philip's careful annexation. Alexander had to make his own decisions. He took command, rode off on Bucephalus into battle, at the head of his own army, and put the rebellion down.

After the triumph, there was no going back. His course was set. The woods and groves at Mieza, empty of Alexander and his companions, went back to being quiet places of no significance. Aristotle's job was done. Presumably, they were free to go, if they wanted to. Alexander and his companions weren't listening any more. They were intoxicated with their first military victory, with Alexander's astonishing skill and daring in the field of battle. Nothing could stop them. They were men now. They had better things to think about. Callisthenes, among them, caught the fever. What might Alexander not do? Great things were ahead and he would need a historian. I will write the history of your campaigns, he offered, and Alexander was flattered. I will be your historian. If Aristotle and Theophrastus were anxious to leave, here was the chance to cut his own swathe. He chose to stay.

But where could Aristotle and Theophrastus go? Athens was so hostile to everything Macedonian, it would be unsafe. Hermias was dead. Lesbos would have been possible but if they believed in their remaining centrality to Philip and Alexander it was too far. Besides, it would be a backwards step, a life of much reduced influence or political involvement. Aristotle had property of his own – he might have gone to where his mother came from, to Chalcis on Euboea, where he had a house. But Chalcis was perhaps *too* close to Athens. Or he might have gone nearby, to Stagira, to his father's house. The estate was ready and waiting for him and according to Diogenes Laertius (the author of the *Lives of Eminent Philosophers*), Aristotle had written a new constitution for its people. From there, he would be able to write, to research, to correspond with Antipater and Alexander and Philip. If he had any purpose in the new order, he would still be in reach. There are, among the list of his writings, nine books of letters to Antipater, a book each of letters to Hephaestion and Olympias and four books of letters to Alexander, so he must still have been exerting influence, although his ability to shape Alexander for the good of his future subjects, at close quarters, was over.

And you, Theophrastus? What about you? Did you go your own way, or did you stay with Aristotle? Here the evidence runs out. History doesn't record his choice. Like a man walking off by himself, quiet, down a road, Theophrastus passes out of my sight; his back, his shoulders, the tilt of his head – carrying all his private thoughts, all his hopes and opinions and secret misgivings – narrow into the horizon and are gone from view.

All of this is history. By which I mean that it's just the things that happened between this date and that, told less as the discipline of History demands and more as history's two syllables suggest – the whole sequence of events nothing more than a story. But history, however it's told, isn't the same thing as a living person – if a person is what you are trying to find. Nevertheless, there is a feeling, sometimes, that if it could be established, if it could be made solid enough, history might work as a backdrop, against which something more shimmering, like a person, might be thrown into visible relief.

Only it doesn't work. The backdrop resists solidity. The events it is made up of are always constructed retrospectively, by other people, all of whom have a position or a purpose or a bias of some kind. If you stitch them together, you get something that wavers, more like a mirage than a backdrop, something complex, something shifting and many-angled, shot through with uncertainty. History is necessarily backward-looking and this is another truth that the Orpheus myth has at its heart: as soon as you look back, the past disappears. It becomes too uncertain to take solid form. It's made of too many memories, some of them false, too many opinions, too many wishes and regrets, too many different perspectives, to be fixable in three dimensions.

In other words, we are back with the problem of time and its effects: its blurring and softening, its numbing, its forgetting. As I said before, it's not an easy thing to move through, or to see through. Its depth is this great accumulated mass of small differences, each one of which is a minute displacement from the beginning. There are differences of detail, of view or of memory, and differences of conditions or customs or agenda. There are differences in material things, such as food, or dress, or roads, or light, or buildings; or in mental things, like structures of belief or knowledge, or patterns of speech. And all of these differences slowly accumulate, gathering weight and mass and shifting the perspective, until life there, wherever it might be, becomes too removed to imagine because the angle of refraction has got too wide, and the distance between then and now is simply too great. That's how we've come to think of time in terms of distance and why we talk about 'time travel'; because this great weight and quantity of time must be passed through, or somehow crossed, if we are ever to reach the people we've lost in it.

Once, in the incubation time of adolescence, I woke up in the dark aware of someone looking at me very intently. It was less than a second, so it was more an impression I had, rather than the actual sight, of dark Victorian looks – the hair, the eyes, the unnerving focus. At the time, I associated it with the vicar who had lived there a hundred years before us and had planted the trees in the garden, and two of whose children had died in the house. As I came to consciousness, the face telescoped away from me, as if vanishing down a tunnel, from face to pinprick, and then extinguished in silence that was somehow so vivid as to be audible. It seemed as though the length of its dwindling and vanishing was spatial, like a path that one might get up and follow. That is how far it is, I thought, from here to 1860. If, rationally, I didn't believe in the vision, still it was odd enough to think about, and it had happened (if it had happened) not in sleep but with my eyes open. It left me with the idea that, perhaps, while we spend all our time peering backwards, trying to look at the past, the past can see us very clearly indeed – that it either chooses not to be, or simply can't be, seen directly in return. Or maybe just that, to those who are living and therefore still caught in its actuality, time is blinding.

Theophrastus, who is human enough to have suffered life, is no help with time, although he agrees with me that it's a medium in which to drown. *An intelligent person ought to deal with time as gently as a non-swimmer who has fallen into a flowing stream deals with the water.*

Aristotle has no such difficulty. His response is calmer, more apparently controlled. Does time actually exist, or not, he asks himself, swatting at it with logic, like you might deal with a troublesome bluebottle.

'One part of it has been and is not,' he reasons, 'while the other part is going to be and is not yet. But time, both infinite time and any other time you like to take, is made up of these two things. One would naturally suppose that what is made up of things which do not exist could have no share in reality.' This is the world of *Alice in Wonderland*: jam yesterday, jam tomorrow, but never jam today. It's a brave try, but despite his logic, Aristotle is, of course, susceptible to the reality of time, as everyone is. His logic does not help with the actuality of time's undertow, either in the individual life or in dealing with the accumulated weight of the past. The experience of life, in the living, is of time's pull as something constant, one-directional and irreversible.

But if time can't be argued away, then maybe it can, as Theophrastus suggests, be dealt with as if it's just another of the world's forces. Maybe it can be harnessed, or cheated, or negotiated in some way, like you might manage water or wind or fire. Maybe it's possible, once we know its effect, to adjust or recalibrate our time-blinded sight. There are tricks to employ, after all. There is Orpheus' music to take us back. There are plays and poems, as true now as they were then, and there's memory, as Proust points out, at the service of our senses of taste and smell. There are also inventions like cameras, for instance, whose images are the result of calculated exposure, which means that they are both a measurement and a picture of time. If you stand in a darkroom and watch your photograph arrive, as its darks and lights float to the paper's surface in the developing bath, you are replaying time, or watching it run backwards.

What if, I would say to Theophrastus, while I wait for him to come back into view, what if you could go on past the image, through all the possible images before – what if, in that case, sitting among the audience at Epidaurus, waiting for a play to begin, I took a photograph, while it is still light, as it would have been 2,300 years ago? What if, developing it, I could hold the paper in the solution so long that the resulting image came from further back? Back and back and back until it found you, sitting as I am in the audience, preparing for Agamemnon to step down again onto the fateful purple cloths, so that, in terms of the story, the time between when his family's first crime was committed and his foot's hesitating descent, could be somehow recalibrated by revenge. Because that's what revenge is: its legacy of anger, passed from one generation to the next, is a foot jammed in a closing door, a refusal to allow time to pass without redress. That, if such a photograph were actually possible, would be a double sidestepping, a double managing of time.

It seems to me that, in order to negotiate time, you first have to acknowledge it. You have to allow it to be there, interposing itself between you and whatever, or whoever, you might be trying to reach, before you can cross it alive in either direction, whether forwards or back. Again, it is photography that provides the most useful example.

Aristotle and Theophrastus drew up a hierarchy of the five senses, and sight they considered to be at the top, by which they meant the most reliable. We still say, 'I can't believe my eyes' on the assumption that what we see is correct, however hard it may be to believe. We still trust our eyes more than any other faculty, so the photograph, as visual evidence, has the status of enshrined truth. The camera never lies, we tell ourselves, although this is only half the story. Photographs can be deceptive. Or rather, they can be both true and not true at the same time.

Look at the first picture ever taken with a person in it. It is of a street in Paris, taken by Louis Daguerre, in 1838. It is strange and very beautiful and it has much to say about our trust in the photograph and much to say about the nature of time and its texture; its necessary relation to life.

At first glance, the picture seems very still, very quiet, lost in its odd mixture of sharp shadows and the fuzz of light at its vanishing point. What time was it taken? Judging by the shadows, early afternoon. Judging by the tall, densely packed buildings, with their many chimneys and their facades softened by use (and presuming you did not know it was Paris), you would say this was a town or city of some age and size, a place where many people must live. But where are they? The street is so deserted. Only two men are in it, one standing offering his foot to the other, and the other cleaning the proffered shoe. The scene is desolate – so desolate, so odd that when I first saw this picture I couldn't forget it. I thought about it all the time, its apparent stillness, its otherworldliness.

The picture is a lie. Perhaps that's why it is so compelling. When Louis Daguerre put down his camera with the copper-plate ready for the light to draw on, the street would have been one continuous stream of people. The light took time to make its picture, about a minute and a half, so whatever didn't stand still would have left no trace of its passing. Only the shoeshine boy and his customer were still for long enough for their image to transfer. Everyone else hurried past. They had things to do and time, as it always is, was in short supply.

So, although the picture, as evidence, is factually inaccurate, it is a truer representation of life than the one we would have seen with our own eyes, had we been walking that street in Paris in 1838. People pass and fall away, and are forgotten. Nothing lasts. It is the absence of those present people that fascinates me, looking at that picture: all the hundreds of people in their stiff and complicated old-fashioned clothes, with their stiff and complicated old-fashioned manners, who are there but not there, who passed the camera, invisible, caught in the thickness of time's unceasing flow.

Words as a medium work less well. It's harder for them to do two things at once. This has long been the ghost-raiser's problem. 'Why should the biographer be limited to one kind of narrative voice, one kind of discursive prose?' Richard Holmes, who is one, asks, restlessly fitting his research into models more fluid than history or straight biography. Because sometimes the conscientious telling of the events of a man's life, and the happenings of history, will make only the flat and cautious and vitally inaccurate picture of a background. It will present the life as a noun rather than bringing it back as a verb. It will take a faithful picture of the empty street where he passed. So there must be another way.

There is, of course. There are 'many different ways in which a "true story" can be told', to go back to Holmes. There is the reanimating of the past that the imagination can effect: the historical novel. So perhaps imagination is the answer – by which I don't mean just making things up. Imagination is a word that seems to degrade every few decades. We need a Coleridge or a Hughes to remind us of what it really is: the slipping of the self for something else, a way to cross divides, whether of time, or kind, or type, so as to experience something under other constraints, other conditions. Because imagination, with its shape-shifting nature, can do that. It has the power to animate research.

But if history flattens, then imagination is too close up. The imagination can bring the conditions of a bygone time vividly and immediately to life but it is too quick to cross over from this shore to that; it flashes over the gap between now and then as if it didn't exist. It doesn't tell you how dizzyingly far back those conditions are, nor how impossible the journey. If you travel to a distant country, not in the eye-blink of an aeroplane but over the earth's slow and difficult surface, you have a different understanding of the quality of that place on arrival. To bring a person not just into view but to life you need to feel, at the same time, both the immediacy of the person's reality and the pressure of the field of passed time, the time to which they belong, holding you away. It isn't possible to know what a bird or a fish is just from looking at a photograph. To really know the truth of its wild self, its essence, you need to see it in its element – to watch it mastering air or managing water. For humans, time is necessary not just because it's part of the context but because it *is* the context.

The jolt that passes through me, every time I look at Daguerre's picture and see the absent throng, is the closest I can imagine to capturing the texture of time itself; the solidity of that absent presence that my mind feels and my eyes deny. Daguerre thought he was photographing a street but what he was actually photographing was time.

Time is our element. It is where we live. It is the stuff that mists our eyes and fills up our minds. The atmosphere of our lives and clothes and thoughts and customs is soaked in it. You absolutely can't ignore it, either as a condition, or as a kind of topographical placement, a location. The feeling of looking back through it for someone like Theophrastus is that of a constant, uncrossable thickness, like an anti-magnetic field, a pressure of dark impassability. If you really want to see him, you have to press your imagination up against that force field. You have to feel the past's resistance to the present build and build until suddenly, in some thought or turn of phrase, like a flash of lightning rooting itself in the ground, Theophrastus will leap the divide. Just for a split second, there he will really be, with all the strangeness and brilliance of how he was in his own time, intact.

IV

The Works

With Theophrastus lost to view, what is left? Just these small green books, where I started, the black and white key pattern around their edges like an old-fashioned picture frame, and the thin paper of their face-to-face pages: English on one side and the glamour of Greek script on the other. These are what have survived, so I leave Greece behind. I return to England, to my books and to libraries. I'm going to look for you there, Theophrastus. Text is a place after all, where we encounter others as real as ourselves. I've met Chekhov in his letters. I've met Lady Macbeth and Okonkwo and Don Quixote and Beloved and Irimiás, and Baba Yaga and the Raven who created the human race out of boredom, and many, many others.

Didn't Aristotle say that active thought was 'essentially actuality'? The persuasive solidity of our structures of thought or imagination, the autonomy of the created thing, these have their own life separate from ours. These are children of the brain and, unlike their author, they persist. In the little green books that I have in my hands, I've seen Theophrastus' shadow moving, like God, behind the mesh of his words. So I know he's there.

Theophrastus wrote so much, and so little of it has survived. But, sometimes, reading through what we still have, there are things – details, images, observations of experience – that are the same now as they were then. The feeling, when you come across one of these, in all that roiling mass of obscurity, is a kind of vertiginous falling into recognition. It takes your breath away. A brief immediate view that pitches you straight into fourth-century Athens as if it were today. So this is another way to drag Theophrastus forwards, or ourselves backwards – a patient, forensic sifting through material to find these little lucent scraps of reality, which might be patched or glued together to make a whole, or just dropped individually, like the markers in fairy tales, so as to light our way back, or light his way forward. There is something fitting about this. It's his own technique after all, this sifting and amassing. You taught me this, Theophrastus, so that's what I will do.

There are lists of the philosophers' works included in Diogenes Laertius' biographical sketches. Aristotle, as expected, is more prolific than Theophrastus, but there are huge areas of shared interest and overlap: the books on animals and plants, for instance, or the books on law or governance, or the traditional preoccupation with logic or mathematics or motion. There are, in both lists, frightening-looking books on dialectical questioning, books called Prior Analytics and Posterior Analytics, books of 'methodics', books of problems and logical divisions, books of syllogisms and definitions, as well as quirkier books on things like love or friendship or the generation of storms. There are books that look like conversations between the two of them: 'eight books of a course of lectures on Politics like that of Theophrastus', or one book 'Of Pleasure according to Aristotle'. In Theophrastus' list, there are six books of 'Lecture Notes either of Theophrastus or Aristotle'.

Both lists are astonishingly wide-ranging. In Aristotle's case the output is, in general, weighty, serious, and both abstract and scientific. It isn't that Theophrastus is frivolous but there is an appetite for life as it is experienced, rather than just for its laws or mechanisms; an eye for the oddness, the variety and whimsicality of forms, or processes, that is irresistible. Here he is. Here is some of the colour and energy of that marvelling mind.

He wrote many books on philosophy: ten on analytics, two on first principles, one on syllogisms. He addressed the philosophy of his Greek antecedents: two books on Anaxagoras, one on Anaximenes, one on Archelaus, one on Democritus, one on Empedocles. He wrote commentaries on both Aristotle and Plato.

He wrote on strange and varied subjects, including: Salt, Nitre and Alum; putrefaction; indivisible lines; the virtues; kingly power; Juices, Complexions and Flesh; Coagulation and Liquefaction; Crimes; Forensic Speeches; Tumult or Riot; Old Age; A Description of the World; and Images and Phantoms, so perhaps he too saw visions. He wrote two treatises on Love. I hope he was happy. He wrote a book on Pleasure and one on Happiness, so perhaps he was.

He wrote one book on Epilepsy; one on Enthusiasm; one on Sudden Appearances; one on the Different Voices of Similar Animals; on Animals that Bite or Sting; Animals that Exhibit Jealousy; Animals Reputed to be Spiteful; and Animals Produced Spontaneously. He wrote seven General Books on Animals, as well as books on Land Animals, Animals that Live in Holes, and Animals that Change Colour. He wrote books on Hot and Cold, Giddiness and Vertigo, and Sudden Dimness of Sight. He wrote on Sweating, on Working, on Illness, on Fainting Fits, on Melancholy, on Solecisms. He wrote on Honey, on Drunkenness, on the Sea, on Suffocation, on Punishment, on Mental Derangement, Acting, Music, and Hair. He wrote on Tyranny, Water, Sleep and Dreams, and Aberration of Intellect; on Smells, on Wine and Oil, and on Astronomy – at least six books.

He wrote at least twenty-four books on Law. He wrote on the Constitution, on Politics. He wrote thirty-four books on Various Aspects of Natural Philosophy – possibly more. He wrote a History of Arithmetic. He wrote two books of Afternoon Essays – I would very much like to know what they were. There were books of lecture notes and books of collected letters written to Phanias, Nicanor, Astycreon. The list isn't finished but it's hard to go on. There is just so much and it's almost all of it lost.

So, besides the books on plants and the notes on metaphysics, what is left? There is a book of character sketches. Otherwise, there are snippets recorded in the writings of others; snippets that have sometimes been so heavily colonized to fit the copyist's own agenda that it's hard to tell how much is Theophrastus and how much not.

A particular case in point is something that became known as the 'Golden Book of Marriage'. Jankyn the Clerk, the Wife of Bath's fifth husband in the *Canterbury Tales,* carries this around with him wherever he goes – as part of his favourite anthology, called *Wikked Wyves.* The anthology is fictional but the extract that Chaucer quotes from it is an actual passage he found in Book One of St Jerome's treatise *Against Jovinianus,* itself extracted, according to St Jerome, from 'a book of marriage, worth its weight in gold that passes under the name of Theophrastus'. There is no mention of the 'Golden Book of Marriage', or anything similar, in Diogenes Laertius' list of Theophrastus' works. There are books on love, a book on the passions, several books on pleasure, and one book on 'Problems in Politics, Ethics, Philosophy and in the Art of Love', but nothing at all on marriage. All we have is Theophrastus' reported dictum that a man should treat his wife in a fine and loving way.

St Jerome's extract starts with the practical considerations that Theophrastus seemingly thinks necessary for marriage to work. Here they are: *the wife must be fair, of good character and honest parentage, the husband healthy and well off.* Under these conditions, marriage would be possible. But, he continues:

> *… all these criteria are seldom filled in marriage. Therefore a wise man should not take a wife. If he does, his study of philosophy will be hindered. It is impossible for anyone to pay attention both to his books and to his wife. Matrons want many things, costly dresses, gold, jewels, great amounts of money spending, maid-servants, all kinds of furniture, litters*

and gilded coaches. Then all night long come the curtain-lectures. She complains that one lady goes out better dressed than she does, that everyone admires another: 'I am a poor despised nobody at the ladies' assemblies'; 'Why did you ogle that creature next door?'; 'Why were you talking to the maid?'; 'What did you bring from the market?'

I've been listening so hard, down the years, trying to hear this voice. But are these really your words – did you say this, Theophrastus?

Observe that as far as wives go you cannot pick and choose. You must take her as you find her. If she has a bad temper, or is a fool, if she has a blemish, or is proud, or has bad breath, whatever her fault may be – all this we learn after marriage. Horses, asses, cattle, even slaves of the smallest worth, clothes, kettles, wooden seats, cups, and earthenware pitchers are first tried and then bought. A wife is the only thing that is not tested before she is married, for fear she may not give satisfaction.

Our gaze must always be directed to her face, and we must always praise her beauty. If you look at another woman, she thinks she is out of favour. She must be called my lady. Her birthday must be kept. We must swear by her health and wish that she may survive us. Respect must be paid to the nurse, to the nursemaid, to the father's slave, to the foster-child, to the handsome hanger-on, to the fancy man who manages her affairs, and to the eunuch who ministers to the safe indulgence of her lust.

Or if she be a good and agreeable wife (how rare a bird that is) we have to share her groans in childbirth and suffer torment when she is in danger.

> *A wise man is never alone. He has with him the good men*
> *of all time, and turns his mind freely wherever he chooses.*
> *What he can't reach in person he can embrace in thought. And*
> *if men are scarce, he converses with God. He is never less alone*
> *than when alone.*

Again, are these your words? How many of them are your actual words?

Scrabbling around to try to find the comfort I'm looking for – that most of them might not be – there are one or two things to take into consideration. Eunuchs, for instance, certainly existed in Asia Minor in Theophrastus' time but they don't seem to have been routinely present, if present at all, in Greek households.

The second thing to consider is the tone of the passage, most particularly its horror of female sexuality. This feels Early Christian rather than Greek. Sex was written into the Ancient Greek religion. It is everywhere exuberantly present, in the statuary, in the mythology, in the pottery. Theophrastus, like Aristotle, thought moderation was important – nothing in excess – but there is something in the atmosphere of the passage that doesn't ring true to Theophrastus' time. For a start, there was no specific word for lust in Ancient Greek. There were three words for desire, each characterized as a deity: Pothos, Himeros and Eros. It seems in some versions of the myths that these were the children of Zephyrus, the west wind already mentioned; the wind that brings the life-giving rain and that – with his wife Chloris, the green push of spring – is responsible for growth. That puts human desire nicely on a level with all growing things and so makes it unlikely that there was any attendant moralizing. Certainly it doesn't, in any of its three iterations, carry the weight of Deadly Sin that the little word 'lust' has to shoulder. So perhaps some of these were your words but they were lifted from their original context and set up in the harsh light of Jerome's version of Christianity, in support of another agenda. Taken out of context, recast a little, what we say quickly becomes open to colonization by other, later ideologies. We know this now. We do it in our newspapers all the time.

But there are things I do recognize, I have to admit. I recognize the humour, the detail and the sharpness of its observation. I recognize the use of direct speech. I recognize the dedication to work, the practicality of not wanting to be distracted, and I recognize too the sensitivity to the pain of others, of not wanting the torment of a life dependent on some other precious person's wellbeing – the fear for the beloved, sick or labouring in childbirth, or just the responsibility for her, thwarted or unhappy, or in the wrong place. I recognize the drive, the commitment to his own inner life. *There may be in some neighbouring city the wisest of teachers; but if we have a wife we can neither leave her behind, nor take the burden with us.* Theophrastus must often have watched Aristotle pack up his household to move on, even though he himself never married. Added to which, there is a clause in Aristotle's will that suggests marriage was something Theophrastus actively didn't want, the tact in Aristotle's bequest suggesting that he knew this. He is making provision for his own mistress, Herpyllis, and her children. He recommends that his nephew Nicanor might take them into his household and later marry the daughter when she comes of age, but he then tosses it all up in the air, adding almost as an aside, 'if Theophrastus is willing to live with her, he shall have the same rights as Nicanor', that is to say, he could eventually marry Aristotle's own daughter. Twice Aristotle says this, 'if he is willing', 'if he consent and if circumstances permit', as though Theophrastus was known to be reluctant. Perhaps this is where Jerome's distortion started.

But there are many things I don't recognize in Jerome's extract. And I'm suspicious because it is, after all, Jerome who has written it down and Jerome has his own demons to contend with on this topic.

If it were possible to imagine away the whole gargantuan foundation of western culture that is Christianity, if it were possible to go back to a place where Christianity was unfamiliar – a burgeoning cult just beginning to flex its muscles – then Jerome's story would go something like this. He was Illyrian, which would now be called Balkan. He was born in about 347 CE and sometime between the ages of 13 and 19 he went to Rome to finish his education. In the great city, first he discovered women and wine, and then he discovered Christianity – but it was Christianity that grabbed him.

How would it look, if you came across it as a new idea in the freshness of its beginnings, as Jerome did, from a long-established polytheistic culture? Because when Jerome arrived in Rome it would have been as a believer in a set of gods probably similar to, if not directly inherited from, the Greek ones known to Theophrastus. These were amoral gods, whimsically powerful and with little or no particular interest in mankind, beyond occasional favouritism or the diversion of seduction. So, when Jerome first came across the idea of Jesus – a god who is actually human, in whose life and suffering the whole story of God's purpose for man played out – just the drama of it alone must have been astonishing, a drama in which everything turned around mankind. And it was more precise and more mysterious than that because it had not just mankind but each individual human at its very centre. For each one of us there was at last a role, a path, a set of things to fight against and a set of things to become. It fitted our inbuilt susceptibilities – the idea of personal progress, the dream of betterment. We have such a need to believe in our own significance. And if that wasn't enough to turn you, there was the added weight of a debt of blood that is our birthright. If a man has died to set you free, you are involved whether you like it or not. Jerome looked about him. The whole thing was strange and intoxicating. This was Rome, where Peter the disciple came, where he established the Catholic Church, here, in this city. It was all documented. He trod these very stones. Christ's disciple.

And at the same time it was still new, this religion, still in its infancy. There was room for a capable man to make his own contribution. It was an invitation to new thought, new systems, new practices because, with the arrival of Christianity, the central question had changed. It was no longer what is the world, and how did it come to be, but how should we live in it? How treat each other?

Here is where the story darkens. Enter the Devil. If you were an early Christian, the Devil was your familiar deity. God was difficult of access, unimaginable, nebulous, elsewhere. It was the Devil who walked the earth, like the ancient gods, always at your side, always whispering temptation in your ear, always showing you things you never wanted to see but which now you can't, for the love of God, shake out of your mind. This was how it was for Jerome. Almost overnight, life became impossible. Everything he wanted was suddenly wrong. Who could be to blame for this new horror called Sin, and why was it so fatally tempting? How had the world changed from something neutral to something set against us, like a sprung trap? The early fathers looked around, wild-eyed. It must be someone's fault. What about those people over there?

Which ones?

Those ones. Those swathed bodies that breathed like the moon and that out of their intoxicating, terrifying, hideous insides mysteriously produced life, as if they too were gods. What about Women?

Women were to blame. That was the answer. Because they were tempting. Incomprehensible. Powerful and vulnerable, and irritating and fascinating. They were the originators of evil. There were stories to prove it – just look at Eve.

Jerome was very susceptible to women. When he converted to Christianity he absorbed the fact that, as the early church had laid it out, to live a good life you had to be disciplined, chaste, temperate. Perhaps he couldn't. The luxury of guilt had got him by the throat. He was addicted to it, tormenting himself with his own sinfulness after each irresistible encounter. After a Roman night out he would go down to the crypts and catacombs and there he would grope his way, alone in the pitch dark, weeping and shuddering among the mouldering bodies of the saints. He was going to Hell. He was sure of it.

Death held a morbid fascination for Jerome; death and pain and sin and suffering. After a spell abroad, living in caves in the desert, completing his education and confirming his Christianity, Jerome settled back in Rome, took some kind of office in the Church and began writing. His main focus was how such a thing as a woman could live a Christian life. A little coterie of self-punishing Roman ladies began to gather around him. He wrote open letters, in which he encouraged them to become consecrated virgins. He must have had great appeal because he had quite a following.

Among his followers was an immensely rich widow called Paula. When she was in the first sharp misery of her bereavement, casting around for comfort and support, she came across Jerome. She became a fanatical disciple, and soon so did her eldest daughter. The second daughter, a beauty called Blaesilla, did not. She resisted. She watched her mother and sister fasting and praying, hating and denying their bodies, as Jerome instructed. It was puzzling. She loved her own. I mean, it was so beautiful. She stopped sometimes and stood still in the marble house, where the rooms and pattering passages had fallen into such sudden silence. She listened with her head cocked, and her eyes wide with concentration, but all she could hear was the hurrying of her own heart. Then she clapped her hands loud into the silence, to summon her companions. 'Bring the litter.' And she went out to find herself some life.

This went on for a while and then Blaesilla fell dangerously ill. Perhaps, as she lay glassy-eyed with fever, Jerome sat at her bedside and terrified her with the intentions of the Devil, because as soon as she was better, as soon as she could sit up again and sup a little soup out of a spoon, she too became a disciple. Jerome went to work devising a programme of punishment to save her soul. She had so much to say sorry for, so much shame to sup up with her soup, and because she had been disobedient and slow to convert, because she had been beautiful and pleasure-loving, she was put on a particularly strict diet of mortification. She must kneel on the cold floor. She must fast. No more silks and jewellery. She must wear coarse cloth. She must pray long hours and never rest. If it hurt or tired her, she must thank God for her suffering. But she was only barely recovered and her body wasn't strong enough. She died.

Maybe this is not how it was at all – or not quite how Jerome thought he was presenting it. Imagine it another way. Imagine that Jerome, following the track of his own fear of sin, found that fasting and praying expanded his mind in ways he could not otherwise have accessed. Imagine the visions he saw. Angels blazing at the entrance to his room. The Watchers watching. They guard him, just him, his own precious soul, beloved of God, day and night with their wings sweeping to the ground and their flaming swords aloft. Imagine, among the vast terrors of the desert where he lived alone in a cave, the lion stopping in the doorway. The ragged mane and the appalling blood-smelling tongue. And imagine, instead of it bounding in and slashing at him with its teeth and claws, it stops, gentled by God to sit peacefully by his desk while he translates the Bible. Even if he just hallucinated it, wouldn't it be hard not to find yourself wanting to persuade others that they too could find these things through abstinence: bliss and power and safe protection?

Perhaps.

Whatever the truth of it, Rome was distressed at Blaesilla's death. She'd been its darling. It went into angry mourning and Jerome was chased from the great city. Rome accused him of murder at one remove, of having illicit relations with the widow Paula. He doesn't say anything at all about this in his own account. He tells us, instead, of Paula's life, how she left Rome 'unaccompanied' for a pilgrimage to the Holy Land. He tells us how her children wept on the quay, how her little boy stretched out his arms to her, and how Paula turned away. He doesn't say that he too was on the boat – that they went together. They lived side by side in neighbouring religious communities in Bethlehem, and Jerome, by his own account, was at Paula's bedside when she died.

So that is how Jerome was. Those were his beliefs. I don't know whether he was telling the truth about Paula but that is how he thought a woman should live, perhaps for her own happiness and benefit, or perhaps only to save himself from temptation. Either way, when I came across his extract from Theophrastus' supposed book on marriage, I assumed that he had doctored whatever he had found to fit his own ends. This is characteristic of what happened overall to the thinking of the ancients. Small passages are often gathered up and taken out of context. They have been cannibalized, extended, warped in different directions, commandeered by later minds – not in open discussion where they could be countered immediately, but cemented for the rest of time in writing. Then others, who didn't have access to the originals, took the extracts to be the workable truth and, in the different light of their new contexts, built on them. And so we have staggered onwards, losing sight of our starting point, in growing confusion.

Some have claimed that, in this case, the extract is entirely Jerome's invention, but that doesn't make sense. If Jerome was looking for classical authority to support his thinking, he would have been more likely to use someone better known. He would have used Aristotle or Plato, if he could. So it's likely that, in all of this, there is some kernel of original text. And the text that the extract, when it does ring true, is most like is Theophrastus' *Characters*. It has the same satirical energy, the same detail of observation, only it isn't levelled, as the other sketches are, against an avoidable quality like ambition or pride or stinginess, it's levelled against one whole gender. There are no women in the *Characters*. Was this once part of it – or did it belong in something else, something that is gone? There is no way of knowing. Almost everything in Diogenes Laertius' list is gone without trace.

Here is how it happened, Theophrastus. According to your will, you left all your books to Neleus. Some of the records talk about you inheriting 'Aristotle's library'. What was that exactly? I know Plato nicknamed him 'the reader' but I can't see where the idea of him as book collector comes from. I've looked at Aristotle's will and I can't find anything. He makes several quite specific bequests. Antipater is to be his executor. He leaves houses and estates. He leaves furniture. He leaves money, both for his consort – one silver talent (about £15,000) – and for individual slaves. Ambracis, for example, is to be set free and given 500 drachmas and her own handmaiden. He leaves instructions concerning the welfare of his various children. You are mentioned but he seems to think you may not be able to fulfil his wishes – 'if he consents and if circumstances permit him', he says. Do you remember this at all? He offers you his daughter.

But where is the library? Where is the collection that Strabo applauds for being so far ahead of its time? Diogenes makes a point of mentioning the 'very large number of dishes' found among Aristotle's possessions but there is no mention, not one word, about books. Nor is there even any reference to the famous school he started with you in Athens, the school at the Lyceum. Nothing. I've been listening to the chain of whispers passed down among the philosophers and writers who came after you. Strabo heard it from Diogenes who heard it from Andronicus, or possibly Ariston, who might have heard it from Lyco, and so it goes on, back and back, for three hundred years. Aristotle's library, whisper whisper, so many books, so carefully collected, whisper whisper, all left to Theophrastus.

What library?

And where does it say that you inherited it?

Surely, if the books had been important to Aristotle, he would have mentioned them specifically. You do in your own will, after all. I also notice that when you leave your books to Neleus you use the definite article, not a possessive. *All the books.* So perhaps you were including Aristotle's collection? Perhaps you meant all the books belonging to the Lyceum library. But that doesn't necessarily make sense because after dealing with the books you go on to the buildings – those were definitely yours alone – and again you use the definite article: *the garden, and the promenade, and the houses which join the garden, I give all of them to any of the friends whose names I set down below, who choose to hold a school in them and to devote themselves to the study of philosophy.* This, by the way, is interesting to me: your gift is conditional, it seems. They may only live there equally, in fellowship *– no one is to claim them as his own private property; but they are to use them in common as if they were sacred ground, sharing them with one another in a kindred and friendly spirit, as is reasonable and fair.* Neleus is one among the fellowship you name although you gave him the books outright. Perhaps you hoped he would become head of the 'school'. Perhaps you thought he would stay.

I can tell you he didn't.

Strato, if you believe the whispers, took over. Strato of Lampsacus – do you remember him? – became Scholarch (Director) of the Lyceum after your death. And Neleus put the library, which was now his, into a boat and sailed the several days and nights it must have taken to Scepsis, to his home below Mount Ida, in the country I now call Turkey. Perhaps, as the son of Coriscus and a member of your first school at Assos, he went with your approval, or even at your suggestion. Perhaps it seemed to you that a city where philosophers could be poisoned, like Socrates, or exiled like Aristotle, wasn't the place for a library. Perhaps you thought taking them back to Asia Minor, where you and Aristotle started, was a better bet.

It either did, or didn't happen, like this. There are, inevitably, several versions of the story.

Either Neleus took them home to Scepsis, where he came from. And if so, they lay in a cellar in the house of Neleus' descendants for years, degrading slowly with damp and being eaten by moths. At one point, so they say, they were even hidden, in a trench, from the Attalid kings who were building a library at Pergamon, in north-western Turkey, and who had a peremptory attitude to the books of other people. And there they mouldered until, somewhere down the years, a dubious character called Apellicon of Teos got wind of them and bought them from Neleus' descendants and took them back to Rome, which was by that time the centre of the 'civilized' western world.

Or Neleus didn't take them home at all, or took them home only for a while, but then sold them, himself, to Demetrius of Phalerum, your old friend and pupil who had moved, as you know, from Athens to Alexandria, that burgeoning centre of learning then under the rule of Alexander's general, Ptolemy Soter. That's what Athenaeus says happened. He was an Egyptian Greek who wrote a book called *The Philosophers at Dinner* (*The Deipnosophists*), full of gossip and small detail. He says Neleus sold the books to Ptolemy's son, Ptolemy II, who had started to collect together a library for the school his father had established. I mean, in some ways, this version makes sense to me. After all, Ptolemy Soter had tried to persuade you to go, hadn't he? – to set up the school in Alexandria. That's how it's told now. Demetrius went and you stayed. Once you'd made your way back there, all those years after Pella, you were happy in Athens. So in some ways Alexandria could be seen as an extension of your school at the Lyceum. Ptolemy and Demetrius were both your friends. I know that the scholars there held all their possessions in common, as you insisted that they did at the Lyceum – Strabo the geographer tells us so. If your books had been sold to Ptolemy's son then the library would just have been moving about within the tradition that you and Aristotle established.

But still, it's hard to know. You can see, I can't tell the story properly because I don't have all the facts. That's your phrase, isn't it? *We don't have all the facts.* It's possible that both versions are true: that some of the books were sold to Alexandria and that some went back to disintegrate in a cellar in Scepsis. Perhaps the important ones, like Aristotle's lost finished dialogues, went to the library and the ones that were just field-notes for lectures were kept by Neleus.

I'm aware you may be puzzled by the detail of this, by why it matters so much to me – to us. I've tried to make you see what is lost. I've tried to explain how much of your thought, and Aristotle's, is erased. Silent. Think of all that Aristotle did and wrote. Think of the books. We have one-fifth of what he produced. That's all. We have none of his formal writings, only his notes. When we look at the extracts people have copied into their own works none of them (or remarkably few) match what we have in his surviving works. This is unusual. Almost everything we have of Plato's matches or corresponds exactly. For someone so important to us in his thinking, Aristotle's sources are worryingly questionable. So you see it does matter. We imagine this huge library of works by you and Aristotle, and no doubt by many others as well, and we look for it down the ages. We puzzle over it. How could it be that this incredibly precious haul got lost? Who could have allowed this to happen?

*

We have machines now, Theophrastus, with memories, that store all our knowledge but even so, we are still obsessed by the idea of books. They have a sacred mystique. They embody learning and scholarship and literature – some of our best achievements. For many centuries, they have been the way we keep track of our progress, so we treat them with a kind of religious awe. We have libraries in all our universities. We have national libraries, local libraries, private libraries. We have archives. We don't really use our memories so much. We keep our brains in books and now increasingly in the machines I mentioned. There's too much information out there and it's too complex. That way we think it is safe. The worst thing that could possibly happen, we think, would be to lose what we've so painfully learned.

So, you can imagine, we see the loss of your library as something catastrophic, a kind of intellectual and aesthetic horror. This is perhaps a very big difference between us. We have a writer who died only recently, who trod a dangerous line between what he understood to be the essence of things and the actual facts of the matter – he was a Polish journalist called Ryszard Kapuściński. You perhaps wouldn't have approved, but if he disregarded detail, still he saw the structure of many things very clearly. Here's what he said about how we look at the past – I try to keep it in mind when I'm talking to you:

> Every human being has his own particular web of associations for identifying and interpreting reality, which, most often instinctively and unthinkingly, he superimposes upon every set of circumstances. Frequently, however, those external circumstances do not conform with, or fit, the structure of our webs, and then we can misread the unfamiliar reality, and interpret its elements incorrectly.

On such occasions, we move about in an unreal world, a
landscape of dead ends and misleading signs.

I only say this, I suppose, because I'm assuming that the almost total
loss of all your work must matter to you – or maybe, if I'm honest,
because I'm angry and incredulous that it clearly didn't, or you would
have tried harder to safeguard it. I'm trying to keep in mind that this
may not be the case for you. You, perhaps, think of books differently.
We can replicate them, again with machines, absolutely exactly,
many thousands of copies at a time – infinitely, if we don't need the
physical copy. I can imagine that, for you, books are in themselves
more precious – because they are unique – but also, at the same time,
because of that uniqueness, less practical and therefore, oddly, less
precious. They have less authority – you can't rely on them. They
are fragile. They degrade. They are wearying and time-consuming
to copy because each copy must be done by hand. And then, since
they are done by hand, by humans, they are less reliable. There will
be mistakes. There will be little sections copied out and preserved
that will have got out of context – as happened with Jerome and your
book on marriage. So they aren't much help for teaching. And there
aren't enough of them to go around, in any event.

They also embody a new approach. A shift from the use of
collective memory – presumably well established as a reliable
method of teaching and also of recording where you had got to in
your thinking. I know you had different schools of thought among
the philosophers in Athens. I suppose that the Academy, where Plato
taught, had its own defined and entrenched positions from which
to argue. I used to assume that's why you and Aristotle broke away;
because you thought differently and so didn't fit. I know now that it
was possible that this wasn't altogether the case – that you remained

Platonic in much of your thinking, that you tried twice to put into practice his ideal of good governance through education. I know, too, that there were Stoics and Epicureans, and I know that you had your own school at the Lyceum, so I'm imagining that the body of your thought was kept, as we keep ours in our computer machines or in our books, in the heads of your own group, the community of your pupils and colleagues, as you say in your will.

What I'm picturing is a system that is still largely oral in tradition. You taught what you knew by word of mouth rather than from writing. I'm assuming that your writings were mostly a form of private noting, a way of ordering what you thought so as to be able to deliver it later, in the form of a lecture. So that makes your 'school' something organic: a body of scholars who are evolving a position in relation to the world based on inherited findings. In which case, the thing that matters most is the current position – where we've got to now, for instance. The tradition is live and being taught daily, so it is both preserved and embodied in the teaching. That way a school is a kind of living organism, with a defined position that is established, in opposition to and in the context of, the other schools around it at the time. And all these places, together, make up one flexing mind that is working out its philosophy and advancing knowledge daily and in the round.

If all of this is correct, it makes our mania for recording, for books and libraries, appear backward-looking and even dead – as if they were just different types of cupboard. Perhaps, too, this is an attitude that goes with the approach of the scientist. I was talking about you once to a friend of mine, a professor of renal physiology, from Canada. He teaches a course on scientific rhetoric, starting with Aristotle, and I thought he would be interested in your ideas about persuasiveness in speech. In passing, as we talked, he described the scientist as being very like an explorer. 'What we know, what we've proven,' he said, 'is much less interesting than what we've still to learn. The scientist is like someone standing in the doorway of a lit room, looking out into the dark ahead of them and saying, "Now, where next?"' I have never forgotten it. Perhaps that's how you feel. I can see, if so, why the library mattered less to you – if it did. It answers some of the questions we ask, like, 'why would the school allow the library to leave without copying it first?' Well, I would say, in the light of this, perhaps because things were continually evolving and because the important teachings are already preserved in the intellectual tradition of the school. Perhaps, too, like my friend the professor, you felt that the work still to do was more important than preserving the work that had been done. Perhaps it didn't occur to you, in your dawn of discovery, that knowledge is mortal in every sense; it can die.

Whether you thought the books were important or not, you should, at any rate, know what we think happened to them.

*

The library that Ptolemy Philadelphus (Ptolemy's son) had started in Alexandria grew and grew and, in time, became so famous that of course it attracted notice. He had amassed a great collection of works, the basis of which – I imagine – must have been either the original texts, or copies, of everything that you and Aristotle had produced as formal writings. I think this because I see the school at Alexandria, at its outset, as an extension of your own school in Athens – as Assos might have started as an extension of the Academy for you and Aristotle, all those years before.

So, time passed, and whereas in your day Alexander the Great had an empire, by now Rome had taken over and become the dominant western power. About 240 years after your death, there was civil war among the Romans. Rome was trying to be like Athens so it was organized as a republic – however, by this time it had lost some of its stability. The power which had previously been split between three men was now being fought over by two of its most prominent generals: Julius Caesar and Pompey. They had ranged across the empire chasing each other back and forth, and had taken the war as far as Greece. Caesar beat Pompey at the Battle of Pharsalus and Pompey then fled to Alexandria.

Caesar is, in our eyes, a man of great note because he invaded and subdued our country. He was a man hardened by soldiering. He is supposed to have been very fond of his wife but on the evidence of his many statues he looks dour and decisive, his face and body so spare of softness, so free of any plumpness or fat, that he seems to be made of something other than flesh. A man made of wood perhaps. Light and dense and dry. Besides this hardness, what Caesar's statues also all show is the size of his forehead; the housing for a mind of extraordinary ability. He wasn't just a fighting man. He wrote histories. He is known to have been so able that he could dictate a letter while writing some complicated, different thing – like a history – at the same time. That's the story. We have it from Plutarch, a Roman writer and historian, that 'Caesar disciplined himself so far as to be able to dictate letters from on horseback, and to give directions to two who took notes at the same time' and we have it from Pliny, another similar Roman, that Caesar 'used to write or read, and dictate or listen simultaneously, and to dictate to his secretaries four letters at once, on his important affairs—or, if otherwise unoccupied, seven letters at once'.

By rights, after the Battle of Pharsalus, Caesar should have been exhausted – he'd been campaigning solidly for over a decade, pitting his ingenuity against whatever conditions came along, keeping going, building bridges, marching, sleeping the wily and flickering sleep of the strategist, thinking it out, damming rivers to water his army while parching his enemy downstream, and never once relaxing. After the battle, many of his troops were too wounded and worn out to do anything, so with a unit made up of only those fit enough, roughly two legions – in his own words, a 'feeble force' – he set out for Alexandria to harry Pompey.

He was too late. Pompey was murdered, almost as he put his weary foot to the ground, on the orders of the Ptolemy in charge at the time. He was hoping that Caesar would be pleased. But Pompey had been Caesar's son-in-law. Some say Caesar wept over his death. Others that he only pretended – and that it suited him to take sides against Ptolemy, which is what in the end he did. Because Egypt, like Rome, was having its own problems. Ptolemy's sister was Cleopatra, and she was fighting her brother for control.

So Caesar occupied the city, offering to settle the dispute between the siblings by acting as a 'common friend and arbitrator'. We have his own account of events, which obviously isn't the same as knowing what happened. He writes that Ptolemy, being badly advised, raised an army and instead of coming back peaceably to Alexandria, knowing that Caesar's force was much reduced, attempted to overwhelm him by sheer force of numbers.

The intelligence that Caesar's agents had gathered was good. Ptolemy was on the march. Caesar took over the palace and deployed his men in the streets and waited for Ptolemy's army to arrive. Perhaps it was then, while waiting, that he thought about the library. For a man of such brilliance and learning as Caesar, and with Rome now the centre of the 'civilized' world, it must have seemed lopsided to house the greatest library ever known in some foreign outpost, however majestic a place Alexandria might have been. Obviously, such a library should be relocated. He was a man who was hungry for knowledge as well as power and there were all those books, the works of the great philosophers, the mathematicians, the historians, sitting there in the Mouseion, only just back from the harbour. It was too tempting. He had his soldiers move some 400,000 of the library's scrolls down to the docks, into grain stores, ready to be shipped back to Rome. Back and forth they went, with armfuls of the precious scrolls, stacking them in towers in wooden crates. It was only fair after all and they would be better looked after in Rome.

Then suddenly Ptolemy's army was upon him, funnelling down the streets towards the palace, and Caesar switched his attention from books to tactics. The fighting was close and the places of engagement were narrow, and because of this – despite their inferiority in numbers – Caesar's army managed to hold their own. And then the word went out that Ptolemy was trying to take the Roman fleet, currently at anchor in the great harbour. If Ptolemy's men made themselves masters of these ships, they would control the port. They could close off Caesar's access to reinforcements and supplies. He'd be besieged. Caesar's mind goes scudding ahead, watching the battle in the streets, calculating, weighing up different outcomes. He needs to send a detachment to the harbour. But how to make a detachment with so small a force? His force is too small to protect everything at once. What to do? What to do? Quick! There is no time. What is best to do?

Fire the ships!

The momentary confusion of the little handful of men given this order, the split-second hesitation. What? Our ships? Because these were not just small vessels for fishing and trading. These were the grand Roman galleys, Caesar's fleet, the triremes and quinquiremes, with their banks of oars and their underwater battering rams. These were the pride of the Roman navy. Not to mention the twenty-two other vessels always kept at Alexandria to guard the port – and besides all of which, the army was far from home and home was across the sea.

Fire them, I said! And the order is rasped out most dangerously, the small veins in Caesar's temples pulsing.

So the men run with torches, dripping burning pitch, down to the harbour and push a boat out into the midst of the fleet and set it alight. And ship after ship after ship, these great wooden castles, leap into flames. The sound of it just like its opposite – the roar of a waterfall. Deafening. So that Ptolemy's men, who had been ready with poles to grapple aboard and take the fleet, back away from the harbour with their faces protected in the crooks of their arms. It's so hot and there's so much smoke. The heat spreading and intensifying and the fatal sparks swirling upwards, sailing overhead.

Fire is a hungry force. Caesar raises his restless eyes briefly skyward. Alexandria, in its splendour, is made of stone and marble so it will be quite safe. He has taken no particular risk. But everything, in the heat of Egypt, is so dry. And it isn't as if there is no wood at all. There are beams and doors and floor supports. In the grain stores, the stacked parchment scrolls contract in their wooden crates, as if by shrinking they could somehow escape their fate. And down from the sky above, bright with energy, the sparks fall, raining on the harbour buildings. They catch. The grain stores burn and with them go the words, all those carefully chosen millions of persuasive words that have lain so quiet for so long. As if in agony the parchments flex and open. They make one final roar in unison and the letters show black in the flames. And then?

Gone. There is nothing there any more – just a snow of ash, which shifts and settles on silence.

*

Caesar doesn't mention this in his account, the burned books. Why would you? He just makes a brief defence of his orders. He had to do it. He couldn't afford to let the harbour fall. He had to focus his forces. He couldn't have defended so many places at once with so small a handful of men. Battles are made of such events.

So, in that case, who is this? Who is this man I can see, walking softly out through the streets, in the stunned aftermath of battle? This severe man with his mouth set hard like a crack in a board. Caesar. He is listening to the click of the cooling embers. He is watching the ashes, picked over by the light winds, dance their grey dance, swirling and drifting and settling again; darkness falls on the day, in every sense.

And maybe his wooden heart is briefly breaking.

I wish only to remind my reader that the naturalist, too, was a professional storyteller, a public demonstrator of new and interesting species.

Osip Mandelstam, *A Journey to Armenia*

V

Patterns

We worked and thought together very closely for a number of years so that I grew to depend on his knowledge and on his patience in research. And then I went away to another part of the country but it didn't make any difference. Once a week or once a month would come a fine long letter so much in the style of his speech that I could hear his voice over the neat full page.

This is not Theophrastus. This is the voice of another, speaking with the stop-start, lifted intonation of someone unrolling his thoughts as he goes along, in a light drawl that is furred with nicotine, and in phrases punctuated by the catchy breath of the dedicated smoker.

John Steinbeck. He is talking about his friend and collaborator Ed Ricketts, killed when a train hit his car on a railway crossing. Ricketts was a charismatic marine biologist who made his scant living out of a specimen laboratory, squashed in between canning factories, on California's Monterey Bay. He was a compulsive collector and categorizer, a descriptive scientist who was one of the first to consider marine animals environmentally instead of just taxonomically – that is, in terms of their habitat, their communities, and the way these two things co-depend and interrelate. All of this was at the wider service of his other abiding interest, which was philosophy.

Ricketts was compelled by the patterns his researches produced – patterns which he saw everywhere in life. He came to believe in the notion of the pattern as an indication of essential similarity or belonging – 'participation' as he calls it. 'I think that participation,' he writes, 'is, if not the most dramatic, at least the most deeply interesting thing in the world. To the degree of its intensity or depth, it's "all things" not superficial or spread out – diffused, but deeply participatingly, all-things.' In other words, he found in the endless repeat and correspondence of one life form to another, not just belonging but something deeper, as if everything, ourselves included, were simply porous to life; as if the same life flowed equally, and unhindered, through us all, regardless of type, or species or kind. This was a philosophical principle that Ricketts embodied in his own life, socially, spiritually and scientifically. When Steinbeck first met him – surrounded by his specimens, his charts of geniuses and composers, his books of poetry, and his ragtag, impoverished, urchin band of collectors – this life seemed hugely significant and attractive. He fell under Ricketts' spell and they began a friendship that, with small interruptions, lasted until Ricketts died. 'He was my partner,' Steinbeck said once, in conversation, 'for eighteen years – he was part of my brain.'

Steinbeck would stop by the laboratory most days and watch Ricketts at work, or help with whatever it was he was doing, or afterwards sit and drink and talk in Ricketts' bedroom-cum-library-cum-music-room, where the walls were floor-to-ceiling shelves, lined with precious biological books, books on philosophy, art, literature and music. There were gramophone records by the hundred: Monteverdi and Mozart, Bach and Benny Goodman. And there were piles of papers and heaps of pamphlets and the many, many stacks of field notebooks containing Ricketts' notes and thoughts and researches, his whole life's work of categorization and observation.

On the night of 2 November 1936, something overloaded in the Del Mar Cannery's electrical circuit, next door, and a fire broke out. The fish oil that was stored in tanks and saturated in the wooden flooring flashed immediately into flame and the factory was engulfed. The fire leapt the walkways into the warehouses. The packing materials caught. Fanned by the November winds, Cannery Row was soon an inferno. Great billows of smoke, black against the fire's fierce light, rose into a blacker sky. All night, the fire department battled to get the blaze under control but the heat of the fire was such that the water from their hoses evaporated, the hiss of steam adding to the fire's roar. By morning the cannery and the little Western Biological Laboratory that hunkered under its shadow, together with Ricketts' library, his records, his specimen collection, both commercial and scientific, and all his life's notes and researches, had been burned to the ground.

*

Ricketts' essays were saved by being in circulation among his friends, in manuscript form, at the time of the fire, while the typescript of his seminal book, *Between Pacific Tides*, was already safely with the publisher. Slowly, Ricketts rebuilt his life and Steinbeck's visits, when he was at home, resumed. In 1939, *The Grapes of Wrath* was published, occasioning a perfect storm of combined adulation and fury. Europe was several months into what would become a world war and Steinbeck's marriage was failing. He was exhausted. Casting around for something other than fiction to occupy his mind and time, he found marine biology and began to retrain under Ricketts' direction, reading, studying mathematics and learning the practical detail of collection and preservation of specimens. He wrote to a friend:

The world is sick now… There are things in the tide pools easier to understand than Stalinist, Hitlerite, Democrat, capitalist confusion, and voodoo. So I'm going to those things which are relatively more lasting to find a new basic picture. I have too a conviction that a new world is growing under the old, the way a new finger nail grows under a bruised one. I think all the economists and sociologists will be surprised some day to find that they did not foresee nor understand it.

What Ricketts and Steinbeck were planning was a book of marine biological research that they would co-author, whose results would underpin their joint philosophical project: a 'non-teleological' view of the world as a single interconnected, fighting and flourishing whole, in which mankind is simply one of its integrated parts. They would look closely at individual specimens. They would find and catalogue and name. They would look, of course, for the patterns that Ricketts was so fascinated by, both in the physical structures of things and in their relationships with each other, and they would broaden their thinking outwards to encompass human nature and society and their place in the rest of the natural environment. Ricketts' and Steinbeck's researches were done by boat in the most species-rich waters they could find – another gulf – the Gulf of California (also known as the Sea of Cortés). You once suggested, Theophrastus, that whatever causes we might find for the world, the first principles, are likely to be nothing more than imaginings, just something our minds are inclined to create. So you'd be interested in their conclusions. They decided that life was made not out of causes and effects but out of an infinitely varying and repeating series of relationships between things. Life is a pattern, they said, and, 'in such a pattern, causality would be merely a name for something that exists only in our partial and biased mental reconstructing. The pattern… goes everywhere and is everything and cannot be encompassed by finite mind.' In other words, we are a tiny but integral part of an infinite organism whose nature and structure is a repeating and co-varying pattern. If we can't intellectually grasp the exact form of the patterning, it is because we are too tiny a part to comprehend the whole.

Steinbeck knew that *Sea of Cortez* (the joint account of their researches) was likely, initially at least, to be a 'flop', but he had hopes that it would nevertheless turn out, in time, to be a great work of lasting philosophical and scientific importance: 'Gradually it will be discovered that it is a whole new approach to thinking and only very gradually will the philosophic basis emerge. Scientific men, the good ones, will know what we are talking about.'

The trip took six weeks but the discipline of biology stayed with Steinbeck, in his writing, for many years to come. He had taken the trip, in part, because he felt he had come to the end of the novel and needed something new. He was wrong – or else he couldn't stop – but in the different discipline of research a new way of writing became clear, a particular dispassionate way of looking at the world, an absolute outwardness and an absolute attention to what is there, in all its individual but intricately connected life. He went on writing novels, of course, but in *Cannery Row*, the second novel he wrote after the trip with Ricketts, he is still meditating on the difficulties of translation at its most literal. That is, how to carry the phenomenological world across an impossible divide: how to put actual things into words in such a way that they stay alive. He observes:

> When you collect marine animals, there are certain flatworms
> so delicate that they are almost impossible to capture whole,
> for they break and tatter under the touch. You must let them
> ooze and crawl of their own will onto a knife blade and then
> lift them gently into your bottle of seawater. And perhaps that
> might be the way to write this book.

Between novel-writing and science it seems there is only a narrow divide. At some point, in his daily work of looking – or with that long habit of observation still working in him, because he, too, couldn't stop – Theophrastus glances up from the samples assembled on the bench in front of him, perhaps to rest his neck, or ease out his shoulders stiff from long stooping. Maybe something has caught his eye outside, some man in slipshod sandals, crossing on his way to the Agora, or a messenger hurrying up from the harbour, bursting with important news. Whatever it is he sees, in that moment his electric mind makes a leap that is entirely new – to a written form yet to be invented, something halfway between science and story. Just as a man who had been at his desk since dawn might allow himself a moment of inattention, dreaming into the middle distance and watching the people passing, and then – only half intending to – in a sudden moment of inspiration might start to write. And this time, writing not something carefully formulated but just automatically, without thinking, just to see what would happen, and for fun. So that even he himself was surprised by the result. Did it happen like that, Theophrastus?

However it happened, Theophrastus started a description of types of people, observing and classifying neutrally, just as he'd classified plants: the man who is such a bumpkin he goes to town in slipshod shoes, the man whose currency is news, the man who flatters, the boastful type, the coward, the penny-pincher. The familiar blizzard of fine detail swirls onto the page. So-and-so goes to the market with his toenails black and uncut. Someone always whitens their teeth. Someone's cloak is always shabby; their best one is always 'with the cleaner'. Someone mean gets up naked in the night and goes shivering and tripping to check that his storehouse door is locked. And in the dining room, among the ladies, someone hitches his tunic too far up and sits with his legs spread wide.

*

The *Characters* may not have been written all at once. It may have been added to, as his plant studies were, over time. It is certainly incomplete but it was most likely written in the later part of the century, around 319, when he was living again in Athens. Nothing else is at all like it. It is astonishingly vivid in its observed detail – alone among the classics for its impartiality, its existence apparently just for its own sake, as a catalogue of types, without any apparent message or literary purpose. Its people aren't in the service of anything else – they aren't ciphers for some vice or virtue; they are just their quirky, ordinary, conversational selves. Reading them, all the smallness and business and habits and clutter of Athenian life, all the impossible-to-imagine day-to-day stuff of the ancient world comes suddenly and clearly into view. Something long obscured at last fully visible, like the moon sailing clear of the clouds. It isn't myth, or drama, or allegory. It's just a bit of life, wriggled, still breathing, onto the page. Why did you do it, Theophrastus? What was it for?

No one really knows. Slowly the street life of Athens rolls itself out, unexplained, before our eyes. Over there, for instance, looking as if he's made of leather, that man with his hair like a gull's nest, picking his nose by the kipper shop. What on earth kind of person is that?

The country bumpkin is the sort of man who drinks up a bowl of gruel before going to the Assembly and claims that garlic is as sweet as any perfume. He wears shoes too large for his feet and talks at the top of his voice.

He takes no interest in anything in the street until he sees an ox or a donkey or a goat he likes. Then he'll stop in front of it and stare.

He raids his own larder, drinks his wine undiluted and makes passes at the girl who does the baking.

He fodders his plough animals while he's eating his own breakfast.

> He answers the door himself, calls his dog and grabbing it
> by the snout, says, 'this is the one that guards my home'.
>   If he's lying awake at night and remembers lending someone
> a plough, a basket, a sickle, or a sack then he gets up right then
> and there and asks for it back.
>   He sings at the baths and hammers nails into his shoes.
>   On his way to town he stops a man he meets and asks him
> how much hides and kippers are going for and then he tells him
> that as soon as he gets to the city he means to have a haircut
> and, while he's about it, have a look at the shops and pick up
> some kippers from Archias's.

Or over there, someone completely different, hurrying along in the columned shade of the Stoa: that man, whose beard looks expensively oiled and trimmed, and who turns his head this way and that, as if he were afraid of missing something. That man who smirks as he walks – I don't know at what – what kind of a person is that?

> The toady is the sort of man who says to a person he's walking
> with, 'Have you noticed what admiring looks you're getting? No
> one else in the city gets as much attention as you.'
>   While he's going on like this he removes a flock of wool
> from his companion's cloak, or picks from his hair a bit of straw
> blown there by the wind, adding with a laugh, 'See? Because I
> haven't run into you for two days you've got a beard full of grey
> hairs, although I must say no one has darker hair for his age
> than you.'
>   When his man is speaking he shushes everyone else, telling
> them to be quiet and then praises him loudly so he can hear. At
> every pause he adds an approving, 'Well said!' And at a feeble

joke he bursts out into hysterical laughter, stuffing his cloak into
his mouth as if he can't control himself.

Anyone they meet along the way he orders to wait until the
great man has gone past.

He buys apples and pears and brings them to the man's
house and gives them to his children making sure their father is
watching. Then he kisses them and calls them 'little chicks of a
noble sire'...

At dinner he's the first to praise the wine. He's sure to be
sitting by the host and he says to him, 'How luxuriously you
entertain!' And then he takes something from the table and
says, 'How exquisite!'

Next he asks the host if he's chilly and if he'd like to put
something on, and before the words are out of his mouth he
leans over and wraps him in a blanket. Then he leans forward
and whispers in his ear.

In the theatre he takes the cushions from the slave and
spreads them on the seat with his own hands.

He tells the man his house is a masterly piece of
architecture, that his farm is superbly planted and that his
portrait is an excellent likeness.

I know these people. They are real. It doesn't matter whether it is
then or now, whether I am sitting looking out over the green gardens
of a small town in England, or whether I'm in Athens in the fourth
century BCE. I can see them. I can see the encounters, like that one,
there! That person on the street corner who shifts from foot to foot,
with a look of despair on his face – he's been caught by someone who
insists on talking, who just won't let him go. Too polite to move on,
he is trapped. Every now and again he looks up with that particular,

half-impatient, half-agonized look on his face. If only someone else he knew would pass so he could make an excuse. What on earth kind of person would impose themselves on a fellow citizen like this?

> *The chatterbox is the sort of person who sits next to a complete stranger and first sings his own wife's praises, then recounts the dream he had last night, then describes in every detail what he had for dinner. Then, as no one has managed to stop him, he continues with talk such as this:*
>
> *People nowadays are far less well-behaved than in the olden days. Wheat is now selling in the market at a bargain price. The city is crammed with foreigners... More rain would be good for the crops.*
>
> *He goes on about what land he will cultivate next year. He says life is hard and that Damippos set up an extra large torch at the Mysteries. Goodness me, he says, how many pillars there are in the Odeon! I threw up yesterday. What day of the month is it? The Mysteries are held in September, the Apatouria in October, the Rural Dionysian in December.*
>
> *If you let him go on he will simply never stop.*

So now you catch his impatience. As if you, too, were suddenly in the narrow gravelled streets of ancient Athens, in the heat, with all the strange smells of the marketplace pricking in your nose, and as if, here, right in front of you, this thickset man with almost no neck is dawdling in your way, scratching at his head, as if he were cartoon thinking. Who could possibly be so obtuse as not to notice your presence behind him, standing in your way as he ferrets around in his pouches and pockets for something he's misplaced? Who would be so maddeningly time-wasting as that?

*The slow-minded man is the kind of person who counts
something up on his abacus and then turns to the person next
to him and asks him, 'what does it come to?'*

*When he should be appearing in court over a lawsuit
against him he forgets and goes to the country.*

*At the theatre, when everyone else has left, he is found alone
asleep in his seat.*

*When he wakes at night, having stuffed himself at supper,
he has to get up and go out to relieve himself, and while doing
so he gets bitten by his neighbour's dog...*

*When he buys something and puts it safely away he then
spends hours looking for it and can't ever find where he hid
it ...*

*In winter he gets cross with his slave for failing to buy
cucumbers.*

*He exhausts his children by insisting they wrestle and run
races with him.*

*In the country when he's boiling lentil soup he salts the pan
twice and makes the soup inedible.*

And now who is this, beyond him, this sallow-faced person, raking
about in the gutter, tutting with irritation, as if he's lost something
important?

*The penny pincher is the kind of man who, at a communal
dinner, counts how many cups each guest has drunk and makes
the smallest preliminary offering to Artemis. When the bill
comes he complains that everything he's had, no matter how
little it cost, was too expensive.*

*When a slave breaks a dish or a pot he deducts the cost
from his food rations.*

When his wife drops a penny he shifts the kitchenware and the couches and the chests and rummages through the rubbish for it.

He won't let you eat the figs from his garden or walk over his land or pick up a fallen olive or date.

He inspects his boundaries every day to see if they have been tampered with.

When he goes shopping for food he comes home without buying anything.

When his wife wants to lend something like salt, or a lamp-wick, or cumin, or marjoram or barley meal or fillets, or sacrificial grain, he forbids it saying that little items like these add up to a tidy sum in the course of a year.

That's how people are. That's how they have always been, since there have been towns to live in and shops to shop in and money to make or to lose or to drop in the gutter by mistake. You'd see them just the same if you went down to the financial district in New York, or the City in London, or anywhere similar. You'd see the entrepreneurs, the traders, the sharks and the chancers. Down at the harbour, then or now, watching the shipping come and go, someone showily dressed would be shooting his mouth off to his companion in a voice loud enough to be overheard.

The kind of person who stands in the market at Piraeus and tells foreigners that he has a good deal of money invested at sea. He will tell you how vast the money lending business is and how much he personally has made and lost.

While he is talking he'll make a show of sending his slave to the bank even though there isn't in fact a single penny in his account.

He will boast that during the food shortages he spent
more than five talents on handouts to the poor because he just
couldn't say no.

He will go up to the dealers selling thoroughbreds and
pretend he is a customer.

He will go to the clothes stalls and look for an expensive
outfit and then be angry with his slave for coming out without
money.

Even though the house he lives in is rented he will tell the
listener that it belonged to his father. He will say he intends
to put it on the market because it is too small for the scale at
which he likes to entertain.

What were you doing, Theophrastus?

What was it you were thinking, or intending, when you made these strange and vivid and anachronistic studies?

*

I'm in a colder place than you ever inhabited. I'm a long way north, in what you would have called 'Prettania', looking out of the upstairs window of a house. My house, to be exact. I am far, far into the future, looking down at my garden. This is a new garden. I am still making it. Two neat beds dug out of the lawn. Crows pass over the lines of winter vegetables sown. Rocket, lettuce, perpetual spinach, Italian chicory. You can't see it from up here but already there's a dusting of seedlings showing pale stooped heads. As if hauling themselves upright from the waist, their little green crowns still half under soil. They have come up so quickly they've taken me by surprise. What a marvel. Look at my seedlings, Theophrastus.

*Not all herbs germinate within the same time, but some are
quicker, others slower, namely those which germinate with
difficulty. The speediest are basil, blite, rocket, and of those sown
for winter use, radish; for these germinate in about three days.*

I share your love of plants and I like the fact that a seedling now looks
the same as it did to you. But everything else, every single thing else is
different. So tell me, why are these characters of yours so alive? How
is it they are so familiar to me? Why do they ring such a bell in my
head, as though you were doing something I recognized, something I
know from trying to do it myself? What is this hunch that so possesses
me? Why do you seem to me to be almost a novelist?

Ever since I first opened this little green book and found your
characters moving about among their clattering possessions, I have
had the feeling that something has gone unnoticed, some line of
connection that stretches still live – although unacknowledged –
between us. And I'm not alone. If I follow the journey the characters
took from your hand to now, there are many, many who feel the same.

*

There are thirty or so of these character sketches, minutely observed.
No one really knows what they were for, or why Theophrastus might
have done them. In terms of immediate precedent, aside from various
characters in comedy, the only possible influence is a contemporary
life of Philip, the *Philippica,* written by Isocrates' pupil Theopompus.
This is an account of Philip himself, as a king and as a man. It is
unusual in that histories up to this point had centred around individual
places like cities, or single events like the Persian War. Theopompus is
interested in something different – he is interested in one individual,

his reason being, as he says himself, that there has never before been such a man as Philip. And he's interested less in what he did than in what made him do it. The word he uses is 'toioutos', which is the word Theophrastus uses at the beginning of each character sketch, 'such a man as would…'. Theopompus' portrait is almost vindictive in its criticism but nevertheless it was praised by Dionysus of Halicarnassus as having the original ability 'to see and express in each action not only the things that are clear to all observers but to examine also the hidden motives of actions and all the states of the soul which are not easily discovered by most men, and to reveal all the mysteries of seeming virtue and undiscovered vice'. Perhaps the *Philippica* triggered something in Theophrastus. Perhaps he thought action an interesting index of nature, in the way that growth habits tell you something about the nature of a plant. Perhaps he just thought it was time he turned his taxonomic mind to cataloguing people. Whatever it was, the *Characters* are interesting for the fact of their concentration on evidence, on how a characteristic trait, like meanness, manifests itself actively, in speech or behaviour or body language.

Their title in Greek is *Charakteres Ethikoi*, where 'character' means something like stamp, or imprint, and 'ethics' are customs or habitual behaviours. Neither word carries the moral weight it carries today. So the *Characters* might possibly have come into existence as observational field notes for Aristotle's work on ethics, much in the same way as their studies of plants or animals were the basis for formal treatises, or lectures, written later – a catalogue of behavioural types. There are identifiable crossovers with Aristotle's *Nicomachean Ethics*, in the table he drew up of virtues and their corresponding vices. Aristotle's understanding of virtue was of a point of balance in the emotion generating any given behaviour, a halfway mark between the absolute lack of something and the having of it in excess. For instance, at the mid-point of fear comes the courage or bravery to overcome it – while still being careful about possible dangers. At one end, where the fear is paralysing, is cowardice, and at the other, where it is not felt at all, foolhardiness. He lists thirty-six qualities in all, of which there are nine replicas in Theophrastus' *Characters*: the dissembling man, the oaf, the shameless man, the dullard, the mean man, the coward, the con-man, and the obsequious flatterer. In his sketches, however, Theophrastus is interested in the surface only, in what he sees and hears, not in either establishing the morality of the person, nor in understanding the underlying motivation. He is essentially neutral in his method.

So it's quite possible that they started out as illustrations or fieldwork for the *Nicomachean Ethics*, but this seems a cold and unsatisfactory approach in context of the *Characters* as they are, or as they feel to read. Because they are so enjoyable, so full of life and so free of judgement or moralizing – and they are odder and more varied than a philosophical treatise has room for. There are things among them, for instance, that couldn't quite be classed as vices but that are more an indication of Theophrastus' own cast of mind. These are the people he saw in the streets and wanted to poke fun at, like the Oligarchic man, strutting about in his expensive cloak, with his hair trim and smooth and his hands manicured – the sort of man who says things like, *we must meet and discuss this privately and be rid of the mob and the marketplace.* Or, *you mustn't expect thanks from the common people. They soon forget where the handouts come from.*

According to Hermippus, who wrote a life of Theophrastus now lost, every morning 'bright and early, Theophrastus would appear at the place of lecture, finely groomed and apparelled, and taking his seat, proceed to discourse with such perfect abandon of movement and gesture that on one occasion, to illustrate a description he was giving of the gourmand, he put out his tongue and licked his lips before the whole assembly'. In other words, he was performing and this was a thing unusual enough to be noted.

So, however they started, it seems that the *Characters* soon became something else, something designed for performance or, at any rate, entertainment. They were popular. Theophrastus drew big audiences; among them, his student Menander, the drowned playwright from the Mytilene Museum with his Al Pacino looks, lapped up Theophrastus' character sketches and turned them over in his mind and later made them the basis for his plays. There were over a hundred of these, almost all of which are lost but, in keeping with the *Characters*, Menander chose to write only about the ordinary citizen, about private instead of public life – the old misery who stands in the way of his daughter's marriage, for example, or the slave that is too clever, or the girl with short hair. Some, like *The Toady*, and *The Superstitious Man*, seem to have a direct correspondence with types in the *Characters*. These plays were enough of a break with tradition to become known as New Comedy.

And for all their antiquity, new is how the *Characters* still feel. All this time they've been continually strange enough and original enough to be noticed. They've survived because of it, catching the eye of different writers for different reasons. They've been copied, co-opted and used, hitching a ride in other texts, until they arrived at today.

Indeed, the very first people to co-opt them, because of their performative quality, were the rhetoricians. The other, possibly more likely, purpose the *Characters* might have served – if they weren't, in fact, examples of types of behaviour for works on ethics – is as illustrative material for the lectures Theophrastus is known to have given on the art of rhetoric. Speech-making, even in non-democratic Athens, was the centre around which civic life turned. Eloquence was admired but it was persuasion that really counted, not least because a speaker's ability to sway an audience to his way of thinking was often literally a matter of life or death. This meant that pleading your case against accusation became a gladiatorial exercise. In fear of their life, the speaker would stop at nothing. Many speeches, although they might look like lofty, ordered argument, had something much darker at their core – complete character assassination. At a certain point, as Demosthenes says, it simply 'becomes necessary for the defendant, no longer to speak merely about the facts of the case, but about the character of the speaker as well, and to show that he ought not to be believed on account of his reputation'. Demosthenes goes on to shred his opponent, not in the crude mud-slinging of generic insult but in carefully observed detail, detail that made what he was saying appear true even if it wasn't, or wasn't quite. His attack on Aeschines, for instance, framed him as his mother's assistant in her role as initiator of a female mystery cult. In a society as male as Athens, it is a devastating account:

> At night it was your duty to mix the libations, to clothe the initiates in fawn-skins, to wash their bodies, to scrub them down with the mud and the bran, and… to set them on their legs, and give out the hymn…
>
> In day-time you led your gallant throng of bacchanals through the public streets, their heads garlanded with fennel and white poplar; and, as you went, you squeezed the fat-cheeked snakes, or brandished them above your head, now shouting your Euoi Saboi! now dancing to the measure of Hyes Attes! Attes Hyes!—greeted along the way by all the old hags, with such proud titles as Master of the Ceremonies, Horn-blower, Ivy-bearer, Fan-carrier; and at last receiving

your payment of sweets, and cakes, and currant-buns. With such rich rewards who would not truly rejoice, and think himself blessed with good fortune?

In other words, Aeschines is childish, superstitious, part of a hysterical cult, and not even as a priest but as a servant, a servant to his own mother. Was Theophrastus' *Characters* written as a textbook on rhetorical attack? I don't think so. Demosthenes' attack is a slander that is vivid and hard to forget. It is also vicious and personal, neither of which qualities are present anywhere in the *Characters*. For all the sharpness of its observation, there is nothing so snide in tone, nothing that has the sting of that sneering final line. Theophrastus disliked Demosthenes and the way he spoke. He and his pupil, Demetrius of Phalerum, are supposed to have agreed that Demosthenes' oratory was overly contrived, 'not simple and of noble fashion, but inclined to what is weak and mean'. As a naturally kind man, a man universally liked, it's hard to imagine him following Demosthenes' example – however, from time to time, no doubt even kind men find themselves with their backs against the wall, in which case character assassination as a technique might be a last resort.

This difference in tone is important. It marks the first small refraction away from Theophrastus, through his *Characters*, to now; the first displacement from the original. From this point, whatever their original purpose, the *Characters* were commandeered by rhetoricians who saw the usefulness of the character study as an attribute of persuasive speaking or writing. This is how we might follow them, down the centuries of their long transmission. Closest at hand, Ariston of Keos, Theophrastus' successor-but-one at the Lyceum, was known to use them in his lectures. Then, in the first century BCE they appear again on a piece of papyrus found among the charred remains at Herculaneum, quoted in the work of Philodemus of Gadara, and by now, even this early, the first mistakes in transmission have been made. Things have already been lost and jumbled and miscopied.

Then, for a few hundred years, the *Characters* disappear from view. Although, even so, they are slowly multiplying somewhere out of sight, like a root system – or perhaps not like roots but like the copyists themselves. Because manuscripts breed and die. They create little families of copies with recognizable traits. From the offspring of whichever source it might be you can trace the parent. The same idiosyncrasies or mistakes replicate down the generations like genes. If, as indeed happened to the *Characters*, someone slapdash only manages to copy half the sketches, then a series of copies branch out that are similarly incomplete. Texts, like people, quickly become what scholars refer to as 'corrupted'. If someone else gets distracted and loses his place, then picks it up again, yawning and half-asleep, and misses something out, and then perhaps, noticing his omission, adds it in later where it looks like it will fit, then a whole family of manuscripts will follow that disjointed order.

Like families, manuscripts, too, migrate from place to place. By the late tenth or early eleventh century the *Characters* have made it as far as Byzantium, now triple fortified with majestic pink-striped, pink-capped crenellated walls. This is a Christian city now and it goes by the name of Constantinople. Here, the *Characters* reappear again to be pored over by Christian thinkers, who are troubled by what they find: that problematic mix of paganism and undeniable, indispensable brilliance. All the sheen and dexterity of thought, and all the authority of classical Greece, is now shadowed by the amoral polytheism of its origins. What to do? A second refraction occurs. The *Characters* acquire a long and prosing prologue about the need to teach children the difference between good and bad behaviour.

Moralizing introductions to each sketch are added, along with heavy-handed definitions of the type of behaviour about to be anatomized. The *Characters* are firmly bedded into their putative rhetorical and ethical origins. They are added, incomplete, into the backs of the handbooks on rhetoric.

There were originally a number of these. They were collections of practical precepts and exercises known as Progymnasmata, used right up until the seventeenth century to teach style in writing and speaking. They were taken from the work of several thinkers from the intervening period, men like Theophrastus' contemporary, Aphthonius of Antioch, and Aelius the commentator, and the later, sad, second-century CE child prodigy from Tarsus, called Hermogenes the Polisher, who suffered a brain-damaging disease in early adulthood and lived out the rest of his long life much impaired and unable to look after himself. Into the backs of these men's writings, the *Characters* were added, as an appendix, a collection of useful stylistic models, copied out slowly in quiet rooms, under the glitter of mosaics and the real-life gaze of those heavy-browed Church Fathers in their sweeping chequered robes.

In this way, they were finally tacked onto a tradition that they may, or may not, have been originally intended for, and in this form they survived. This is where, every now and then, someone would find them and be struck again by the odd, immediate, untarnished people that jumped so lively out of its pages.

Most of the time they sat, forgotten, in monastery libraries, or mouldered away in someone's damp lodgings, or were torn up and used to kindle fire or, as wrapping, to pack something more valuable than themselves. Or else they just slowly degraded, cobwebbed and eaten to holes by insects. They crumbled to dust in the corners of whatever rooms there were in the Dark Ages, sifting down until the little piles of their remains were found one day by someone who clicked their tongue and swept them away – without ever knowing what a precious thing it was they had lost.

Now, today, there are just over seventy manuscripts still extant. Some of these somehow crept their way north to Italy where they eventually arrived, in the fourteenth century, just in time for the dawn of humanism. At this point, partly because Petrarch, the great Italian scholar and poet, said so, ancient texts were suddenly highly prized. If these fragile, increasingly scarce manuscripts weren't actively sought for and preserved, then the door to the great storehouse of ancient thought would close and there'd be no way to open it again. That whole world of thought would be gone. To Petrarch, this was a horrifying prospect. So now ancient texts were hunted down, collected, copied, translated into Latin (if they were Greek) and passed reverently from hand to educated hand. Travelling at home or abroad, no opportunity was missed for inspecting known libraries, both private and monastic.

When Petrarch, on his way to Rome, stopped in Florence, he made the rounds of the major collectors: Boccaccio, for instance, and the powerful lawyer and politician Lapo da Castiglionchio, both of whom had large private libraries they were happy to show off and share. Only recently, Boccaccio had given Castiglionchio a manuscript of Quintilian's *Instituto Oratorio*, which Castiglionchio then passed on to Petrarch. He also lent him some Cicero, a rare copy of some speeches that Petrarch hadn't come across before. Four years later, Petrarch still hadn't returned it. He wrote to Castiglionchio to apologize. The problem was that Cicero was his most beloved author, and he'd found he couldn't bear to do without it so, since there were no trustworthy copyists nearby, he'd set to copying it out himself. He writes:

> What was left to me but to rely upon my own resources, and
> press these weary fingers and this worn and ragged pen into

the service? The plan that I followed was this. I want you to know it, in case you should ever have to grapple with a similar task. Not a single word did I read except as I wrote… from the very first it was enough for me to know that it was a work of Tullius, and an extremely rare one too… the only difficulty which I experienced in reading and writing at the same time came from the fact that my pen could not cover the ground so rapidly as I wanted it to, whereas my expectation had been rather that it would outstrip my eyes, and that my ardour for writing would be chilled by the slowness of my reading. So the pen held back the eye, and the eye drove on the pen, and I covered page after page, delighting in my task, and committing many and many a passage to memory as I wrote.

Four years – for a careful, non-professional copyist – gives an idea of just how long a labour and just how slow the dissemination of classical texts could be. It was, in practice, back-breaking work. Petrarch records feeling 'the sort of fatigue that springs from excessive manual labour'. Why had he even started? Why did he think himself able to do better than a professional copyist? He began, as he says, 'to regret having undertaken a task for which I had not been trained'. But just as he faltered, suddenly he came across a place 'where Cicero tells how he himself copied the orations of – someone or other; just who it was I do not know…'. His beloved Cicero engaged in the very same laborious task, bent over some similar but unimaginable ancient desk, straining his eyes and his hand and, in poor light, inching out his copy. The echo was enough to spur Petrarch on to the finish.

Lapo da Castiglionchio was a powerful force in fourteenth-century Florence but he managed to make an enemy of the Medicis and when they rose to power he found himself as good as ruined. By the first half of the following century, his grandson, Lapo the younger, was living in such reduced circumstances as to find himself constantly petitioning influential men at the Papal Curia, in the hope of finding employment. The accepted method was to send a letter, accompanied by a translation of an ancient text, so elegantly done as to attract notice. What hadn't been done before? What would make them sit up? He needed something new, something noticeable. Searching along the shelves, perhaps, of his grandfather's library in Florence – I like to think – he found the *Characters*. His was the first translation into Latin.

So there were copies of the *Characters* in Italy in the mid-fifteenth century, slowly, slowly proliferating and slowly making their way northwards. Just short of a hundred years later, they reached Nuremberg, that town of turrets and pinnacles and cobbles and little red weathervanes that you can see if you look at the illustration in the *Nuremberg Chronicle*. Here, something important happened. For just short of a century, Germany had been printing rather than hand-copying books. Here, the *Characters* finally made it into print, both in their original Greek and again in Latin, this time in a translation by Willibald Pirckheimer. In their new paper and print dress, between boards bound in calfskin, they were safe, or if not completely safe, then at least more numerous and more durable.

Pirckheimer was a distinguished German lawyer who spent his life's spare time translating the classics. He was another humanist, waist-deep in the waters of Aristotelianism, although – as he told his friend and correspondent Erasmus – he preferred Isocrates. Isocrates' style was so admirably ornate and he lent himself better to Christianity. His writings, Pirckheimer thought, 'contained most suitable admonitions, and the holiest precepts, agreeing very much with the Christian religion'. In the engravings of his neighbour and best friend Durer, he looks as weighty as his literary tastes, prosperous and well fed, his jowls like dewlaps, disappearing into heavy furs. 'Nothing makes me more angry,' Durer wrote to him in a teasing letter from Venice, 'than when anyone says you are good looking.'

The original from which Pirckheimer translated the *Characters* was an Italian manuscript given to him by Giovanni Francesco Pico Della Mirandola, nephew of the famous philosopher by the same name. Pirckheimer's volume appeared in 1527 with a dedication to Durer, 'once preeminent in the art of portraiture', so that he might learn something from an 'old master'. Because here was an example to follow – here was a gallery of portraits executed with all the wisdom and artfulness of the ancients.

Necessarily, because of grand reasons like the wider culture of Christianity and modest reasons like style and taste, as the *Characters* made their way down the ages they started to take on a different emphasis. It wasn't so much that they began to accrue a purpose that hadn't been there in the original; more that, as they moved towards us, both topographically up the map of Europe, and temporally through the ages that followed, their perceived purpose began to outweigh in importance the detail of their observation. Morality became increasingly front and centre. It was the driving force behind aesthetics and philosophy, and it was a constant anxiety in religion and daily life. The *Characters* had come a long way since Theophrastus acted them out with such relish to his Athenian audience. Their aim was now more solemn: to teach, to improve, not so much to entertain or enlighten. They became part of textbooks on rhetorical style; dry manuals for use in schools and universities, serving a high moral purpose. Because rhetoric too had suffered a refraction. It still held in view the manipulation of an audience in one direction or another, but where previously its aims were predominantly civic, it now had moral persuasion in its sights. It was still useful, as it always had been, as a training for politics, or the law, but it was becoming increasingly necessary for the priesthood. So Thomas Wilson, the sixteenth-century English judge and diplomat, who wrote a famous treatise on rhetoric, echoing Theophrastus, offers his reader the sketch of a miser to use as a pattern for a Demosthenes-style assassination of character, not just in public debate or in a court of law but every Sunday from the pulpit, in order to persuade people towards better lives:

> As in speaking against a covetous man, thus: there is no such pinch penney on live as this good fellow is. He will not lose the paring of his nails. His haire is never rounded for sparing of money, one pair of shoon serve him a twelvemoneth, he is shod with nailes like a horse. He hath been knowne by his coate this thirtie winter.

The bumpkin's nailed shoes and the miser's single cloak have been put to a new end but, however solemnly they are surrounded, however weighted with moral purpose, still they come fizzing and glittering to the surface. They can't help it. They are still alive.

*

In 1592, rocking and shivering their way across the Channel, the *Characters* finally made it to England. This time, it was in the ferociously scholarly edition by Isaac Casaubon, in the original Greek, fully annotated and with a Latin translation. The book was an immediate success, and eight years later, Casaubon himself, with his widow's peak and his needle-thin face and the terrifying hospital-white of his Calvinist collars, followed them across the Channel at the personal invitation of James I. Despite his hungry and forbidding looks, Casaubon was a sociable man and a keen correspondent. He was very much liked by James and for several years he was dined and fêted up and down, from London to Oxford and back again. But the attention and the lavish dinners had come too late. He had the meagre body of a workaholic; no amount of luxury or attention could cushion him now. And, besides, he couldn't change the habits of a lifetime – work and more work.

Part of the reason for this was that he'd had a slow start. As a hunted Huguenot, he was almost always in hiding, unable to attend a school. Up until the age of nineteen, his father was his only tutor, teaching him wherever they happened to find themselves, and in the snatched moments that he was able to do so. Casaubon's first Greek lesson had been taken in a cave in the Swiss mountains. When he was finally able to stop hiding and go to university, he worked assiduously, as if to make up for lost time. But even though he started late, by his early twenties he was a professor at Geneva, and by middle age he was generally considered the most learned man in Europe. He knew ancient Athens as closely as if he'd been a citizen – its literature, of course, but also its habits and odd traditions, the geography of its streets and even the whereabouts of its occasional markets. His edition of the *Characters* was for a very long time definitive. It was immensely popular. Suddenly, it seemed as if everyone wanted to try their hand at character writing and a new genre was born: the genre of the character sketch.

*

What kind of people were these – the new writers of characters? Well, to use Theophrastus' own form, 'toioutos tis', such a one as the poet Thomas Overbury, whose mind was buzzing with business but who sat neatly at his books, his eye sometimes darting out to notice what was important around him – that boy with the silken whiskers, for instance, or that court dodderer who might die and leave a vacancy; the sort of man who applied himself until he saw he'd outrun everyone else, more or less, in brilliance. The kind of person who gathers up his brilliance and takes it to where it will have most effect – the court of James I. Such a man as couldn't help but notice his own superiority, on a daily basis and in public. His looks, his mind, his fitness to control things – his everything, in fact – seemed to him better than those of anyone else around, so that his few friends would argue behind his back over who was more proud, he or Sir Walter Raleigh. He always won, by quite a margin. He beat Sir Walter and Sir Walter was a man who was 'damnable proud'.

So, a haughty man. A man who held his head high, floating almost, above its delicate cow-parsley collar. A man whose movements were graceful but only minimally so, and who – if you watched closely – sometimes fidgeted with irritation, as if to swat something away, as if a fly had got in behind his eyes. Or snapped his head round for no reason, halfway through someone talking, and tutted and picked at something invisible on his cloak.

A man who liked women to keep in their place and told them so, even the ones he wanted. Go, read my poem to Lady Rutland for me, he commanded his friend Ben Jonson – while the lady listened. No matter that she's married; I have the greatest desire for her. This is what women are:

> But physicke for our lust their bodies be,
> But matter fit to shew our love upon:
> But onely shells for our posterity,
> Their soules were giv'n lest men should be alone:

So the kind of man who had limited success with women. The kind who overstepped and talked peremptorily to his friends, demanding favours, waving them about his business with one impatient hand, until his friends, the great Ben Jonson included, became his enemies. So that at last he found himself imprisoned, ulcerated and hungry, in the Tower of London. There he died, poisoned by his best friend's mistress, who sent him tarts she'd baked with 'arsenic, aqua fortis, mercury, powder of diamonds, lapis costitus, great spiders and cantharides' bought from a corrupt apothecary. That kind of man.

*

Or, a hundred years later, when the tradition of character writing was still in full flow, the kind of pale, almost translucent person, who has often not had enough money for food, so has eaten words instead, whose genteel clothes and shoes and arms and legs and the features of whose face are all worn as thin and fine and rubbed as a pencil drawing. Such a one as Jean de La Bruyère, sitting in his one room on a top floor in Paris, watching society pass under his window, in its preposterous wigs. Watching them pass, and thinking, hooped over his manuscripts, while the single curtain that divides his bed from his desk blows in the breeze. The kind of man who persists until his scholarship is such that it attracts the notice of royalty – the Prince de Condé in his case – who invites him to tutor his son and heir so that, ever after, he lives no longer in his one room but in two apartments, in Fontainebleau and in Paris, moving about, surprised at his fortune, among green and gold furniture, and carrying the great cataract of someone else's hair gingerly aloft on his own head. That kind of man.

*

Or, maybe not a man at all, but a nineteenth-century woman – albeit with a man's name; such a woman as slips in and out of French, German, Greek and Latin as easily, and with as little attention, as she slips on and off her shoes but who is, even so, happy to spend her days bent over the rock pools on Ilfracombe beach, looking for marine animals to collect in buckets of seawater. A woman like George Eliot, stopping for lunch of sherry and biscuits, in bare feet and clothes that 'won't spoil', sitting on a rock with George Lewes, the philosopher, writer and naturalist who was her life's love and soulmate. The kind of woman who wants to know the proper, scientific names for things – a woman after Aristotle's own heart – who makes a paper box for a caterpillar so as to watch its behaviour when cut in half. Or who writes happily of her seven weeks of marine biological research, 'You would laugh to see our room decked with yellow pie-dishes, a footbath, glass jars and phials, all full of zoophytes or molluscs or annelids.'

Such a woman as has read both Casaubon's *Characters*, and La Bruyère and who, herself, writes novels that will be more widely read and admired than either. A woman, even so, whose mouth is too heavy and masculine for what she's been told is correct, whose nose is too hooked and too bony and behind whose pale eyes the ghost of the woman she isn't, and can't be, struggles with the woman she is. In the street, going back to her specimen-filled hotel room, she walks with a long stride. Her chin is forwards and her rear is out. She carries in her hands her buckets of specimens and she looks about her, as she goes, with complete absorption. But if you stop her and greet her, recalling her back to herself, something crosses her face like the shadow of a bird, before the warmth of her conscious attention settles itself on you, whoever you are and whatever you happen to be doing. She can't help it, because her mind keeps company with men. Clever men who, whatever their mouths say, have told her, or she has thought they have told her, silently, just with their eyes, that she is herself a specimen, a bizarre biological fluke, a gender anomaly. 'Behold me', Henry James wrote to his father, 'literally in love with this great horse-faced, bluestocking.' That kind of woman.

*

Or, maybe again, such a man as is blown all his life from place to place like a leaf. A man like Elias Canetti who was born in Bulgaria and came to Manchester and then went, in quick succession, to Vienna, Zurich, Frankfurt and back to Vienna before taking shelter in England again and, in his last years, back to Zurich, where he died. Whose profusion of hair stands upright, as if astonished at it all, and whose face has concentrated itself inwards, receded behind his spectacles and behind the waterfall of his moustache. There, like Overbury, he held council with his own brilliance, sitting in judgement on his country of exile and its favourite poets, while seducing its female philosophers. England's intellect was decaying, he mumbled, as he made love to Iris Murdoch. The kind of man, a moment later, who adjusts his trousers, shaking his head and muttering, 'No, I don't think there's anything that leaves me quite as cold as that woman's intellect.'

A man who sat in cafés stirring his bitterness into his coffee, cursing England for its cultural parochiality while watching and wishing for the doe-eyed English girls, who crossed their legs just so, and sat at other tables reading *Four Quartets*, with softly parted lips. Ach… T.S. Eliot is 'a libertine of the void, a foothill of Hegel, a desecrator of Dante'. He is 'thin lipped, cold hearted, prematurely old… armed with critical points instead of teeth, tormented by a nymphomaniac of a wife'. They must be stupid – all of them – because they hadn't read his own book, his great novel – or worse, if they had, they hadn't said anything about it.

However, Canetti was also the kind of man to notice that, for all its rootedness in observation, the *Characters* was full of overheard speech. A man who, when he wrote his own acid sketches, decided to call them not *The New Theophrastus*, as planned, but *Earwitness*.

That is just a handful of the figures, one for each century, who were inspired by Theophrastus' form and wrote their own versions of the *Characters*. There were many, many others – bishops, moralists, playwrights, pamphleteers, satirists, essayists, poets and novelists. Addison and Steele wrote them for the *Tatler* and the *Spectator*. Thackeray wrote them. Dickens wrote them. See how they feed into the development of the English essay, the academics say, looking at their underlying message, their short form, their showcasing of razor-blade intellect. This is the well-trodden path that the *Characters* has traditionally taken, the path of the literary sketch. But this is a form that seems very limited for someone of Theophrastus' breadth, for his generosity and gentleness of temperament, 'ever ready to do a kindness'. It seems too dogmatic, too judgemental, for someone so accepting of the mixed nature of things, someone so aware of the necessity for compromise. It seems too moral, too abstract. There is none of the oddness or clutter of ordinary life in any of these later versions. Where, for instance, are all the pots and kettles, the ploughs and baskets, the nailed shoes and threadbare cloaks, the kippers, the honey, the twisted Spartan walking sticks? Where are the markets and the barbers, the expensive theatre seats and the hot water tanks at the public baths? Where, in short, is Theophrastus' profusion of observed data – all that detail, all that solid materiality of things? Where is the gossipy direct speech? And where the actual life?

As the *Characters* slowly disseminated, with each new version something was repeatedly overlooked. Each time it was passed on, something about the atmosphere of the original characters – their essential, scientific neutrality – was sacrificed to the observance of later obsessions. Something about the absence of message or obvious purpose, something about observation for its own sake, was overruled and replaced with judgement, or the neurosis of moralizing, or satire's personal and very public sting.

But all this time something else had been happening, something more hidden, something winding secretly forwards all along, towards a different flowering. Something that appeals to a gentler type of writer, or a different type of writing, was being passed from hand to hand. Like John Hoskyns in 1599, for example, a lawyer and a poet, who gave a pupil of his in the Temple a copy of Philip Sidney's *Arcadia*. Along with it, to help his protégé with his writing, he gave him a copy of his own treatise, *Directions for Speech and Style*. 'Men are described most excellentlie in *Arcadia*,' he says. Much of this he had previously assumed to be a result of Sidney's knowledge of Aristotle, both the moral philosophical and the rhetorical works, 'but lately' he had changed his mind: 'I thinke alsoe that he had much helpe out of *Theophrasti imagines*'. Casaubon's *Characters* arrived in England in 1592. The *Arcadia* was first published, after much revising, in 1593. In 1598, Ben Jonson's play *Every Man in his Humour* was first put on in London, with its debt to Theophrastus on its sleeve and Shakespeare on the cast list. So, when Hoskyns made his present to his pupil, character writing was very much in the air.

Much later, another John – John Buxton – picked up Hoskyns' trail. He was an ornithologist and a Renaissance literature expert at Oxford, who died in 1979. He had in his collection a seventeenth-century manuscript index to the *Arcadia* which referenced all the passages descriptive of character. Whoever it was who made the index explained their reason for doing so in a note, 'were all ye choice pieces gathered out and sorted generally by themselves, they would make as good a booke of characters as is yett extant'. The Coward, the Skinflint and the Bumpkin are all there, in ways that echo Theophrastus' own versions of them so many centuries earlier, in their manner of speech and their small actions, not as a book of characters but as something else, a form not yet officially invented. Buxton ends his observations on the same thoughtful note: 'The importance of the Character books in the development of the English essay has long been recognised; perhaps it is time to consider their relevance to the early history of the novel to which the *Arcadia* gave so vital an impulse.'

John Hoskyns, who noticed it first, met his end when Theophrastus' Bumpkin walked right out of the *Characters* and into a crowd at the Assizes. There 'a massive country fellow stepped on his toe' so heavily in his self-nailed shoes that it had to be amputated. The wound went bad and Hoskyns died of gangrene – a homely echo of the death of his mentor, Sidney, who died from a gangrenous thigh-wound at Arnhem. The *Characters* went on into the future without them, looking not down the closed little cul-de-sac of the character sketch but away to something more expansive, something more mysterious and wide-ranging and far into the future, to the long reaches of the realist novel.

*

Or this is how it seems. This is how it feels even though the thinking is wildly anachronistic. It isn't possible. The gap is too wide. The forms are too irreparably different. Theophrastus' *Characters* is a minor work. The similarity, if there is one, is a mirage, an accidental repetition, a trick of the eye which is not to be trusted.

Unless it isn't. Unless a link can be found so that the journey can actually be traced back from end to end. Because words are in essence anachronistic, or, more accurately, diachronistic. Men and women sink under time's waters and are lost but their words bob to the surface like paper boats and continue, carried on by the current, for as long as there are eyes to read them or the paper itself allows.

Puzzling over the echoes I hear – however faint, however unlikely – it seems I am not alone. There is a pattern to this puzzlement that repeats over the last few centuries. Virginia Woolf, for instance, didn't altogether like the *Arcadia* but she couldn't help noticing that it was apparently ahead of its time. She calls it 'a luminous globe' in which 'all the seeds of English fiction lie latent'.

At almost exactly the same time, G.K. Chesterton looks out at the Buckinghamshire rain, scratching his enormous head over a similar problem in an earlier author. Why does Chaucer feel like 'the grandfather of all our million novelists', he can't help asking himself. He is looking particularly at *The Canterbury Tales*. Why does it feel like 'the first true novel in history'? He works his way round and round the subject. He knows it's anachronistic. It must be an accident. Even so, he can't stop feeling the connection. 'He was a novelist when there were no novels,' he repeats in puzzlement. 'I mean by the novel the narrative that is not primarily an anecdote or an allegory but is valued because of the almost accidental variety of actual human characters.' In other words, why are these people made of words, these pilgrims, so vivid? Because look, there is a break in style between everything Chaucer wrote up to and including *The House of Fame* and the work that came after it, culminating in *The Canterbury Tales*. There is a shift, he can't help noticing, from the 'purely rhythmic decorative style' of medieval writing that Chaucer has mostly used before to 'something suggestive of the realism of modern novels'. Why is that? What are the models? Where might a link or an explanatory influence be found? He turns to the classics. He thinks about the dominance of classical thought in medieval literature. Any man of Chaucer's time who had the luck 'to hear the right lectures, or look at the right manuscript... looked straight down the ages into the radiant mind of Aristotle'. But that is as far as Chesterton goes.

Well, GK, what if Chaucer saw something specific that changed his style? What if he looked right past the radiant mind of Aristotle and into the equally radiant mind of his friend? What if he came across the *Characters,* in manuscript somewhere? It isn't altogether impossible.

*

The earliest image we have of Chaucer is in the margin of the Ellesmere manuscript of the *Canterbury Tales*, just at the beginning of Chaucer's Tale of Melibee. It was painted in 1420, twenty years after the presumed date of his death and it is oddly out of proportion. Chaucer has a large, carefully painted head and torso, much too big for the horse he is riding, let alone for his own little dwindled legs. Nevertheless, the features are so characterful it is thought to be an adaptation from a panel portrait painted in his lifetime. Hoccleve the poet, who was a young and aspiring man about town when Chaucer was writing the *Canterbury Tales*, made a copy of it for his *Regement of Princes*, saying:

> The resemblance
> Of him hath in me so fressh lyflyness
> That to putte othir men in remembraunce
> Of his persone I have here his lyknesse
> Do make, to this end in sothfastnesse,
> That thei that have of him lost thought and mynde
> By this peynture may ageyn him fynde.

There wasn't, at this period, any tradition of portrait likeness so if the picture bears a resemblance to Chaucer himself it is almost accidental. What is more likely is that it catches Chaucer's atmosphere, his soft inwardness, the feeling of his 'thought and mynde', of being in his company. He is plumpish, well wrapped in woollen garb and with a short, silken, forked beard. His eyes are cast down, his mouth is pursed and his face is wistful as if he were lost in thought. Even his horse, in its little black slippers, tiptoeing forward across a smudge of green, seems to be trying to be inconspicuous. But at the same time, if you could reach out and prod him back to himself, he looks teasable, temptable, fond of comforts, as if he might wake into some kind of performance, a funny story, or a gently self-mocking anecdote. He has the look of a medieval Buster Keaton.

Obviously, Chaucer was many things. He was poet, father of our literary language, and at the same time he was a wool man, working at the customs office on the wharves of London. He was an occasional, circumspect diplomat, a loner and a courtier. He started out, in his teens, on the upwardly mobile track of life in service at court. Dressed in tight tights and a bum-freezing doublet, he must then have looked good enough and been witty enough to be taken into the retinue of Prince Lionel's wife, Lady Elizabeth de Burgh. Perhaps he thought he was going places. He then married, relatively young, at about twenty-two, a woman who was socially a little above him. There are, in his various poems, little snippets in which he appears to be self-mocking, as if he had what might now be called a complex relationship with himself, as if he was disappointed by something, his original choices, his marriage, or his inability to resist – what exactly? – the compromises that his life required perhaps, or the envy of comparison, or his frustrated literary ambition?

'What man artow?' the Host of the *Tales* asks Chaucer, as if he was deliberately unsocial, or different in some way. What kind of man do you call yourself? And the answer is, such a man as always looks at the ground, staring 'as thou wouldest finde an hare'. The sort of man who is not to be taken seriously, who is to be shaken out of his introspection by his companions, precisely because he might take himself too seriously; the kind of man who has private dreams, perhaps of his own fame or perhaps just of the folly of the world, himself included. A man round in the waist, 'a popet in an arm to embrace/For any woman, small and fair of face'. A man whose own looks are 'elvish' and who won't join in unless he's forced. Tell us a story, Chaucer. And he tells us a story so boring that he is the only one of the pilgrims to be interrupted and not allowed to finish. In the worlds he creates, his little avatar is solemn and comical and without audience. A 'drasty' rhymer, whose rhymes are 'nat worthe a toord' and for whose nights of study there is no recompense beyond an aching head and a fool's dazed expression.

Chaucer spent his whole life on the periphery of the court, and at the wool excise, in both of which places he would have had to make the kind of compromises that Theophrastus had to make at Pella. The wool men were notoriously corrupt and self-seeking and he held his position among them for a dozen years or so. If he couldn't bring himself to profit from it personally, he had to turn a blind eye while everyone else did. Wool, in the fourteenth century, was the equivalent of coal in the nineteenth or oil in our own. As such, it attracted a sharp and predatory company of sharks: speculators, price-fixers and profiteers, all of whose eyes were made to be turned blind at wrongdoing, whose fingers were strong for scratching, and whose backs were broad for receiving, and all of whose pockets were ready for lining, because huge fortunes were there for the taking if you weren't too scrupulous about your methods. And here was Chaucer, an ungreedy, undangerous man who would be Controller of Customs without complaint and without asking for anything for himself in return.

For twelve long years, Chaucer managed these dark waters. He couldn't have failed to notice the corruption but he never hindered it. He must so often have been tempted to take a bite here and there for himself but it seems he never did. He just bent over his desk and kept his quiet. He made his accounts, his records, his comprehensive and exhausting 'reckenynges' and then he walked home through the teeming streets, perhaps asking himself in a troubled way why he did it. And why hadn't he the energy to profit himself? Did he think his conscience was clean just because he kept quiet? What hypocrisy. He knew well enough what was going on. He was exhausted by it. It took such energy not to look, to turn away, to smile while these things were done, to look at the figures that screamed corruption at him, to arrange them nonetheless in their little ordered columns. What a farce. What weakness to be a frame for such a tapestry but to be neither in nor out, neither for the outright good, nor wholly for the bad. Why was he like this? What did he want? He walked a little awkwardly because he carried with him the pitcher of wine that was, by royal decree, his allocation and that he had to collect each day from the Port of London. On he went, vaguely trying not to spill the wine, thinking his back-and-forth thoughts and watching, as he did so, the scurrying people in the streets about their business, all the different degrees of them, high and low, all the different ways you could be half-good or half-bad, or both.

Chaucer lived, for the period he was at the Wool Customs, in lodgings above Aldgate, the easternmost gate to the city of London. This was probably not much more than one fortress room, in the south tower, whose walls were at least six feet thick and whose windows, buried in the six-foot walls, were not windows at all but arrow slits. Here he lived alone, apart from his wife, a separation that seems to have been his condition for most of his marriage, aside from the time it took to father three or four children. Here, when his work was done, he returned, instead of going out to socialize or to better his state in any way, choosing instead to strain his eyes in the dust-laden shafts of what remained of the day, or by the flickering light of candles. Here 'also domb as any stoon' he read whatever books he could lay his hands on, or wrote, through the night, so many of his own.

In the room below him, the gate's guard were housed and he would have heard them, through the watches, clanking and clattering, talking, and occasionally shouting. In summer, the gate was not shut until nine at night, so he would have felt the thrum of all that human activity, coming and going in carts, clip-clopping on horses, or pushing and pigeon-stepping in crowds, or in processions, or just alone on weary foot, the constant tide of people of all kinds and all ages, in and out of the city's great heart. So much was happening. So many stories. He would have felt it and heard it, but in his twilight inside the south tower he wouldn't have seen very much. He would have sat in his room like a blind man sits in his own skull, listening, thinking, smelling, feeling, imagining. Maybe, along with his complex position at work, that too explains his inwardness, his feeling of remove.

The people Chaucer wanted to measure himself against were not at the court or the customs. They were his contemporaries abroad, on the continent. Before his job at the customs, he'd been to France on some kind of diplomatic business; he'd fought and been taken prisoner in the Hundred Years War; he'd been to Spain and, although Italy didn't yet exist as a nation, he'd been to the city-states of Genoa and Florence. It was these last two places in particular that seemed to lodge in his head. Dante had been dead for half a century or more but he had left his work behind him; his greatest work, the *Divine Comedy*, was written not in literary Latin but in his own Tuscan dialect. Petrarch, crowned laureate one year after Chaucer's own birth, was still alive and writing. Boccaccio had completed his *Decameron*, also in Tuscan dialect. The Renaissance had begun, with the rediscovery of the ancient worlds of Greece and Rome at its heart. Manuscripts were being traded and translated, new things being found and preserved all the time. The humanists were in a ferment of activity, writing letters to each other, discussing philosophy and morality and science, translating manuscripts, and writing new works, and in all this where was muddy-brained England? The continent was where Chaucer's imagination was. This was what he thought mattered.

One of the things he was labouring over in the evenings was a translation of Boethius' *Consolations of Philosophy*, from Latin into contemporary English. Translation had three functions. The first two were preservation and dissemination. The third was social, even political. In England, with the notable exception of Langland's *Piers Plowman*, literature was written in French or in Latin. These were the languages of the court and of scholarship. Writing in English immediately widened your audience. Books were not readily available. Printing hadn't yet been invented, so they were still in manuscript form. This meant that although, as a culture, we were no longer strictly oral, we were not yet strictly literate either. We were somewhere in between – an aural culture perhaps, a culture of ears. Even reading to yourself was done out loud. If Chaucer was sitting dumb as a stone, reading his books, then he was in a minority. Poems were 'published' by being read aloud to an audience. If you were writing for entertainment, or to hold a mirror up to nature, to make people aware of themselves, or to make people better, whether morally or educationally, you needed to be understood. How much wider, how much longer-lasting would your audience be if you addressed it in the language everyone familiarly spoke? If you wanted society to better itself, how much more could you achieve if everyone could understand your message?

These are tricky narrows to negotiate because it would be wrong to imagine Chaucer as egalitarian in any modern sense. He was a medieval man and he believed in degree. You were born to a certain position in society, and the structure of society was hierarchical, just like the structure of heaven. It was almost sacred. Nevertheless, there was room for adjustment and improvement within your allotted place, or within the confines of your own self. Chaucer had subtle views on women, for instance. The Wife of Bath is a woman who has made what improvements she can to her own condition – she is someone who has fully realized her own talents and capabilities. As such, she is a mouthpiece for female strength; strength not just of character but of will, of vivid intelligence, sense of adventure, self-reliance, profit and desire. She may not be man's equal in society but she is his match, his other necessary half. It is her will that wins, outwitting her husband in the end. Through her will, and only so, lies the route to a happy marriage.

So much for the material things of life. After that, there was religion, and religion encouraged you to lift your eyes, to mend yourself internally. Improvement, within your allotted position, was part of the road to heaven, and in this education was the greatest help. Or so Chaucer must have reasoned.

That this – even so modified – was a political position is clear from the prologue to *A Treatise on the Astrolabe*, which Chaucer wrote for his son, 'lyte Lewis'. In it, he goes to some length to explain why he has written it so simply and in English. He has simplified it because in all the other treatises there are concepts too abstruse, 'to harde to thy tender age of ten yeer to conceyve'. And he has written it 'under full light reules and naked wordes in Englissh' for the reason that 'Latin canst thou yit but small, my litel sone'. But Chaucer knew that the treatise wasn't private, that it would reach a wider audience –

perhaps that was, in fact, his intent after all. 'I preye mekely', he says, that anyone else 'that redith or herith this lytel treatise' will excuse its simple language. Perhaps Lewis is a screen for the fact that what he intends is to educate more widely, to demystify something that has been the closely guarded preserve of the educated few. Knowledge is enlightenment. It is the way people better themselves in every sense. And knowledge is power, as Alexander complained to Aristotle, his former tutor. Making it widely available shares it out and as such necessarily diminishes the power of those who previously had it all to themselves. 'Alexander to Aristotle, greetings,' his peremptory letter runs. 'You have *not* done well to publish your books of oral teachings; for what is there now that we excel others in, if those things you privately taught us are now laid open to all?'

Whatever his intent, Chaucer knew he was on dangerous ground, not just politically but linguistically, and he felt it necessary first to make a defence on behalf of English as a fit language for scholarship in its own right. These English instructions will work as well and be as true, he says, as the Greek instructions were to the Greeks, and the 'Arabiens in Arabik, and to Jews in Ebrew, and to Latyn folk in Latyn… And God woot that in alle these languages and in many moo han these conclusions ben suffisantly lerned and taught… right as diverse pathes leden diverse folk the righte way to Rome.'

To write in English was subversive. It took away from the clergy and the academics who preferred Latin. It took away from the court, which preferred French. It might be judged revolutionary, in the literal sense, a turning upside down of the sacred order and, as Alexander worried, a lessening of influence in both spheres. Just in case anyone might be tempted to accuse him of that, Chaucer closes his prologue with a caveat that sites his treatise squarely and unarguably within the established hierarchy of society. English is the king's possession, his treasure, at the service of his glory and upholding the divinely ordained structure of his own society. There is no threat here: 'I ne usurpe'. Chaucer is talking about copyright but he lets the word ring with all its full range of associations:

> God save the king, that is lord of this language, and alle that him faith berith and obeith, everich in his degre, the more and the lasse.

The humanist project was utopian. It looked to a society that was improved simply because its populace was improved. It believed in education and science and method, in the cultivation of practical, civic qualities, of active virtue. Whatever your lot in life, you were the master of your own mind and temperament. The humble country parson and his brother the ploughman are both among the lowest in degree and the most admirable of Chaucer's pilgrims. By the time he came to write the *Canterbury Tales* (probably in the mid-1380s), character, for Chaucer, had become an energy, an expression of individual personality, not just a way of describing someone's position in society.

The question is: how did this idea come to him? Because it was by no means the norm. No one else, at this date, was interested in personality. No one else was interested in the texture of reality, in what life is actually like. The closest parallel to the *Tales*, for instance, Boccaccio's *Decameron*, which Chaucer certainly knew and used, has characters all taken from the nobility, all of roughly the same age – between eighteen and twenty-seven. These are barely more than ciphers for various virtues. They are disguised in names that reflect their qualities. When they speak, they don't talk so much as make speeches. They address each other formally, in ornate and literary language. They are all beautiful, graceful, modest, of 'matchless charm' and ready wit and they are all incapable of managing simple tasks like getting dressed, or washing, without the help of a servant or two. They retire (with their servants), in order to escape the plague, to a palace on a hill outside Florence where, on arrival, they find to their great relief all the necessary housework has magically been done:

> The cellars were stocked with precious wines... the place
> had been cleaned from top to bottom, the beds in the rooms
> were made up, the whole house was adorned with seasonable
> flowers of every description and the floors had been carpeted
> with rushes.

Boccaccio was writing with the Black Death still a recent trauma. Florence, that ant heap of mercantile, artistic and literary activity, had seen its population halved. But it wasn't just that. The plague had destabilized something deeper. People hadn't known how to make sense of it. Nothing worked against it. Nothing stopped it or helped it or explained the savagery of its attack. All the sacred bonds had been broken: husbands had fled and left their wives to die; mothers had abandoned their children. Some people had given up and spent their days and nights riotously drunk. No one had been properly buried. People had died alone like wild animals, and now servants and urchins, those who had by some miracle survived, were parading in the clothes and jewellery they had pillaged from their betters. One of the things the *Decameron* sets out to do is to reorder, to control, to put civilization back on its legs again. The cleanliness of the palace that Boccaccio's travellers find is a balm for the chaos of rotting bodies in Florence's streets, for the horror and squalor of the unattended death. It isn't designed to be believable. It is designed to soothe and improve, to salvage something from a world turned upside down. Boccaccio was writing to re-establish a certain order of society, to entertain an audience that was small, noble, educated, conditioned in the same ways as he was – but also to wake them up to the vitality of the natural world and to celebrate love as one of its most irrepressible motivations and expressions. He was writing away the chaos of civic breakdown and the anxiety of superstitious morality and making new again. It is presented as a highly wrought and self-consciously artistic whole, of which he is necessarily in complete and cool control.

Chaucer chooses otherwise. What material he borrows from Boccaccio, like the Miller's Tale, he subverts. Instead of returning to order and reinstating a lightly modified ideal, he allows the story to spool out of control, descending at last into sexual chaos and farce. It is as if the text blows with a stormy force all its own, in the face of which even Chaucer himself is powerless. He presents himself plunged up to his neck in the flood of his own work, bobbing alongside his fictional pilgrims, like a cork on a surging tide. When he comes to take his turn and tell his own tales, they are muddled into the middle, buried in among the rest. What's more, his first is boring, badly shaped and barely in control of its material. He has, in fact, to make two attempts because he is the only one of the pilgrims who can't manage the business of storytelling. At the meta level, this is obviously as self-conscious, complex and artistic as anything Boccaccio is doing in the *Decameron*, but at the simple level of experience it creates something that feels as whimsical, uncontrollable and engulfing as life itself. In other words, it feels real.

If Boccaccio, artistically, is interested in love as an ideal, Chaucer is interested in marriage. Perhaps this is because his own was so complex, or so lonely. Women were impossible. They were completely different from how men had told them to be. They were problematic and vivid and wilful when they were supposed to be meek and demure and chaste. They gave roaring birth to bloody babies out of unmentionable parts of their bodies and that was terrifying. It made them powerful when they were meant to be weak. And they wanted things. Chaucer, so close a watcher of human behaviour, couldn't have helped but notice the strain that women were under, the different and impossible standards they were held to. He couldn't have helped but see the difference between expectation and reality, not just men's expectations of women – and vice versa – but also women's expectations of themselves. It was unfair and it was impractical. There was so much disappointment on both sides. Perhaps in his work at the Wool Office, perhaps in the context of his advancement, or lack of it, or of the expectations of his wife, Chaucer felt for himself how falling short in the eyes of others can chafe – how easily life can become a trap and how being trapped affects the character, how it can stoop and cripple and distort.

Added to this, he had before him the example of a particularly powerful and determined woman in the shape of his sister-in-law, Katharine Swynford. Katharine was governess to John of Gaunt's children and more importantly his long-term mistress and eventually third wife. She was born noble but in all other respects she was a useful prototype for the Wife of Bath. She was clever, manipulative, ambitious, free of small shame, full of appetite and very beautiful. She must have been challenging, if not fascinating, to Chaucer. Was she good? Or bad? She was certainly a million miles from any ideal. Whatever she was, she was effective. She wanted money and power and John of Gaunt and she got all three.

So, for Chaucer, women are not quite what they are for Boccaccio. 'Women,' Boccaccio has one of his ladies say, 'when left to themselves, are not the most rational creatures, and… without the supervision of some man or other their capacity for getting things done is somewhat restricted. We are fickle, quarrelsome, suspicious, cowardly, and easily frightened.'

In the context of contemporary thinking on the nature of women, this was mild. Women, through Eve, were the source of sin. Sitting and looking out from behind the Wife of Bath's eyes, Chaucer has her ask herself softly, having heard the litany of woman's wickedness read out to her by her fifth husband: 'Who would wene, or who wolde suppose/ The woe that in myn herte was, and pyne?' In other words, who could imagine the grief and pain, the insult in her heart? Was she so much worse than any number of men? Why the double standard? And why was there no public redress for this, the view that men disseminated about womankind?

> By God, if women hadde writen stories,
> As clerkes han withinne their oratories,
> They wolde han writen of men Moore wikkednesse
> Than all the mark of Adam may redresse.

Into the mouth of the venal Wife of Bath, Chaucer puts the case for women, not as the saints that contemporary literature demanded, but as the muddied and managing equals of men. How complicated it was, to be a woman. You were allied to sin in a way that it seemed men weren't. Then you were instructed to be spotless.

Up in his tower room, at night, Chaucer has been reading Jerome's treatise *Against Jovinianus*. In the inconsistent light of the candle, he listens to Jerome's voice and Jerome's voice is grating. His judgements are harsh. He presses for virginity as a woman's only hope. Then, in the middle of Jerome's text, there is suddenly something else, something that Chaucer recognizes absolutely as a match for what he sees around him. In the middle of the text, there is the Theophrastus fragment, describing his imagined wife. *She complains that one lady goes out better dressed than she does, that everyone admires another: 'I am a poor despised nobody at the ladies' assemblies'; 'Why did you ogle that creature next door?', 'Why were you talking to the maid?'* From this, another voice rises clear. It is the voice of a woman caught in a cage. He can hear her thrashing about, savage like a cat, clawing through the bars at her captors. Why is she like that? Is it just because she's confined? Would she be the same if she were free – or not? Chaucer draws back the bolts and opens the cage. Out steps the Wife of Bath, haranguing.

She is the same woman. She still lays about her, raging word for word with the same complaints. 'Why is my neighboure's wyf so gay?' asks the Wife of Bath:

> She is honoured overal ther she gooth;
> I sit at hoom; I have no thrifty clooth.
> What dostow at my neighboure's hous?
> Is she so fair? Artow so amorous?
> What whisper ye with oure mayde?

Whether what he wants is a screen to hide behind, in order to say what might not otherwise be sayable, or whether he sees its potential not just for showing character but for making a person in the round, Chaucer fastens on to the materiality of Theophrastus' images. He catches the vividness of a particular voice as a literary strategy, the idea of dialogue. He spins the Wife's character out of the extract's cloth entirely: the vigour of her thwarted will, the determination of her logic, her force, her physicality and all the heat and energy of her desires. The extract is quoted almost word for word, and almost completely, the only changes being to the order of the original, along with the fact that he puts all of it into the mouth of the Wife herself, either as her own or as her own report of her husband's speech. For example, Theophrastus says:

Observe that as far as wives go you cannot pick and choose.
You must take her as you find her. If she has a bad temper, or
is a fool, if she has a blemish, or is proud, or has bad breath,
whatever her fault may be – all this we learn after marriage.
Horses, asses, cattle, even slaves of the smallest worth, clothes,
kettles, wooden seats, cups, and earthenware pitchers are first
tried and then bought. A wife is the only thing that is not tested
before she is married, for fear she may not give satisfaction.

The Wife, accusing her first husband, repeats back to him:

Thou seiest that oxen, asses, hours and houndes,
They ben assayed at diverse stounds;
Bacyns, lavours, ere that men them bye;
Spoons and stooles and al switch housbondrye
And so ben pottes, clothes and array;
But folke of wyves make none assay.

Chaucer is interested in character, in how much is circumstantial and how much is innate, and that is very new, but he is also interested (as Boccaccio is) in how much, and in what ways, writing feeds into life. How, he seems always to be asking, do these two very different realities interact? In this regard, he makes of Theophrastus' fragment a whole repeating world which opens itself out, through the spaces of the Wife of Bath's Prologue, like a hall of mirrors.

It is a book in a book in a book. When the Wife steps so unforgettably into the *Tales,* she is the archetypal woman of Theophrastus' treatment incarnate. She is alive enough that we feel her anger. We see its cause and we see the end it holds constantly in sight. At the same time, Theophrastus' original treatment is also present in its own right, as text, exerting its relentless influence, in the Wife's day-to-day life. It is her husband Jankyn's favourite book and constant companion, the book of *Wikked Wyves*. This is an anthology of female vice that Jankyn calls his 'Valerie and Theofraste' and it contains, among many other things, Jerome's *Against Jovinianus*.

Jankyn reads it day and night, sometimes out loud to his wife, gloating over its judgements and berating her for her congenital immorality. It is a torment. In the end, the Wife destroys it. She snatches at the offending pages and tears them to shreds. She and Jankyn resort to violence. They beat each other until she loses consciousness and is close to death. Terrified that she will die, Jankyn utters frantic apologies over her body, only for her to revive and smack him in the face. Exhausted, equally culpable and equally reduced at last, they live happily and truly ever after, against all of Theophrastus' predictions. Literature's destructive influence is destroyed by literature, and life – real, messy, compromised life – is made not only possible but happy.

Chaucer's discovery of the Theophrastus fragment is something that fires him with a new approach. The idea of creating character in the round, rather than just offering the flat coordinates of a single quality, is for Chaucer a revelation. We experience the Wife in the same way we experience the people we meet in life, that is, on her own terms, at the first hand of her own voice and opinions. She has a weight and an unknowability and an authenticity to her that is entirely new. She is much more than we can grasp, however many times we read her.

*

It's impossible to know when Chaucer read Jerome and found the nugget of Theophrastus' nagging wife but, in the *Tales* at least, Theophrastus seems to be at the forefront of Chaucer's mind, both indirectly, in his influence on Chaucer's approach to his pilgrims, and directly by name. Beyond finding a new way to characterize, beyond creating what looks like a catalogue of society's various types, Chaucer names Theophrastus repeatedly, four times in all, in the *Tales*, although he mentions him nowhere else in the whole of his work before that. It is as if, having found him, he couldn't get him out of his head.

Did he ever come across the *Characters* in manuscript, somewhere among his book-collecting friends? It's impossible to know. In December 1372, Chaucer went on some kind of diplomatic mission to Italy and was away until the following autumn. He was detailed to go to Genoa and possibly to Padua to meet Petrarch, whom he greatly admired. The expense accounts show that he then went on to Florence, probably early in the spring of 1373. Here lived Lapo da Castiglionchio, the prominent politician, a banker, and a known collector of manuscripts, whose grandson, of the same name, was the first to translate the *Characters* into Latin. Lapo the elder was a stiff and self-important man but he prided himself on his library. I like to imagine him turning to the king's envoy – this 'popet' of a man, in his English wool, so quiet, who people said was so keen on learning, wafting a hand in Chaucer's direction, as if he didn't care either way, offering with nasal condescension – I have a few classical manuscripts that you might like to look at. Do come by, if it would interest you.

So, I can get Chaucer to the right city, and even to the right family, but I am a generation away from the first Latin text and Chaucer didn't read Greek. I'm left with the feeling that, like Theophrastus' *Characters*, there is something taxonomic about Chaucer's pilgrims, something different from the monoculture of Boccaccio's youthful nobles. Is it just chance that there is something much closer to science than established literature in the neutrality of his descriptions? His types are characterized, not through descriptions of the abstract qualities of a particular virtue or vice, but through the character's relation to the matter of life: to their possessions, bodies, food or clothes; or to the food, bodies, clothes or possessions of others. Is it coincidence that, as in Theophrastus' *Characters*, there is no judgement here, simply the presentation of observed data and the solid materiality of things? Or is it just chance that there are thirty pilgrims in the *Canterbury Tales*, including Chaucer, just as there are thirty character sketches? Or that the pilgrims speak each with their own distinct and idiosyncratic voice, like Theophrastus' characters, in direct speech?

These are important questions. Chaucer is the father of the English canon. Is this perhaps why I followed you, Theophrastus, without really knowing – going on instinct – answering the pull of your shadowy presence as the waves follow the shaping force of the moon? All of us, Chesterton, Woolf, Buxton and I, sitting at our desks, looking out of our windows, puzzling away at the same thoughts, feeling the same odd hunch. We sense you, Theophrastus, deep in the DNA of our own literature.

*

For Chesterton, shifting his bulk around his Beaconsfield study and feeling his way backwards from the nineteenth-century novel to Chaucer, his instincts, like mine, make no sense. The jump is too big and too unprecedented. Nevertheless, like Chaucer and the Jerome fragment, the thought won't leave his head. What is it that connects Chaucer with the modern novel? Why do I keep feeling there is a connection? And how does Chaucer stumble on this unusual thing, this anachronism, this way of making real, meetable people out of words?

I am offering you a gossamer line of chance, GK, something as thin and invisible as the first brave thread that the spider throws across the impossible span of a future web. I'm offering something made a little bit out of science, with its demands for the dispassionate and meticulous discipline of observation; and a little bit out of the desire to catalogue and to order, to pattern-make; and a little bit out of style and rhetoric and the ear for dialogue. I admit I am biased. I am looking for a line that I can throw securely back and along which I can haul Theophrastus into the present. I stick it to its stepping stones, through the early Christians to Chaucer and through Chaucer to the novel, to George Eliot, whose last work, *Impressions of Theophrastus Such*, is nothing if not a tacit tribute to his help with her chosen form.

The world is full of such repeats and patterns. Wind flows like water, which flows like wood-grain. Trees grow in the same patterns as rivers. Their roots map like our veins, or mesh like our nervous systems. Maybe the patterns mean nothing. Maybe they are just fractal coincidence, just the forms that life happens to take, as Steinbeck and Ricketts would have it. And why should patterns of thought be any different – their repeat any more indicative of meaning, their recurrence any more consequential?

Whether or not the repeat is significant, whether the connection is there or imagined, there is something in the *Characters* that has always appealed to the novelist. While Steinbeck read up on marine biology and stooped – as George Eliot had at Ilfracombe – over the seabed, concentrating all that masculinity, all that bulk of shoulder and brow, on tiny translucent creatures, at the same time on the other side of the Atlantic, Virginia Woolf was sitting among the packing boxes in her new house at Mecklenburg Square. She was trying to steady her mind. She was trying to distract herself from despair at the coming war by reading Greek because, as she says, 'The Greek has his eye on the object.' She was, as it happens, reading the *Characters*. 'It's a long distance', she observes, 'that one has to roll away to get at Theophrastus and Plato, but worth it.'

Or maybe it was not as impossibly long as she thought. Maybe it could be done bit by bit, travelling back, as if following a thread, across stepping stones.

VI

The Teacher

I'm back in Athens, in a flat in a house with a turret, in a potholed street, where in the evening tall Somali couples stroll arm in arm, the women swathed in patterned fabric. Downstairs, during the day, the granddaughter of the man who designed the turreted house plays Mozart on the flute. She is a member of an orchestra but there is no work for flautists, since the crash. Over and over she spills her music through the mornings, like a trapped bird. In the afternoons, I walk to the American School of Classical Studies, where I take Greek lessons.

I learn that in Modern Greek, to make the future tense, you have to go backwards in time. You take the present-tense endings and add them onto the past-tense stem. So the future is simply the past by way of the present. The connections are all intact – in the language at least. Walking around Athens in January, this seems, for some reason, a blinding insight. The sky is the palest blue and the light has a stillness to it, an unearthly clarity, as if everything was resting from winter. These are the halcyon days, the seven days of respite from storms that Aeolus gave his daughter Alcyone, once she'd turned into a kingfisher, so that she could hatch her eggs in safety. It's warm and still and, walking the potholed streets in sunshine, it does feel as though someone is holding their breath.

Up above, all the balconies have blossomed with washing. Coloured sheets. Someone's long-johns, several identical pairs of them. Aprons. Skirts. Enormous underwear. And among it all, the little caged birds, like mechanisms sprung at the touch of the sun, trill their song at a sky they will never again reach.

It is a sign of rain or storm if a chaffinch kept in the house utters its note at dawn.

And just like that, in his clean garments, stepping his light step, Theophrastus walks back into view, here, in Athens. He must have come back, with Aristotle, sometime after Athens officially surrendered to Alexander. Most likely they returned in 335.

*

Between now and where we left them, in Macedonia, much had happened. Philip's siege of Byzantium failed, his plan to make a night-time sortie frustrated by the city's dogs. Vigilant while the city slept, they heard his army, its muffled clanking under the walls, its siege ladders. They set up a barking that didn't stop until it had awakened their owners, alerting them to the attack. Philip left, fighting his way north into Scythia instead, which was easier. There he met little resistance, taking 20,000 horses and as many women and boys as prisoners. But on his way back, through Thrace, he was attacked. A Thracian spear, thrust up through his kneecap into his thigh and rammed on into the belly of his horse, caused him serious injury. Alexander – so the story goes – saved his life, but Philip was forced home to convalesce. Respite for Athens which, urged on by Demosthenes, was by now preparing for war.

It came on 2 August 338 BCE, when Athens and its allies met Philip, with Alexander on his left flank, on the road to Chaeronea. Carnage. Athens was thoroughly routed, and among the thousands of the dead was the entire 300-strong Sacred Band of Thebes, the paired lovers who were Thebes' elite fighting force. Athens, decimated, fled back inside its walls to prepare for siege. Desperately, they tried to shore up their defences, strengthening the walls with whatever came to hand. Would Athens be fired and its temples rubbled once again, as it had been by the Persians? They had grown so proud and so powerful. Surely Philip would raze the city to the ground?

But in the end and to everyone's surprise, Philip dealt with them very lightly. Some say Aristotle had a hand in moderating his response – that Aristotle persuaded him to be merciful, thereby saving the city. Whatever the truth, it suited Philip tactically to be forgiving to Athens. He still wanted to subjugate Persia and a unified Greece would make a stronger base for his campaign. Besides, he needed the 300 Athenian triremes – Athens' navy was incomparable. He returned the dead under an escort of honour. He freed their prisoners and he sent the young and graceful Alexander, educated in Athens' own Academy's tradition, to talk through the terms of a surrender.

Philip never got to Persia. He was murdered, stabbed at close quarters, possibly by the order of his own wife, at his daughter's wedding, barely two years later in 336, and Alexander, Aristotle's pupil, became king. He took up where his father had left off. The inevitable rebellions that a change of rule always provokes were put down decisively and with devastating speed. Thebes, which dared to rally, was razed to the ground as an example and its 30,000 inhabitants sold into slavery. Athens, which had been preparing to do likewise, crept back home, shivering into submission, and Alexander was able at last to turn his attention to Persia. Behind him, in overall command of all the conquered Greek states, he left Aristotle's friend, Antipater.

At this point, Aristotle's Macedonian connections were an asset. He would be useful as an intermediary. He would be able to plead Athens' case if ever the need arose, so the city he'd left over a decade before made a show of welcoming him home. But if some were resigned to Macedonian rule, there were many in Athens who weren't. Demosthenes still prodded at the bees' nest of nationalism in his speeches, and if Aristotle was now seen as useful, the old rules still pertained. He was an outsider, a metic, and always would be. He was still barred from owning property.

Nothing had changed though, in the dedicated approach of Aristotle and Theophrastus to their chosen work. They found a public place, the Lyceum, which had a covered walkway – or 'peripatos' – where lectures could take place and, as they had done so often before, they set up their community and began their teaching. When they weren't teaching, they were writing. While Aristotle gave his lectures on rhetoric, ethics, metaphysics and logic, Theophrastus amassed his researches into natural history:

> *If the wind is from the south, the snuff of the lamp-wick indicates rain. If the snuff is small, like a millet seed, and of bright colour, it indicates rain as well as wind.*

> *It is a sign of rain when a toad takes a bath, and still more so when frogs are vocal. It is a sign of rain when swallows hit the water of the lakes with their belly. It is a sign of storm or rain when the ox licks his fore-hoof; if he puts his head up towards the sky and snuffs the air, it is a sign of rain.*

Above my head the sky is still its soft, unbroken blue but something feels like change. Theophrastus has been scoffed at for his observations on weather. How primitive and how superstitious they look. *It is a sign of rain when a crow puts back its head on a rock which is washed by waves.* But peel yourself down to the nub of knowledge that exists pre-science, pre-meteorology, and look at the number of things he is observing. Even if he's wrong, look at how much he notices, the absorbed gaze, and the continual silent question behind it: why? Always, why and what does it signify? The head cocked, the almost suspended breath of attention. Everything signifies. Everything is worth noting. Always he makes a note of it, for later and just in case, because maybe, when you add these things up, they will come to something. *When a number of millipedes are seen crawling up a wall, it means rain. A number of cobwebs in motion means wind or storm.*

If while a south wind is blowing, glued articles make a cracking sound, it indicates a change to north wind. But how very close you have to be listening, how very far you have to lean into silence, to hear the glued joints in a chair or a door-jamb cracking. *If the feet swell there will be a change to a south wind. If the land looks black from the sea it indicates a north wind, if white, a south wind. A halo about the moon signifies wind more certainly than a halo about the sun.*

If the lesser Mt Hymettos, which is called the Dry Hill, has cloud in its hollows, it is a sign of rain. In the distance I check the long ridge of Hymettos and there are no clouds, and anyway I'm going to spend my day in the National Archaeological Museum, looking at the things that Theophrastus looked at. All the way there I try to notice, to pay attention, to look with other eyes than my own. I borrow his principle, which is to look not just at the detail but also at the reason, the 'why' behind things. The beauty of Athens – which is its mad mix. Notice its peculiarity. The collapsed neoclassical mansions around here, fallen because they are owned by too many members of the same family for any agreement about sale, or repair, or occupation ever to be reached. The ugly replacements rising up out of their ruins, when finally they fall or are pulled down: brute concrete blocks, each floor owned by a different sibling.

The grandeur of Aristotle looms over our thinking now. We have elided it with our idea of the grandeur of Athens. But the Athens that Theophrastus and Aristotle returned to, after their spell of absence, was a city in the process of slipping from the centre of the world's stage, an outmoded city whose fabric was, even in those days, starting to show signs of wear. Herakleides, a follower of Aristotle and Theophrastus, a Peripatetic of a generation or so later, left a description of how faded and cramped Athens seemed, compared with other places at the time. He was writing about fifty years after their return.

> The city is totally dry and not well-watered, and badly laid out on account of its antiquity. Many of the houses are shabby, only a few useful. Seen by a stranger, it would at first be doubtful that this was the famed city of the Athenians.

Notice the tilted pavements, the sudden corners with their patchwork of architectural styles: a piece of ancient masonry, a nineteenth-century kiosk, an art nouveau front, a 1970s bank building, railings, the surprise of the markets, the street full of bookstalls, of antiques, of pots and pans hung up like scales outside the shop that only sells things that clatter. Then, suddenly, in a break in the buildings, opposite a booth selling gyros, a little sunken Byzantine church whose windows are level with the pavement. Then elegant houses again. All of which variety reflects the city's complex history of ideology, or occupation, or financial straits. Only yesterday afternoon, I passed a street which was all graffiti, right up to the first storey – not just scribbles but great flourishes like complex tattoos, coloured cartoons and, across one whole building, an angel with her back turned and her blue and green and purple wings spread wide. A white van, parked too long, had been absorbed into the general flowering, the graffiti simply flowing across it like water. While I looked, a small child across the street pointed and marvelled at the sudden colour. Her Canadian father pulled her away: 'It's dirty. Come on. Don't touch. It's dirty.'

The little girl swivelled her head like an owl so she could go on looking. 'Why?'

'They don't know not to draw on the walls here, honey,' he said, not answering her question. There was disgust in his voice and in my head I couldn't help echoing his child. Why?

It's vibrant. It's so irrepressible, so energetic. There's something not so much angry as simply refusing to be ignored or silenced. Like a plant that comes up whatever ground it finds itself in, something that insists on expressing itself. The pictures are not unlike the marginalia in medieval holy texts: the obscene monkeys, the birds and monsters and flourishes of tree or flower, the devils, the mooning clowns, the nuns harvesting penises out of trees. It's the same insistence on life's variety, the same childlike gaze, a gaze that doesn't look away, that refuses to be corralled or cleaned or ordered. Don't you like life, I wanted to say to the angry Canadian father in his pressed shorts, but he was already marching his honey round the corner, into a place of cleanliness and safety. I watched, until it was out of sight, the ribbon in the little girl's hair, bobbing in time with her trotting steps.

The pale ruins that we all so prize – their skeletal, bleached grace, their artistic discipline – would have been painted with a riot of graffiti colours. The statues that have schooled our restrained taste would have had coloured clothes and gemstone eyes. Hermes, just like the building-sized angel, would have had coloured wings on his feet.

Athens is beautiful, don't you think, Theophrastus? Whenever you return, after however long, Athens is always the most beautiful mix of everything, old and new, good and bad, ugly and most exquisite. These ancient stones. These potholed streets. These inexplicable, maddening doorsteps that project out across the narrow pavement so that it's impossible to walk comfortably anywhere except the middle of the road. Everything feels surprising, anarchic, alive.

Even if, when they left Athens, Theophrastus and Aristotle had felt that they were taking the spirit of the Academy with them, by the time they came back their thinking had progressed so far in its own direction it was no longer compatible with the Academy – which had stayed true to Plato's tradition all this time. It was necessary for Aristotle to set himself up as the head of something new. As he writes in *On Generation and Corruption*:

> Those who have lived in close contact with natural phenomena are better equipped to formulate broad generalisations. Whereas those who debate at great length and are not observant of the facts are easily shown to be limited in their views. Witness the difference between those who do research empirically and those who do it dialectically.

Research gathering was still central to what they were doing. Theophrastus was, among other things, still amending and adding to his catalogues of plants, helped by samples sent back by Alexander's army as it pushed east. In fact so much material was sent back, unloaded from the ships arriving at Piraeus and ferried up to the Lyceum, that he was sometimes scrabbling to keep up. There were so many plants, such a profusion of new types of tree and herb and flower, many of which were not even named.

Besides plants, there were maps and accounts of different ways of life in different places, other laws, other traditions; all information was important. There were also, of course, accounts of Alexander's campaign. History was being made. Aristotle's nephew, Callisthenes, whom they had left behind in Pella, was travelling with the army as Alexander's historian, and his letters were full of the stories of Alexander's exploits – of mock naval battles fought with apples instead of shot, of desert sandstorms, of how a little party of them got lost by night, among the steepling rocks and crags, on the way to the oracle at Siwa, and of how they were rescued by two crows who flew overhead, showing them again the path. The boy on the boat had grown up but he was still dreaming. 'Alexander's fame,' he is supposed to have boasted, 'depends on me and my history.' He was doing more than just recording events, he was busy creating a myth – a myth in which the name of Alexander, Greece's second Achilles, would be forever twined with his own.

'Callisthenes', Aristotle observed drily, 'is a perfect speaker but he lacks common sense.' How often had he told him 'to speak as seldom and as pleasantly as possible in the presence of a man who had, at the tip of his tongue, the power of life and death.' Theophrastus was softer. He was very fond of Callisthenes. If he was sitting, as he often must have been, at his writing table, answering the letters from Egypt, from Persia, from Herat, or Kandahar as they passed through Afghanistan, or further still, from Bactria…

Or, if he was not writing at all but returning home through the streets, with the quiet order of his thoughts stirred up by the hot din of the market, like muddying a puddle, if at that point the comforting remembrance of his friend flashed through him…

Or, if he glanced up, walking out in the morning, and saw the light strike the angles of the Parthenon above him, and everything cut clear and separate in outline, so that its clarity energized his mind and his thoughts were full of radiance…

If, in any of these moments, he thought of his friend, adventuring in the train of the great conqueror, he would have failed to imagine correctly. He couldn't have helped but fall short in his thinking because the gap between them was now impossibly wide. He wouldn't have known how it was.

He couldn't have guessed as he walked through Athens how the wheel of destiny, in its round, had caught Callisthenes' cloak and was now this minute, while no one knew it, while people stood around discussing things as small as the price of dates or herrings, even now, dragging him horribly under. And Callisthenes himself – how quickly did he notice? He was so slow to react. So lacking in common sense. Because in the east Alexander's temper had taken on the harsh and blasted quality of the landscapes he'd been crossing: the deserts, the plunging passes. If Callisthenes noticed, he kept putting it down to this or that, excusing it, because the descent afterwards into softness, the sweetness of Alexander's old ways, capping each other's quotations and talking philosophy, still lulled him. He didn't realize.

Aristotle was the greatest thinker and Alexander was his creature. That's how Callisthenes saw it. He didn't see that, although in his own mind philosophy, not power, was the thing that mattered, to Alexander the order was different. He didn't see that Alexander was beginning to find him irritating.

One night, in the heat of a post-battle drinking orgy, Alexander fell into argument with one of his older generals, Cleitus, who was head of the cavalry and who some said had saved Alexander's life at the Battle of the Granicus. Days before, Cleitus had been offered the satrapy of Bactria, a sort of semi-retirement post. But he was still active. He didn't want to be told he was too old.

For days, Cleitus smarts with the insult but holds his tongue. He tries, after the battle, to drink it away, but even through the fog of alcohol he feels the sting of Alexander's decision. He starts to over-praise Alexander's father, Philip. He does it loudly, looking straight at Alexander. It was Philip and his generals, the old guard, who really did the work. They laid the foundations for everything that Alexander was doing. Children. This generation of fighters were just a bunch of ill-disciplined children. They made mistakes that almost cost them their lives, like at Granicus. Cleitus' old head swaying like a bull at a gate. They had to be saved by their father's friends. Let that not be forgotten.

And Alexander feels the slight. He feels each sentence like a pebble thrown at his head. He lets one pass. Two. He waves his hand in irritation and turns away. Three. Four. Enough. This is beyond toleration. The little switch inside him flicks, click, at no notice. Alexander picks up the nearest thing to hand, an apple, and hurls it at Cleitus' head.

The general ducks and the apple crashes among the litter on the table. Cleitus reels away, laughing. You see what I mean? Throwing apples in temper. This man is nothing to the men of before. He's a child. Just an angry child. In rage Alexander rises to his feet. Everyone is so drunk. They move with the slowness of nightmare. Falling forever over a stool to land with your head in a dish of meat. Someone's laughter goes black and sounds like something else, crying perhaps. Alexander is laying about him looking for Cleitus. He goes for his sword. Someone through the fog manages somehow to snatch it away from him. Someone else lurches forward to hold him back. Scarlet, blind with drink and fury, Alexander shouts in Macedonian dialect for his shield bearers. Cleitus is dragged still laughing from the room. Everything is crashing and tipping. They let go of Alexander once the general has gone but Alexander is now lost, plunging forwards towards the door, shouting Cleitus' name.

'Here's Cleitus,' Cleitus himself answers, swaying once more in the doorway, having freed himself from those who had removed him from the room. Alexander wheels round. He grabs at a sarissa propped against the wall and rams it into Cleitus, right through. He hears the bones of the man's chest crack like breaking sticks.

He has murdered his own general.

Wake up, Callisthenes. Look where you are. Look at these people. What possible purchase can your logic, your ideals, or your temperance have among the savagery of these berserk war lords?

But Callisthenes believes in his teaching. He is sure of his inherited role, as the guide, the substitute mentor, Aristotle's place-marker. Alexander retreats to his tent. For three days he won't eat or speak. For three days he lies there, like a man caught unaware, rolled by a breaking wave, his feet swept from under him. For three days he is sodden with weeping. Drowned. Tumbled and wrecked in the bitter shame of murder.

Who can get him out of this? He'll die if he doesn't eat or drink. The whole army is at a loss. Send in the philosophers to counsel him. For god's sake. What else are they here for?

So Callisthenes and Anaxarchus of Abdera are ushered into Alexander's tent. Callisthenes speaks of restraint. He comforts him with quiet arguments. Perhaps Alexander had omitted to propitiate Dionysus. Perhaps this was a punishment. He speaks about moderation, about discipline, about the qualities of the king as exemplar. Anaxarchus' approach is very different. He accuses Alexander of self-pity. Get up. He is a king. He claims to be a god, doesn't he? Who, then, is to say what is right or wrong? Get up, son of Zeus Ammon. Lead your army like the warrior you claim to be. Anaxarchus' path is the easier one. It's too far back now, the way of Aristotle. In his slough of self-loathing, Anaxarchus' voice is the one Alexander hears. Anaxarchus' authority, his insulting taunts, answer Alexander's need for punishment. He gets up from his bed. As Plutarch tells it, from this moment on, Anaxarchus 'made himself wonderfully liked by the king, and brought the intercourse of Callisthenes…, which had always been unpleasant because of the man's austerity, into additional disfavour.'

The army moves on, through the mountains of Koh-i-noor, hauling themselves on ropes, slantwise across snowy screes, to attack the rock-top strongholds, and on to Balkh; dry, boulder-strewn, sparse places that take extreme measures of resilience to travel, on foot and on horseback, the column moving among the rumble and scrape of its own passage, breathing its own dust day after numbing day.

Among them went Callisthenes, whose star, though he couldn't see it, was falling. One night, at dinner, when it came to his turn to speak, he praised the Macedonians. The company was delighted. They showered him with garlands taken from their own heads. But Alexander was irritable. How easy it was, anyway, to praise something already noble. Callisthenes would be showing his skill to better effect if he could argue the opposite. He was so serious. So self-important. And how the young men were taken in by his eloquence; they fluttered around him, sucking up his speeches when they should have been looking at Alexander. His restraint was irritating, his commitment to moderation. He still refused to drink his wine unmixed. He was unbending and still the old men thought he was dignified. Already Alexander wanted rid of him. Come on, show us your precious dialectic. Give us the contrary case. And Callisthenes, fool that he was, obliged. In eloquent detail, he shredded the Macedonian culture. The room fell silent.

Then at Balkh, having realized his long-held ambition and to conquer Persia, Alexander, in the interests of integrating the Greek and the Persian cultures, decided to try out the practice of proskynesis. To the Persians, this was a gesture of respect, paid to anyone superior as a greeting, in which you bow before someone, kissing the tips of your fingers as you do so. To the Greeks, this was something only performed to the gods – it was never offered to a human. Alexander set it up, as a trial, in a small group of chosen friends. Each person was to drink, then make obeisance, after which he would be kissed by Alexander, thereby removing any suggestion of hubris on Alexander's part, or any insult to the status of his followers. But to someone like Callisthenes, unable to see beyond the gesture's Greek associations and unable to make diplomatic compromises, the suggestion was offensive. When it came to his turn, he simply omitted the gesture, going up as everyone before him had done, to receive Alexander's kiss. Alexander refused to kiss him. And now, Hephaestion, always quick to pick up his lover's dislikes, was watching.

A plot among the fifteen-year-old pages was uncovered. A boy who had made the mistake of out-classing Alexander in the hunting field had been flogged and deprived of his horse. Brooding over his humiliation in the days that followed, he decided to take revenge. He would kill Alexander. There was a period during the early part of the night, up to midnight, when the pages stood guard while Alexander slept. It could be done then. But on the appointed evening, Alexander spent the whole night drinking, only staggering back to his tent at dawn, by which time the watch had changed and the pages no longer had access.

When the intended plot was leaked, Hephaestion, his cold eyes darting as he listened, saw his chance. Wasn't Callisthenes always preaching to the children? Didn't they have an absurd regard for his powers of speech, his intellect? They were a bunch of spoiled pretty boys. It was unthinkable that they would have the ability to come up with such a plan. Surely someone more experienced, someone more calculating, was behind it. Alexander listened, catching his drift. What, Callisthenes? That's hardly likely. Not the philosopher. But Hephaestion's eyes, so cold, so silent, were full of suggestion. You know you want rid of him. Alexander, silently – I do. Well then, the eyes seemed to say, take this chance. There may not be another.

Alexander wrote to Antipater, telling him of his narrow escape. 'The youths were stoned to death by the Macedonians. The sophist I will punish, together with those who sent him to me.'

So, while Theophrastus makes his way so comfortably around Athens, thinking now and then about Callisthenes' adventures, Callisthenes is in fact confined in a cage. He is bumped and dragged like a dog among the retinue's dust-cloud. He is starving and covered in lice and sores. He is held in fetters for seven months, awaiting trial. Or he has in fact already been hanged by the army. Or crucified. Whichever it was, he was condemned unfairly, held in vile conditions and then shamefully put to death.

How much later is it that the news arrives in Athens? Months perhaps, before a letter comes, from Antipater to Aristotle, telling him as gently as he can what has befallen his nephew and protégé. The horror of it. Was it possible? That boy. That complex, persuasive boy they had tutored, how could he have come to this?

Theophrastus and Aristotle never forgive Alexander. In Theophrastus' head, denial presses like a thundercloud. He can't hear what is being said to him. His mind is turning so slowly. And then for the next days, how to work, how to pick up things that by comparison seem so trivial? He writes, instead, a treatise on grief which he titles simply, *Callisthenes*. It is luck, he says in it, not wisdom, that governs men's lives. *Callisthenes came across a man who was most powerful and most fortunate, but who didn't know how to wear either condition.* He was just fatally unlucky.

*

This all happened in 327 BCE. By 323, anti-Macedonian feeling was again running high. In the June of that year, Alexander the Great, after several months of intensive drinking, and aged only thirty-two, died in Babylon. For a brief moment, the nationalists – men like Demosthenes and Lycurgus – were back in power in Athens, and Aristotle's popularity, which had always been contingent on Macedonian power, declined. A memorial to his intercessions on Athens' behalf, twice preventing Philip from sacking the city, was torn down and pitched over the side of the Acropolis. He was indicted on charges of irreligion. He wrote anxiously to Antipater, 'It is dangerous for a Macedonian to live in Athens… In Athens the same things are not permitted to an alien which are proper for an Athenian citizen.' He was afraid he would be put to death, like Socrates. So he fled to Chalcis, to his mother's house, leaving Theophrastus behind him, in charge at the Lyceum.

'What is a friend?' someone is supposed to have asked Aristotle. 'A single soul dwelling in two bodies,' he answered. He was lonely on Chalcis, watching the tide and trying to busy himself with charting its ebb and flow. He was listless, and work, always so sustaining before, suddenly seemed empty and without comfort. 'The lonelier and more isolated I am,' he wrote, again to Antipater, 'the more I have come to love myth.' What a cry from the soul this is, a cry from the other side of the monumental structure of the newly built natural sciences, as if, gazing out at the sea from Chalcis, he felt that in his lifetime of wondering, of studying and anatomizing, still the heart of things had somehow slipped free of his enquiries. As though the essential thing remained unexpressed, except as it always had been, in myth.

I imagine him watching the water that he'd tried so hard to fathom, all the life it contained that he'd tried to categorize. And as he listens to the waves and remembers with longing the wonder that started him off, I am listening to the echoes in my own language, because the word 'wonder' is a little world of echoes. If you listen, you can hear wander and under and won and one, filling and rounding it out, or grazing its edges with different ideas, although it still maintains its overall meaning. That, it seems to me, is how writing works, ghosted with association and echo, and made of carefully articulated parts, but still whole. And that is perhaps how Aristotle, at the end of his life, saw the world, despite the science he had invented to try to explain it. As he stood looking out at the sea, after all his anatomizing of its parts, he found the world was still mysterious, still somehow magically intact. Is that what I was looking for? A way of living in the world that searches and finds and understands and adds to our ever-increasing knowledge, but that keeps the world itself always in view, as one whole, inviolate mystery, into which we and all our knowing, time-bound lives are seamlessly rolled.

The following year, in 322, Aristotle died. His will (as already mentioned) named Antipater as his successor. He made careful provision for those he loved. None of his slaves were to be sold and when the time came, and if they deserved it, they were all to be given their freedom. Theophrastus, if he wished, was to marry his daughter – if Nicanor didn't want her – and take care of his little son Nicomachus. And so Aristotle exits the stage.

There is no record of what Theophrastus thought, or felt. He went on quietly among his students, in Athens, doing the work that Aristotle had taught him how to do. Only, among his listed works, there is something incongruous, a book called *Achicarus*. Achicarus, or Ahikar, was an eastern story, a version of which appears in Aesop's Fables. It tells of Ahikar – the wisest man in the world – who adopts and educates a son. The son is wilful and degenerate and, in the end, plans his adopted father's murder. The plan is thwarted and instead of being killed Ahikar is imprisoned. Years later, when the king, Sennacherib, is in such trouble that no one can help, Ahikar is revealed to be alive. He is brought to Sennacherib with 'the colour of his face changed, his hair matted like a wild beast, and his nails like the claws of an eagle'. He solves the king's problem. The story of his imprisonment at the hands of his adopted son is told and now the son is brought to him for punishment. Ahikar beats him, shuts him up in a room and tries to instruct him in better ways. The son swells up and before Ahikar can get to the end of his teaching he bursts.

Nothing is left of Theophrastus' treatise so no one knows what he said in it but the story rings with private echoes. Perhaps he was remembering Alexander's boyish admiration for Aristotle, whom he loved 'like a father'. Perhaps he was thinking of Alexander's intemperate letter to Antipater, his threat to punish Callisthenes 'together with those who sent him to me', in other words Aristotle and Theophrastus himself. Perhaps in Ahikar's final triumph, perhaps in the shame and physicality of the son's death, the swelling and bursting that sounds so like the death of an alcoholic, he found some hidden comfort.

After Aristotle's death Theophrastus' life became settled. He was now in his fifties. He was a prominent figure, closely associated with Aristotle and therefore, by extension, with Macedonia. This should have made his position precarious but somehow, in whatever power struggles ensued, he managed not to become over-identified with any particular party. He kept his opinions on the administration to himself. Occasionally, he would make a sharp comment about his chosen home but somehow he would be forgiven. Somehow, although he was an outsider, he was accepted. He buried himself in his work. He brought up and educated Nicomachus, Aristotle's son. He taught. And he was known and respected; it was said that he had 'two thousand students'. Athens suited him and Athens loved him, for his tolerance perhaps. If he was sharp-eyed in his characterizations of people, still he was accepting. He was urbane. Athenaeus, in *The Deipnosophists*, characterizes the Athenians – rightly or wrongly – as quiet, frugal 'eaters of salads', compared with the northern tribes, who think nothing of presenting each individual guest with a whole roast boar. 'You who never go out of Athens,' he says, 'think yourself happy when you hear the precepts of Theophrastus and when you eat thyme and salads and nice twisted loaves.'

Philosophy was flowering. Besides the Academy and the Lyceum, there were now other major traditions in Athens and there was much debate among the different schools. Epicurus had set up in what was known as the Garden, where he taught both women and slaves, one of whom, Leontion, engaged in a written debate with Theophrastus. Xenocrates, now an old man, was in charge of the Academy. Diogenes the Cynic died in the year that Aristotle left for Chalcis but his ideas survived. Crates, his pupil, had taken on his mantle and was now teaching Zeno, who would by the turn of the century set up the Stoics in the Agora, in the shade of the Painted Stoa. Between these different schools, as well as ideas, there was a vivid exchange of pupils, who moved about from one master to another in an atmosphere of hothouse thinking and charismatic, sexually charged teaching. Arcesilaus, who ended his life as a sceptic, started as a pupil and lover of Theophrastus, and was wooed away by Crantor, an Academician. The exchange between the new master and pupil was conducted in quotations from Euripides' *Andromeda*. 'O maiden,' Crantor wrote, 'if I save thee, wilt thou be grateful to me?' To which Arcesilaus replied, capping his quotation with the line that followed, 'Take me, stranger, whether for maidservant or for wife.'

Theophrastus was left to regret his loss, saying sadly, 'What a quick-witted and ready pupil has left my school.' Sometimes the changes worked the other way. Bion of Borysthenes, a colourful figure who had spent some time as a slave, left the Academy because he didn't like the teaching of Crates and went instead to Theophrastus.

So his students were a widely varied and often changing group. He taught them not as a master, like Plato, but on an equal footing, on the understanding that they were all of them, himself included, advancing together towards knowledge. He demanded equality between them, dedication and kindness. And he had certain idiosyncrasies. His students were to be clean and well presented. Above all things he liked quiet. They were to wear shoes. They were not to come barefoot. And their shoes must be 'unstitched and without nails'. He didn't want them clattering along the paths of his garden. Many of those who stayed were artistic, sometimes flamboyantly so. Among the most notable were: Menander, the future playwright, known as 'the beautiful'; Demetrius of Phalerum, a rhetorician and future governor of Athens who liked to have seasonal flowers scattered under his feet; and Polystratus the Tyrrhenian, who 'used often to put on the garments of the female flute players'.

When the soul casts off the weight of worldly thoughts which hinder its movement towards the excellent object then it takes up philosophy with the least amount of trouble and effort. It becomes like a lamp, both luminous in itself and illuminating others.

What on earth did they make of your thought, Theophrastus?

Because if in their habits and their dress his students were extravagant, Theophrastus' precepts must have seemed incompatibly spare and disciplined. *The soul is able to fly. With its hidden wings the soul can alight on anything it wishes. It can observe anything it wishes without being itself observed. It's like a bee, which flies and descends upon a tree filled with the honey of fruits.* And his students sat listening to his voice, in their fine clothes and their nail-free shoes, trying to focus through the mist of worldly distraction.

*

When Demetrius of Phalerum became governor of Athens in 317 BCE, he made Theophrastus the present of a house of his own, near the Lyceum, and with it a piece of land on which Theophrastus could have a botanic garden. So, even though he was officially still a metic, he was settled at last and he had somewhere he could grow the plants he liked to collect. This, as he grew older, became his chief pleasure. He had property in Stagira, possibly inherited from Aristotle, but it was here in Athens that he was to live, for the next thirty years, until he died.

One evening, in the dark, I go wandering around the city, looking for the Lyceum and Theophrastus' garden. Rigillis Street is what I have been told. In Theophrastus' time, it was outside the city walls, a place of not-belonging. It was a little wooded, green space, between the rivers Ilisos and Eridanos, near a complex of temples, as at Mieza. Now the rivers have turned into roads, like the Euripos on Lesbos. Cars seem to be everywhere. Tall buildings. I drag my feet along Vasilissis Sofias Avenue, a huge dual carriageway which seems never-ending, looking for the right street. The Byzantine and Christian museum, some kind of military club for officers. Perhaps I am lost.

Even when I do eventually find it, it doesn't look like the place. My fingers hook through a chain-link fence. It is being restored, apparently. I stand for a while staring at this dark, open expanse. There's nothing I can see. An emptiness that was once a beloved garden, a library, school, a community of quiet thought.

*

The Greek for gardener is 'kepouros'. It is made of two words, 'kepos', which means garden or orchard, and 'orao', which means to look. So a gardener is someone who watches a garden; how things grow or seed, why one thing does better here or there, or just waiting for the first sign, the green points of bulbs, the pale mist of seedlings raised on stalks so fine that the leaves, open like wings, seem almost to be hovering.

Theophrastus' garden had three named gardeners: Pamphylus, Manes and Callias. It must have been big. *Do not use water from irrigation ditches*, he tells them, as he inspects his plants, because it brings with it the seeds of rank grass. If you want to prolong the flowering time of dropwort, pinch off the flower heads rather than letting it seed. Theophrastus moving slowly now that he is old, passing, in the shade of the afternoon, down the paths of his garden, watching. Set the slips of plants for propagation at an angle, more below ground than above. And if you want to stop your radishes from being eaten, sow between the rows with bitter vetch.

Otherwise we see him, about his business in the city, in occasional glimpses; under the sumptuary laws instituted by Demetrius, for instance, which banned excess of dress, Crates the Cynic, hauled before the magistrates for inappropriately wearing linen, said in his own defence, 'I'll show you even Theophrastus wrapped in linen', and when the magistrates didn't believe him 'he led them off to a barber shop and showed them Theophrastus having his hair cut'.

He must have been happy because he stayed. Demetrius fell into disfavour and fled to Egypt to the court of Alexander's general Ptolemy. Several times, when Theophrastus might have felt uneasy for his own safety, he somehow survived. He waited, keeping quiet among his plants, until the moment passed. In 307 BCE, when there was an edict against 'subversive' and 'alien' philosophers, in other words metics, and he was forcibly banished, Ptolemy, remembering Pella, tried to persuade him to leave Athens and come and set up his school in Alexandria. Theophrastus refused. He waited until the edict was revoked and then he went back to his garden, to his library at the Lyceum, to his colonnades where the maps of his world hung, and the shady walks where he continued to teach his crowds of students. He missed Aristotle and the certainty of their old focus. As old people often do, he mocked his own irrelevance. They won't let me be lazy in my old ways, he complained, writing to his lifelong friend Phanias. It was no longer possible to find an audience willing to align themselves with his thought. People's focus had changed. They wanted his arguments to fit their version of the world. *To get a public or even a select circle such as one desires is not easy. If an author reads his work, he must re-write it. Always to shirk revision and ignore criticism is a course which the present generation of pupils will no longer tolerate.*

If he joked to Phanias, still his displacement was sometimes painful. Most particularly, he was disappointed in the boy he loved, Aristotle's son, Nicomachus. Nicomachus, Theophrastus' acknowledged beloved, was slow and uninterested. He seemed to be tempted by all the worst things. Theophrastus worried that he wasn't honest. *It would be a good thing not only to be the heir of your father's property but also of that man's habits.* It did no good. He was lazy and shirking. He had little application and flashy tastes. How to show him what his father had been, how to provide him with a proper example? Aristotle's second treatise on ethics, called the *Nicomachean Ethics*, is a reworking of his first, but thought to have been edited and put together by a different hand. Maybe, in the moments when he was most at a loss over the education of Aristotle's son, Theophrastus sat, as in time to come Cicero would, and Petrarch and Chaucer and so many others, working at the copying of Aristotle's primary text, putting it into new order, making it practical rather than abstract, to give to Nicomachus as a guide.

And then maybe, when the boy was still bored, he thought up the *Characters* for him, as a companion text, to make the dryness of the subject appealing to a childish mind. If he did, it didn't help. Nicomachus went his own way. He joined the army and went off to a life that had nothing to do with quiet, and was killed in battle while he was still a young man. Theophrastus must have doubly mourned. He'd lost his beloved and he'd failed to keep Aristotle's son in the philosophical fold. Later, when Theophrastus himself died, he left money for a life-size statue of Nicomachus to be made and put into the garden, as if it were possible to keep him, as he hadn't managed to in life, to hold him forever where he should have stayed, in philosophy's safe embrace.

Another bereavement. Theophrastus worked. He worked and worked. He never stopped. Even in his eighties, he was still teaching, still lecturing, gardening and writing. And now, when he went into the city, because of his age, he was carried through the streets in a litter. Surely he should take a rest. He could allow himself a little time off, a day or so. But he didn't. He seemed to be racing something to a finish. He was still thinking perhaps of the non-swimmer, flailing his arms in the fast-flowing water. Then one day, one of his students got married and asked him, 'Please, Theophrastus, take a holiday. Come and spend a few days celebrating with us.' Theophrastus, his eyes misted with concentration, put down his pen. *I'm sorry?*

Come to my wedding. Let us entertain you. A rest will do you good.

So he stopped work. He went.

Whose is this body? Someone is laid out here. Weary. Ancient. Someone has died. I don't know how. Perhaps in his sleep. Someone beloved in the cool of this darkened room.

Just this husk left behind. Just this collection of sticks. The oddness of these stiff bird-legs. Someone should have covered them up. The skin of the feet translucent like tracing paper.

And, oh Theophrastus, I am too late.

May I touch you, just once – even just your garment? I found the link, Theophrastus. I found how you connect. I found that, through Chaucer, the father of English literature, you are family, just as I'd thought, after all.

Nothing answers. I'm talking to myself. Just, somewhere, the faint sound of waves beating, which might be my heart, or might be the sound of time – the only substance in life that really endures – approaching. Something – as I lean in to listen – is coming closer. Something heavy with the weight of numberless lives, rolled under as if they'd been nothing. These waters that swallow us whole; even though you are dead, I'm still trying to hold them back. Whole races, whole generations gone, all those eyes and mouths with all their happiness and pain, all those tongues stopped in the babble of their languages, all the little ghosts of irrelevant prayer, whispered in the moment of crisis, the sweat of work or love or terror, all the hands clutching their talismanic objects, the book or the ring or the final glass of water – all of it, all of these human things, which are of the highest importance and the most utter meaninglessness, are gone. Why would you, or I, be any different?

But look, here's his beard, the soft wool of his barbered hair, and his eyes, those patient observant eyes. I never got to look into them – someone stupidly closed them before they'd finished their seeing. It was too early. He didn't want to go. He still had much to do. He'd lived so long but still he loved life and when the time came he didn't want to go. He thought he hadn't finished. Like Aristotle before him, he felt that life had somehow slipped his understanding. *Men never attained what they wished to attain. What they left behind is beyond their reach, and they perished.*

If you could only have waited. Just a little longer.

I'm not the only mourner. Around him, once the word went out, his students had gathered, had whispered their regret – why did we ask him to come? As soon as he stopped work he died. Why didn't we think? Straining their ears for his last instructions. And how are we supposed to live now, without you? What should we do? Tell us, before you go, the answer. We can't find it without you. What is your advice, dear master?

> *Nothing else but this, that many of the pleasures which life boasts are but in the seeming. For when we are just beginning to live, see! we die. Nothing then is so unprofitable as the love of glory. Farewell, and may you be happy. Either give up my tradition, which involves a world of labour, or step forward its worthy champions, for you will win great glory.*

He mumbles. Had they misheard? He seems to contradict himself, or has someone remembered it wrong? Maybe he was muddled. The breath coming harder and harder, and that liveliness, like something diluting, paling to nothing before their eyes.

> *Life holds more disappointment than advantage. But, as I can no longer discuss what we ought to do, do you go on with the inquiry into right conduct.* And so the great man died.

What is left? Nothing. Just a few possessions. His precise and modest instructions for their disposal. Here are his final wishes; here it is, the beloved voice, one last time:

All will be well; but in case anything should happen, I make these dispositions. I give and bequeath all my property at home to Melantes and Pancreon, the sons of Leon. It is my wish that out of the trust funds at the disposal of Hipparchus the following appropriations should be made. First, they should be applied to finish the rebuilding of the Museum with the statues of the goddesses, and to add any improvements which seem practicable to beautify them. Secondly, to replace in the temple the bust of Aristotle with the rest of the dedicated offerings which formerly were in the temple. Next, to rebuild the small cloister adjoining the Museum, at least as handsomely as before, and to replace in the lower cloister the tablets containing maps of the countries traversed by explorers. Further, to repair the altar so that it may be perfect and elegant. It is also my wish that the statue of Nicomachus should be completed of life size. The price agreed upon for the making of the statue itself has been paid to Praxiteles, but the rest of the cost should be defrayed from the source above mentioned. The statue should be set up in whatever place seems desirable to the executors entrusted with carrying out my other testamentary dispositions.

Let all that concerns the temple and the offerings set up be arranged in this manner. The estate at Stagira belonging to me I give and bequeath to Callinus. The whole of my library I give to Neleus. The garden and the walk and the houses adjoining the garden, all and sundry, I give and bequeath to such of my friends hereinafter named as may wish to study literature and philosophy there in common, since it is not possible for all men

*to be always in residence, on condition that no one alienates the
property or devotes it to his private use, but so that they hold it
like a temple in joint possession and live, as is right and proper,
on terms of familiarity and friendship. Let the community
consist of Hipparchus, Neleus, Strato, Callinus, Demotimus,
Demaratus, Callisthenes, Melantes, Pancreon, Nicippus.
Aristotle, the son of Metrodorus and Pythias, shall also have
the right to study and associate with them if he so desire. And
the oldest of them shall pay every attention to him, in order to
ensure for him the utmost proficiency in philosophy.*

*Let me be buried in any spot in the garden which seems most
suitable, without unnecessary outlay upon my funeral or upon
my monument.*

Silence in the little room. The body empty. The man I came for gone
and the dark waste of human time that glitters between us, closing its
distance, moment by moment by moment.

What should I do – now Theophrastus is dead? Below me, in the turreted house, the flautist cycles and recycles through her tune, the runs of notes getting faster and faster each time, as if she were using the music to launch herself at something, drilling her way through time, whether forwards or back, to a place where musicians get paid to play and life is worth living again. 'Keep going,' I say to her when we pass on the winding stairs. 'I don't believe in endings either,' I add under my breath, as I step out into the street, thinking, as I did at the start of my search, of the myth of Orpheus.

As always, I find the story agonizing: the impossible thing achieved, the precious person reclaimed, only to be lost again through forgetfulness, or impatience, or just stupidity. And turning it over in my head, now as always, I see other possible meanings. Is it, I ask myself as I walk, actually to do with our innate fallibility? The problem is fixable and indeed the instructions for fixing it are there, but we, in our hapless way and for no reason, simply fail to follow them?

Or is it about failure of certainty, some fatal fragmentation that has split us off from our world, the gates of Eden barred against us, and us left anxious and stumbling? Either could be true. The meanings proliferate.

I'm going to the National Archaeological Museum one more time, walking the potholed pavements, between the sun-triggered birds. And, appropriately today, music seems to be everywhere; buskers, birds, frustrated flute-players, everything separately singing back something, or singing itself elsewhere. As I walk, I follow suit, fitting the busker's tune to my steps. In the changing eastern rhythms – the one two three, one two three/one two, one two, one two of Greek dance – I make my way along the broad avenue that runs along the side of the Acropolis. The street vendors have set up their stalls on both sides. They are selling everything – old records and new CDs and art and handmade jewellery, books, pictures, little leather purses and flags, food and coloured scarves. Beside them, in the winter sun, Theophrastus' Characters are strolling by, and stopping and looking. The Chatterer and the Flatterer are here, and the Boastful type, and the Absent Minded person. And the Penny-Pincher, sour-faced and slow, going from stall to stall, picking everything up and putting it down again, tutting over prices because, as he says to anyone who'll listen, it's all a total rip-off. Meanwhile, on the other side, the Superstitious Man has turned into a woman and is busy buying a Dream Catcher.

The Archaeological Museum, when I reach it at last, is absolutely full; not full of visitors because it is January, but full of things that were once on stalls, just like in the streets outside. It is crammed with the products of whole generations of looking, making, building and creating. There are pots, combs, cups, weapons, furniture, little votive figures of leaves, doves, parts of the body. There are fingers, eyes, knees, noses, penises, toes, breasts. There are parts of buildings and all of their contents, broken stonework, pillars, gravestones, coins, fish-hooks, knives, loom weights. And in room after room, standing among their possessions, are the people themselves, the Greeks whom I've loved for so long, Theophrastus' people, who used them, or made them, or left them behind. I walk through crowds of these quiet stone and bronze people, some of whom, with their crinkled hair and their secret smiles and their odd triangular knees, would have looked ancient even to Theophrastus. Wandering from room to room among all this, I am aware of what a culture of looking – of what all this – represents; what an emphasis on the eye to capture life, in all its smallest detail, what energy to record things before they are gone. But it isn't a static image, the Greek line is too flowing for that, and the detail feels momentary. It's a noticing of things as they pass that I sense, a capturing of the fleeting.

Maybe I'm hung up on time but it seems to be everywhere I look. It is here in the horses' raised hooves, in the rider's angled body, in his downcast glance. In the flutter of garments there, I can see the breeze that is passing. Someone here is holding something out, in the moment of offering. Someone else is in the middle of pouring, or arming. Sex is happening everywhere, in every way. People are dancing. Birds are swooping. Flowers flowering.

It seems to me that this is a practice of minute and incessant daily observation in which what is important, what is continually noticed, is the present act of living. These are snippets cut from life, as it's lived by all things, all the time. It's a culture where boys go to their deaths, in the suddenness of a moment. On marble reliefs, they pass out of life in the company of partridges who look intelligently up at them from the ground, or in the trotting company of alert dogs, their heads cocked upwards in inquiry. Gigantic women with absorbed expressions, as if dying with more notice, stretch out a hand in farewell, while the children gathered at their feet look up, like the partridges. Men with thoughtful faces go in swathed garments, riding horses whose necks are curved, nostrils wide with spirit. These images are the stones, or steles, of people's graves. They mark death after death after death – only nothing seems to have ended. Everything, everyone, everywhere, is still vividly going on.

Through the echoing rooms, and in case after case, I find myself looking for dead bodies, on pots – anywhere – as if for proof. But even here, life distracts from death by the detail of its continuance. The mourners tear their hair and raise their hands in rhythmic gestures. Their heads are thrown back. Their mouths are open and wailing. Is something being said or sung? I strain to catch it. They are in a procession so vivid that it seems it too will pass on, as if they might suddenly be gone and the pot I'm looking at be left bare. Things change and pass but in the circularity of life's repeat, as in music, there is the feeling of something perpetual. Everywhere, in the repeated gestures, there is the rhythm of life itself. In the serried rows of prancing horses, I can hear the beat of it in their hooves. In the straining oarsmen and the raised oars, I can hear the hiss of it in the water. It's the same for the thump of the mourning drum and the flying rhythms of the dance.

Every single aspect of life is here. Every matter is, as it must be, minutely covered, minutely recorded – and the adverb is well chosen. It repeats in my head like the tick of a clock, because of its other meaning, because it contains both sound and the measurement of time. Minute by minute, nothing in life is too small or too routine not to be noticed: the eating, the sleeping, the worship, the fighting, the loving, the music, the running, the cooking, the washing, the playing. We have pictures of it all, at its most apparently inconsequential – the crow lifting from its rock, the ox pawing at the ground with his hoof – and even in its most private moments. A man and his wife on their bed. A man fondling a youth at a banquet. Chains of people, half-men, half-animal, in vigorous and comic congress. All this conscious enjoyment. These gestures of abandon, these frank women with their elegant hair who are busy accommodating the phallus in all its variety of modes with such delicacy and such purpose.

There isn't the polarity I'm used to – the modern world's either/or of mind and body, thought and action, inner and outer. Both are visible at once. Everything seems fluid and porous and equally sentient. It's a different world, a world where a child, seeing at the bottom of a Nottinghamshire garden a field of bearded barley with all its heads bent and running like a sea, might go down to the garden's edge and, all alongside, run with their arms in a solemn arc because of that fierce energy, that wildness let loose among unripe barley.

It comes back to me now – the ecstatic, sudden conviction, when the wind and the child and the barley were one and the same, as if the living of that wind-filled day had been found somewhere and kept safe, all this time, in these glass cases, as if it were still an option. I can see these animals' characters, despite their bodies. I can see these people's nakedness, their bodies and how they use and live in them, but I can also see their feelings, their minds. So many of their expressions are thoughtful or internalized. And all of it, the people, and the animals, feel to me like flowerings of the same strange force, continuing everywhere unchanged.

But just as I think I have found what I came for, just as I feel I understand, the parts coalesce into mystery again. This is how it always goes. Meaning eludes us, perhaps because there isn't any – or nothing that lasts longer than a flash at any rate. As if the waters of time, momentarily withdrawn, rise again to the full, so that now the people standing in their glass cases feel suddenly strange to me, less removed from their own context: fierce people whose pointed faces and almond eyes have a directness of address that is unnerving. There is something I want to remember, to think about later, something I feel I can't yet grasp. In front of a case of bronzes, just as I did at the beginning of my search, in the museum in Lesbos, I reach for my phone to photograph a small, votive, bronze head of Zeus. But something happens to the focus or the flash. The little eye-sockets blaze savage at me as I take his picture, as if to say, how dare you? When I look at the image later, it is blurry – a visual proof that I couldn't see it clearly, neither the god nor his people. As if it wouldn't translate.

I carry this with me as I leave, at the end of the day, to walk up through the woods of the Pnyx in fading light. As if for some reason it matters, I race the dark to get to the top and I think as I go that I'm treading in your very footsteps, Theophrastus. You must have walked up here so often, to listen to what was happening, to attend the debate of the day. Almost, in the dusk, I can see your clean tunic swing as you move, ahead of me, among the slim trunks, the bare skin of your ankles flashing. Who is following whom, I find myself thinking. Am I following you backwards – or are you following me forwards?

Every now and then, breathless with my ascent, through the gaps in the trees I catch glimpses of the city below, quiet and glittering in the last of the light: Athens, which has changed so much and yet stayed so strangely the same. Perhaps that's what the museum was saying: that things shift, or alter their condition, but that nothing is lost. It was a failure of will, or of memory, that made Orpheus doubt. Forgetting how to see her, he thought, when he turned round, that Eurydice was gone.

There are different ways of looking at the world and these differences condition our seeing. Theophrastus taught me that. Somewhere, in flashes, changed but the same, if we look hard enough, whatever we've lost is there – the Greece that I first encountered, that fluid, unbounded, halfway place, and my childhood self, caught in the glass boxes of the museum, or Eurydice, forever patient on the lip of the world, waiting to be noticed. You too, Theophrastus.

The path flattens out. The sun has set but its light is still in the sky. Ahead, through a break in the trees, the Acropolis comes suddenly into view, pearly against the first dusk. I catch my breath. From the Pnyx, as I look at it now, there is lightning behind the Parthenon, flashing out from a giant thundercloud gathered out of nowhere, while I was in the museum. Zeus still angry. In the flashes of his eerie electricity, I catch sight once again of that different world. Of that same sharp-bearded, pagan people, of energy and ingenuity. I see momentarily the strangeness of their beliefs. I see, but from the outside, their intricacy of thought and imagination, their secrecy, their fierce purpose and their utter mystery.

Behind me, the trees sigh in a wind that precedes the coming rain. I look ahead at the lights of Athens spread out below me, and out, and further, at the dark of the horizon beyond.

I will not turn round.

Map of the Greek world in Theophrastus' time

ADRIATIC SEA

Phili[

Amphipolis

Pella

Stagira

Olynthus

Potidea

Dion

Larissa

Dodona

Pheae

Corfu

Ambracia

Elatea

Delphi

Corinth

Olympia

Sparta

Byzantium

Perinthus

PROPONTIS

Maronea

era

s

Lesbos

Smyrna

Ephesus

A E G E A N   S E A

Samos

Miletus

etria

thens

Rhodes

CYCLADES

DODECANESE

Rhodes

Crete

0   50   100 km

Notes

A note on the spelling of names

Because the Romans were so influenced by the Greeks, they imported Greek culture and religion almost wholesale into their own. In doing so, they Romanized the spelling of Greek names. These are in general the versions we are familiar with – for example, Theophrastus rather than Theophrastos. This doesn't matter with an unknown figure but it draws unnecessary attention to itself, in a book for the English-speaking general reader, to spell Socrates, Sokrates. I would have preferred to use Greek spellings but, for the sake of familiarity, I have stuck mostly to Roman. In one or two cases, as in the Hotel Alkaios, I have gone with the Greek version because that's what it says on the hotel sign – and matched the spelling of the poet's name, too. Only once, in the case of Theophrastus' given name at birth, Tyrtamos, have I kept the Greek spelling for sentimental reasons. It seemed wrong to deprive him of his origins and it isn't his public name. It's the name his family would have used. Changing it felt like an invasion of privacy.

Place names are very difficult to make fit a system. In general, where they are appended to someone's name, I have used the Roman form – for example, Coriscus of Scepsis rather than Skepsis. Otherwise, I have used the Greek forms.

A note on sources

First, a caveat: this is a book for the general reader written in the tradition of a thieving magpie rather than a scholar or specialist, piecing together details from different sources and attempting to imagine a coherent picture. It aims to look at the past not as a discrete and separate place, but as something vitally connected to today.

I have very limited, very rusty Ancient Greek, so all primary sources are in translation with the exception of Theophrastus' own works. These I read using parallel texts. In the case of the *Characters*, the translations are versions of James Diggle's definitive edition. I have in some cases slightly altered the language so as to make it more accessible to the contemporary reader.

Demosthenes, Athenaeus and Diogenes Laertius are the writers I quote most, after Theophrastus. For these, I used Perseus Tufts online library (as I did for other classical writers too), which is a wonderful resource for the layperson and has a huge number of texts in translation. In the case of Demosthenes' *Speeches*, I also used the Oxford Classics translation for comparison, as I did with Plutarch's *Lives*. Aristotle's works are quoted from the Kindle edition of complete works.

A note on pictures

The black-and-white photographs of Greece throughout the text are not illustrations to the text. They are designed to give the Greek landscape, the source of so much of Theophrastus' thought and inspiration, its own separate and distinct voice in the book. For this reason they are not necessarily typographically relevant. In case it is of interest, the places are as follows:

Plate 1. Palaiopoli, Samothraki
Plate 2. Mytilene, Lesbos
Plate 3. Assos
Plate 4. Gulf of Kalloni, Lesbos
[Plate 5. Eastern Crete]
Plate 6. Lassithi Plateau, Crete
Plate 7. Eastern Crete
Plate 9. Epidauros
Plate 12. The Acropolis, Athens from Filopappou
Plate 13. Irakleia
Plate 14. Kythera

References

For reasons of space, and because this isn't an academic work, I have taken the approach here that I only attribute the longer sections of text. In each case, I have simply indicated the title of the work they come from, without giving either the particular edition, or the page reference. The tiny snippets of text go unattributed. Equally, where the attribution is given in the text I haven't put it into the notes, as for instance in the abstract of Theophrastus' *Metaphysics*.

As far as biographical detail goes, this is obviously impossibly uncertain. I haven't presented reasons for my interpretation of given events, I have just chosen one from among those on offer, in order to tell a story. For example, not everyone thinks that when Aristotle left Athens, Theophrastus went with him. Some, like Jaeger, think he joined later from Lesbos. Not everyone thinks he accompanied Aristotle to teach Alexander, and so on.

Theophrastus' works are abbreviated as follows: *Causis Plantarum*, CP; *Enquiry into Plants*, EP; *First Principles (Metaphysics)*, M; *Odours*, O; *Stones*, S; Theophrastus' *Characters*, TC; and *Weather Signs*, WS.

I. The Man

page 11 – He speaks in dialect… Coming from Lesbos, Theophrastus would have spoken Aeolic rather than Attic Greek. There were snobberies about this.

page 23 – *How would I know…* Taken from 'Sayings of Theophrastus in Arabic' in 'The Life, Works and Sayings of Theophrastus in the Arabic

Tradition', edited by Dimitri Gutas, part of *Theophrastus of Eresus*.

– *It is not possible to stand…* S.

– *Beautiful… greasy* etc. S.

page 24 – 'I am bored…' For information on the literacy levels of ancient Athens and its world, I am indebted to Robert Pitt, expert on ancient Greek epigraphy, in conversation.

References

page 24 – 'But do you…'
Demosthenes, 'On the Crown'
speech.

page 28 – Diogenes and the
Athenian philosophers. Most
of these anecdotes come from
a collection of biographical
accounts called the *Lives of
Eminent Philosophers*, written
by another Diogenes: Diogenes
Laertius (hereafter DL). He opens
his account by dismissing the
Zoroastrians and starting instead
with Orpheus, on the grounds that
Greece was where the human race
started. He was writing long after
all of his subjects were dead, in
the second century CE, so for both
of these reasons his biographies
are hardly to be trusted. However,
even if his work isn't useful for its
accuracy, it's still a vivid account of
the kind of surviving folk memories
of the long-gone philosophers, not
as thinkers but as people. He shows
us how they spoke to each other,
how they lived and dressed and
competed with each other in their
systems of thought.

page 29 – 'As Plato was
conversing… "tablehood" and
"cuphood"…' *The Life of Diogenes* in
DL 6.2.

– 'Be sure and have the second
course…' The descriptions of Greek
dining procedure are taken from
a long account by Athenaeus of
Naucratis, *The Deipnosophists*,

or *The Philosophers at Dinner*.
Athenaeus was born around 170 CE
in Naucratis, a Greek trading port
on the Canopic branch of the Nile,
famous, among other things, for the
beauty of its prostitutes. Sappho's
brother is supposed to have gone
there to purchase the freedom of
one, Rhodopis, a Thracian slave girl.
She was so beautiful that an eagle,
watching her bathe, apparently
snatched up one of her slippers
and dropped it in the lap of the
king of Egypt. The king, smitten,
took the sandal around the country
until he found the foot it fitted. It
is the earliest known version of the
Cinderella story. In other accounts,
Rhodopis subsequently made her
fortune, running a brothel of her
own. She became rich enough to
make a showy offering at Delphi,
which Herodotus records having
seen.

page 30 – Theophrastus said… 'sing
to us of three things…' 'Sayings of
Theophrastus in Arabic'.

– 'Stranger, it is…' From Cicero's
Brutus.

page 31 – Aristotle's character.
There are several non-
contemporary, ancient sources
for Aristotle's life, from each of
which these accounts originally
come. I found them collected in
During's *Aristotle in the Ancient
Biographical Tradition. The Portraits
of the Greeks*, edited by Richter

and Smith, puts some of these descriptions in the context of the various images and portrait busts that exist of Aristotle, as well as of those of his contemporaries.

page 33 – 'If we are ever to know…' Plato, *Phaedo*. Plato's remarks on wonder come from the *Theaetetus*; Aristotle's from Book 1 of his *Metaphysics*.

page 37 – Theophrastus' character. DL 5.2.

– *Intelligent tax collectors…* and *An intelligent person…* 'Sayings of Theophrastus in Arabic'.

page 38 – 'Aristotle did in fact…' From *The Dictionary Historical and Critical of Mr Peter Bayle*, 1697.

page 53 – 'I considered and debated…' These extracts are taken from Plato, *Letters* VII.

pages 55, 56 – 'For you are living…' and 'What is the point of these remarks?' Plato, *Letters* VI.

page 56 – On Plato's scheme of education, as practised at the Academy, which trained men of exceptional all-round ability from childhood in order to produce 'an autocracy of sages', see Professor Michael Tierney in 'Aristotle and Alexander the Great', who observes that the Academy 'already during Plato's lifetime had become the recognised source in all Greece

for advice on political theory and general legislation'.

page 57 – 'Hence all these men…' These observations on Hermias, translated by Werner Jaeger, are taken from his book *Aristotle*. They were made originally by a Greek scholar called Didymus Bronze-Guts who lived and taught at Alexandria.

page 60 – Theophrastus' *Metaphysics* – Perhaps the world… This section draws on the Stanford University online entry on Theophrastus, which bases some of its conclusions about Theophrastus' *Metaphysics* on his use of the word '*sunephe*', which was commonly used to signify close connection of the kind found in 'inseparable parts of a continuous whole, bound by some "partnership" (koinonia) of a hierarchical but also reciprocal nature'.

page 61 – *The ebb and flow of the sea*… 'Theophrastus on the Limits of Teleology', in *Theophrastus of Eresus*.

– On Theophrastus' position in relation to Aristotle's thinking. Quintilian, the Roman author, observed on a particular point of rhetoric that Theophrastus agreed with Aristotle, 'although he is accustomed to dissent from him without timidity', quoted in *Peripatetic Rhetoric after Aristotle* by Fortenbaugh and Mihady.

II. The Invention of Science

page 71 – 'I could exceeding plainly perceive...' All quotations from Hooke come from his *Micrographia*, published in 1665.

page 75 – On Aristotle and Theophrastus' style of writing. Plutarch commented in *Alexander*, in his *Lives*, that Aristotle's treatise on metaphysics 'is written in a style which makes it useless for those who wish to study or teach the subject from the beginning. The book serves simply as a memorandum for those who have already been taught its general principles.'

– *They say that the only dates...* This and all the subsequent quotations about plants in the section come from Theophrastus' two surviving works on plants: CP and EP.

page 94 – 'Why did he turn away...' Philodemus, *On Rhetoric*. Philodemus of Gadara was an Epicurean, later than Theophrastus, writing in the first century BCE, whose philosophical works were thought to be lost until the eighteenth century when they were discovered, preserved in the ash, in the Villa of the Papyri at Herculaneum.

page 100 – Linnaeus was much criticized for using Theophrastus by the Oxford botanists. A furious letter from Johann Dillenius to Linnaeus survives, in which he says, 'we all know the nomenclature of botany to be an Augean Stable... you rush upon it and overturn everything... I think that the names of the ancients ought not rashly and promiscuously to be transferred to our new genera... The day may possibly come when the plants of Theophrastus and Dioscorides may be ascertained; and till this happens, we had better leave their names as we find them.' Taken from MacGillivray, *Lives of Eminent Zoologists*.

page 103 – Theophrastus' comment on the stream at Pyrrha is quoted by Athenaeus in *The Deipnosophists*.

page 104 – 'One needed a bridle...' DL 5.2.

III. The Backdrop

page 114 – 'You who see Philip...' Demosthenes gave four speeches against Philip, known as the *Philippics*. This is from the second of these: Demosthenes 6.

page 115 – 'Philip saw Demosthenes' plight...' Taken from Aeschines' reply to Demosthenes: Aeschines 2.

page 117 – 'I see the plot thickening…' Demosthenes 6.

– 'You want freedom…' Demosthenes 6.

page 118 – On Isocrates and the concept of Panhellenism. This was first proposed by Gorgias in 392 BCE, then celebrated by Lysias in 384. See Markle, 'Support of Athenian Intellectuals for Philip'.

pages 118–21– 'I so impressed…', 'You must realise…', 'Like yourself…', 'You should not honour…' Isocrates' Discourse to Philip (Isocrates 5.4).

page 123 – 'If only he had chosen…' This and all subsequent quotations from Demosthenes in the trial of Aeschines come from Demosthenes, 'On the Corrupt Embassy' speech.

page 125 – But at this point… We know about the audience's reaction to Demosthenes' account of Aeschines' debauchery because Aeschines himself refers to it in his reply. All quotations from Aeschines' speech refer to No. 2 in his collected Speeches.

page 130 – '[H]e has sent you…' Speusippus' letter to Philip is taken from Markle.

page 134 – 'Since I am writing to your father…' and other quotations from Isocrates' letter to Alexander in this paragraph, from Isocrates.

page 134 – 'Aristotle was the man admired…' Plutarch, The Age of Alexander.

page 135 – When the subjects are obedient to their king and their king acts in accordance with tradition and justice… 'Sayings of Theophrastus in Arabic'.

page 136 – 'Now we may drink…' This and the anecdote about the dice both come from Athenaeus, The Deipnosophists.

page 139 – Nothing that is… and Control of desire… 'Sayings of Theophrastus in Arabic'.

page 142 – 'Tell my friends…' Quoted in Aristotle, Fundamentals in the History of his Development by Jaeger.

page 143 – 'To Hermias the Eunuch…' DL 2.

page 144 – Philip's letter about the grain ships. This is quoted in full by Demosthenes in his most famous speech 'On the Crown'.

page 145 – Sometimes it is necessary… 'Sayings of Theophrastus in Arabic'.

– 'Since conduct has to do with…' I have taken this from a digest of Aristotle's Nicomachean Ethics in Humphry House, Aristotle's Poetics.

page 147 – 'Affected these divine possessions…' From Plutarch, Alexander in Lives, 2. Olympias was, some say, responsible for organizing the murder of her husband out of worry that her son would be passed over in favour of the son of Philip's newest wife.

page 147 – *Whereas others sacrifice…* From Theophrastus' lost treatise, *On Piety*, here taken from Robin Lane Fox's definitive life, *Alexander the Great*, p. 45. The longer quotation is from a fragment preserved in a treatise *On Abstinence from Eating Animals*, written by Porphyry of Tyre, a third-century Neoplatonist and vegetarian.

page 154 – *An intelligent person ought to deal with time…* 'Sayings of Theophrastus in Arabic'.

– 'One part of it…' Aristotle, *Physics*.

page 159 – 'Why should the biographer…' From Richard Holmes, *Sidetracks*.

IV. The Works

page 170 – St Jerome's extract… These are all from *Jerome Against Jovinianus*.

page 180 – Strabo heard it from Diogenes… These are all Scholarchs of the Lyceum after Theophrastus' death, in reverse chronological order.

page 184 – 'Every human being…' From Ryszard Kapuściński, *Travels with Herodotus*.

page 188 – Descriptions of Caesar from Plutarch and Pliny. Plutarch, *Fall of the Roman Republic: Six Lives*. Pliny, *Natural History*.

V. Patterns

page 198 – 'We worked and thought…' From 'About Ed Ricketts', in *Steinbeck: A Life in Letters*.

page 199 – 'I think that participation…' Quoted in *Breaking Through: Essays, journals and travelogues of Edward F Ricketts*.

page 200 – 'He was my partner…' Quoted in *Breaking Through*.

page 201 – 'The world is sick now…' John Steinbeck to Carlton A. Sheffield, 13 November 1939, in *Steinbeck: A Life in Letters*.

page 202 – 'In such a pattern…' Steinbeck and Ricketts, *Sea of Cortez*.

– 'Gradually it will be discovered…' Steinbeck to Pascal Covici, 19 June 1941, in *Steinbeck: A Life in Letters*.

page 212 – *Not all herbs germinate…* EP.

page 213 – 'To see and express…' Dionysius of Halicarnassus, *Critical Essays 4*, 'Letter to Pompey'.

page 215 – 'Bright and early…' Athenaeus, *The Deipnosophists*, 1.21.

page 216 – 'Becomes necessary for the defendant…' Demosthenes, 'On the Corrupt Embassy'.

page 217 – 'At night…' Demosthenes, 'On the Corrupt Embassy'.

– Theophrastus' dislike of Demosthenes' oratorical style is based on the work of Craig Cooper in a chapter called 'Remaking Demosthenes', in *Alexander and his Successors*. According to Cooper, Demetrius of Phaleron found Demosthenes' oratory 'overly contrived, intricate and overdone, not simple and of noble fashion but inclined to what is soft and mean'. It was noted that Demosthenes became 'carried away in a Bacchic frenzy when he spoke, swearing once in the assembly a metrical oath as if he were possessed'.

page 221 – 'What was left to me…' From *Petrarch, the First Modern Scholar and Man of Letters*, translated by James Harvey Robinson.

page 223 – 'Contained most suitable admonitions…' Pirckheimer, quoted in James Overfield, *Humanism and Scholasticism in Late Mediaeval Germany*.

page 224 – 'As in speaking…' From *The Art of Rhetoric* by Thomas Wilson.

page 227 – 'But physicke…' From Thomas Overbury's poem, 'A Wife'.

page 228 – 'You would laugh…' George Eliot, *Letters*, 2.

page 230 – 'No, I don't think…' This and the comments on Eliot come from Elias Canetti's *Party in the Blitz*, translated by Michael Hofmann.

page 233 – This account of Sidney and Hoskyns is based on an article by John Buxton: 'The Achievement of Sir Philip Sidney'.

page 236 – 'A luminous globe…' From Virginia Woolf, *The Second Common Reader*.

– 'The first true novel…' This and all subsequent remarks made by Chesterton on Chaucer come from his monograph, *Chaucer*.

page 236 – The background for my observations on Chaucer's portrait is taken from an article by Michael Seymour: 'Manuscript Portraits of Chaucer and Hoccleve'.

References

pages 238–40 – My understanding of Chaucer's life in London is much indebted to Paul Strohm's brilliant *The Poet's Tale*.

page 242 – Quotations from Chaucer are taken from the Riverside Edition of Chaucer's *Complete Works*.

page 243 – 'Alexander to Aristotle...' Quoted by Plutarch in *Alexander*.

page 255 – 'The Greek has his eye...' Virginia Woolf, *Diaries*, 1939.

VI. The Teacher

page 261 – *It is a sign of rain...* This and the following descriptions of weather are from WS.

page 266 – 'The city is totally dry...' Herakleides, quoted in John M. Camp, *The Archaeology of Athens*.

page 269 – 'Alexander's fame...' Callisthenes, quoted in Lane Fox's *Alexander the Great*.

– 'Callisthenes is a perfect speaker...' Plutarch, *Alexander*.

page 275 – 'The youths were stoned...' Quoted in *Aristotle, New Light on his Life and on Some of his Lost Works*, by Chroust.

– *Callisthenes came across a man...* Cicero, *Tusculan Disputations*, quoted in *Theophrastus of Eresus*.

page 276 – 'What is a friend...' DL 4.

page 281 – 'O maiden...' These anecdotes are recorded in DL 4, the life of Crantor, who started as Theophrastus' pupil at the Lyceum and ended as head of the Academy. According to Laertius, the sequence of succession at the Academy after Plato went as follows: Speusippus, Xenocrates, Polemo, Crantor.

– On the changing allegiances of the philosophy schools' pupils, DL 6 has an alarming story about Metrocles who left Theophrastus after having broken wind in one of his speeches. He was so horrified he shut himself up and decided he'd starve himself to death. Crates the Cynic came to see him, gave him a meal of lupins and persuaded him that what he'd done was no more than give in to necessity. Metrocles, as a result, became a Cynic and burned all his notes to Theophrastus' lectures.

page 282 – *When the soul...* and *The soul is able to fly...* 'Sayings of Theophrastus in Arabic'.

page 284 – *To get a public...* DL 5.

314

page 285 – *It would be a good thing... Theophrastus of Eresus, Commentary*, vol. 6.

page 289 – *Men never attained...* 'Sayings of Theophrastus in Arabic'.

– *Nothing else but this...* and *Life holds...* and *All will be well...* Theophrastus' will, quoted in DL 5.

Select bibliography

Classical texts

Theophrastus' works

Characters, James Diggle, Cambridge University Press (2007)

Enquiry into Plants and Minor Works on Odours and Weather Signs, Arthur Hort, Loeb Classical Library, Heinemann (1916)

Theophrastus de Causis Plantarum, Benedict Einarson and George K.K. Link, Harvard University Press (1990)

Theophrastus: On First Principles (known as *Metaphysics*), Dimitri Gutas, Brill (2010)

Theophrastus on Stones, Earle R. Caley and John F.C. Richards, Ohio State University (1956)

Some of Theophrastus' lost writing has been preserved through quotation in the works of other authors, either contemporarily or later. These mentions have now been collected together through an ongoing international effort known as 'Project Theophrastus' and can be found in the two-volume *Theophrastus of Eresus: Sources for his Life, Writings, Thought and Influence*, edited by William Fortenbaugh et al., Transaction Books (1985). There are also, so far, eight books of commentaries with individual editors: *Theophrastus of Eresus, Commentary*.

Works by other authors

Aeschines, *The Speeches of Aeschines*, Charles Darwin Adams, Harvard University Press (1919)

Aristotle, *The Complete Works*, Jonathan Barnes, Princeton

University Press (1984; ebook 2000s)

Aristotle, *Physics*, translated by P.H. Wicksteed and F.M. Cornford, Loeb Classical Library 228, Harvard University Press (1957)

Athenaeus, *The Deipnosophists*, Henry G. Bohn (1854)

Cicero, *Brutus: Orator*, translated by G.L. Hendrickson, H.M. Hubbell, Loeb Classical Library 342, Harvard University Press (1939)

Curtius Rufus, Quintus, *The Life of Alexander*, translated by John Yardley, Penguin Books (1984)

Demosthenes, with an English translation, C.A. Vince and J.H. Vince, Harvard University Press and William Heinemann (1926)

Demosthenes, *Selected Speeches*, Robin Waterfield, Oxford University Press (2014)

Isocrates, with an English translation in three volumes, George Norlin, Harvard University Press and William Heinemann (1980)

Isocrates, *Complete Works*, Delphi Classics (2016)

Laertius, Diogenes, *Lives of Eminent Philosophers*, R.D. Hicks, Harvard University Press (1972)

McKeon, Richard (ed.), *The Basic Works of Aristotle*, Modern Library (2001)

Petrarch, the First Modern Scholar and Man of Letters, translated by James Harvey Robinson, G.P. Putnam's Sons (1898)

Philodemus, *On Poems*, translated by Richard Janko, Oxford University Press (2003)

Philodemus, *On Rhetoric*, Books 1 and 2, translated by Clive Chandler, Routledge (2005)

Plato, *Euthyphro. Apology. Crito. Phaedo. Phaedrus*, translated by Harold North Fowler, Loeb Classical Library 36, Harvard University Press (1914)

Pliny, *Natural History*, Vol. 1, Books 1 and 2, translated by H. Rackham, Loeb Classical Library 330, Harvard University Press (1938)

Plutarch, *The Age of Alexander*, translated by Ian Scott-Kilvert, Penguin (1973)

Plutarch, *Plutarch's Lives*, Vol. 8, *Alexander*, translated by Bernadotte Perrin, Harvard University Press and Heinemann (1919)

Plutarch, *Fall of the Roman Republic: Six Lives*, translated by Rex Warner, Penguin (2006)

Plutarch, *Moralia*, Arthur Richard Shilleto, George Bell (1898)

Porphyry, *On Abstinence from Killing Animals*, translated by Gillian Clark, Bloomsbury (2000)

317

Select bibliography

Secondary sources
On the classics

Barnes, Jonathan (ed.), *The Cambridge Companion to Aristotle*, Cambridge University Press (1995)

Barnes, Jonathan, *A Very Short Introduction to Aristotle*, Oxford University Press (2000)

Bayle, Peter, *Historical and Critical Dictionary* (1697)

Burckhardt, Jacob, *The Greeks and Greek Civilisation*, Fontana Press (1998)

Camp, John M., *The Archaeology of Athens*, Yale University Press (2004)

Canfora, Luciano, *The Vanished Library: a Wonder of the Ancient World*, Random House (1991)

Chroust, Anton-Herman, *Aristotle: New Light on his Life and on Some of his Lost Works*, Routledge (1973)

Connor, W. Robert, 'History Without Heroes: Theopompus' Treatment of Philip of Macedon', *Greek, Roman and Byzantine Studies*, vol. 8, no. 2 (1967), pp. 133–154

Cooper, Craig, 'Remaking Demosthenes', *Alexander and his Successors*, edited by Pat Wheatley and Robert Hannah, Regina Books, Claremont (2009)

Cottrell, Leonard, *The Bull of Minos*, revised edn, Pan Books (1955)

Düring, Ingemar, *Aristotle in the Ancient Biographical Tradition*, Almqvist & Wiksell (1957)

Fortenbaugh, William W. and Mirhady, David C. (eds), *Peripatetic Rhetoric after Aristotle*, Routledge (1994)

Fraser, P.M., *Ptolemaic Alexandria*, Clarendon Press (1972)

Fraser, P.M., 'The World of Theophrastus', *Greek Historiography*, edited by Simon Hornblower, Clarendon Press (1994)

Goldhill, Simon and Osborne, Robin, *Performance Culture and Athenian Democracy*, Cambridge University Press (1999)

House, Humphry, *Aristotle's Poetics*, Rupert Hart-Davis (1956)

Hughes, Bettany, *The Hemlock Cup: Socrates, Athens and the Search for the Good Life*, Vintage (2011)

Jaeger, Werner, *Aristotle, Fundamentals of the History of his Development*, Oxford University Press (1962)

Jerome, *Jerome Against Jovinianus*, translated by W.H. Fremantle, G. Lewis and W.G. Martley, in *Nicene and Post-Nicene Fathers*, Vol. 6, edited by Philip Schaff and Henry Wace, Christian Literature Publishing Co., Buffalo, NY (1893), revised and edited for New Advent by Kevin Knight, http://www.newadvent.org/fathers/30091.htm

Kapuściński, Ryszard, *Travels with Herodotus*, translated by Klara Glowczewska, Penguin (2007)

Kitto, H.D.F., *The Greeks*, Penguin (1991)

Kurfess, Hans and Düring, Ingemar, *Aristotle and his Influence: Two Studies*, Garland (1987)

Lane Fox, Robin, *Alexander the Great*, Penguin (1973)

Lane Fox, Robin, 'Theophrastus' *Characters* and the Historian', *PCPS*, 42 (1996), pp. 127–70

Lynch, John, *Aristotle's School*, University of California Press (1972)

Lyon, Annabel, *The Golden Mean*, Atlantic (2010)

Macleod, Roy, *The Library of Alexandria: Centre of Learning in the Ancient World*, Tauris (2002)

Markle, Minor M., 'Support of Athenian Intellectuals for Philip: A Study of Isocrates' Philippus and Speusippus' Letter to Philip', *Journal of Hellenic Studies*, vol. 96, 1976, pp. 80–99

Millett, Paul, *Lending and Borrowing in Ancient Athens*, Cambridge University Press (2010)

Millett, Paul, *Theophrastus and his World*, Cambridge Philological Society (2007)

Podlecki, A., 'Theophrastus on History and Politics', in *Theophrastus of Eresus: Sources for his Life, Writings, Thought and Influence*, edited by William Fortenbaugh et al., Transaction Books (1985), pp. 231–49

Renault, Mary, *Fire from Heaven*, Virago (2014)

Tierney, Michael, 'Aristotle and Alexander the Great', *Studies: an Irish Quarterly Review*, vol. 31, no. 122 (1942), pp. 221–228

Webster, T.B.L., *Athenian Culture and Society*, University of California Press (1973)

Whitehead, David, *The Ideology of the Athenian Metic*, Cambridge Philological Society (1977)

Select bibliography

On botany and natural history

Al-Khalili, Jim, *The House of Wisdom: How Arabic Science Saved Ancient Knowledge and Gave Us the Renaissance*, Penguin (2012)

Baumann, Hellmut, *Greek Wild Flowers and Plant Lore in Ancient Greece*, Herbert Press (1993)

Farrington, Benjamin, *Greek Science*, Dufour (1981)

Hooke, Robert, *Micrographia: or, Some physiological descriptions of minute bodies made by magnifying glasses*, J. Martyn and J. Allestry (1665)

Leroi, Armand Marie, *The Lagoon*, Bloomsbury (2015)

Lewes, G.H., *Aristotle – A Chapter from the History of Science* (1864)

Lindbergh, David and Shank, Michael (eds), *The Beginnings of Western Science*, University of Chicago Press (2008)

Lloyd, G.E.R., *Early Greek Science, Thales to Aristotle*, Norton (1974)

MacGillivray, William, *Lives of Eminent Zoologists, from Aristotle to Linnaeus*, Edinburgh (1974)

Edward F. Ricketts, *Breaking Through: Essays, journals and travelogues of Edward F Ricketts*, edited by Katherine A. Rodger, University of California Press (2006)

Schrodinger, Erwin, *Nature and the Greeks and Science and Humanism*, Cambridge (2008)

Steinbeck, John, *Cannery Row*, Viking Press (1945)

Steinbeck, John, *A Life in Letters*, Penguin (1989)

Steinbeck, John and Ricketts, Edward F., *Sea of Cortez*, Penguin (2009)

Taylor, Angus, *Animals and Ethics: An Overview of the Philosophical Debate*, Broadview Press (2003)

Thomas, Keith, *Man and the Natural World*, Allen Lane (1983)

Thompson, D'Arcy Wentworth, *On Aristotle as a Biologist*, Clarendon Press (1913)

On the transmission of the Characters and on characters in general

Aldington, Richard, *A Book of Characters* (1924)

Boyce, B., *The Theophrastan Character in England to 1642*, Harvard University Press (1947)

Buxton, John, 'The Achievement of Sir Philip Sidney', *English Literature of the Renaissance*, vol. 2, no. 1 (1972), pp. 779–82

Canetti, Elias, *Earwitness: Fifty Characters*, Farrar, Strauss and Giroux (1998)

Canetti, Elias, *Party in the Blitz*, translated by Michael Hofmann, New Directions (2010)

Eliot, George, *Impressions of Theophrastus Such*, Routledge (1993)

Eliot, George, *The Letters*, edited by Gordon S. Haight, 9 vols (1955)

Gosse, Edmund, *Three French Moralists and the Gallantry of France*, Heinemann (1918)

Gordon, G.S., *Theophrastus and his Imitators*, Clarendon Press (1912)

Gough, Charles Edward, *The Life and Characters of Thomas Overbury*, Princeton (1909)

Haight, Gordon, *George Eliot: A Biography*, Penguin (1985)

Hall, Joseph, *Characters of Vices and Virtues* (1608)

Holmes, Richard, *Sidetracks*, Flamingo (2001)

Horden, Peregrine and Purcell, Nicholas, *The Corrupting Sea: A Study of Medieval History*, Wiley-Blackwell (2000)

Nashe, Thomas, *Pierce Penniless his Supplication to the Devil* (1592)

Overbury, Thomas, *Characters, or Witty Descriptions of Sundry Persons* (1614)

Overfield, James, *Humanism and Scholasticism in Late Medieval Germany*, Princeton University Press (1985)

Pizer, John, 'From Jean de la Bruyère to John Aubrey and Beyond: The Development of Elias Cannetti's Character Sketches', *Comparative Literary Studies*, vol. 44, no. 1–2 (2007), pp. 166–181

Sim, Lorraine, *Virginia Woolf: The Patterns of Ordinary Experience*, Routledge (2010)

Select bibliography

Smeed, J.W., *The Theophrastan Character: The History of a Literary Genre*, Clarendon Press (1985)

Thackeray, William, *A Book of Snobs*, Nelson (1848)

Wilson, Thomas, *The Art of Rhetoric* (1553)

Virginia Woolf, *The Second Common Reader*, Mariner Books (2003)

Virginia Woolf, *Diaries*, 5 vols, Mariner Books (1979–1985)

On Chaucer and the Characters

Benson, Larry (ed.), *The Riverside Chaucer*, Oxford University Press (1987)

Boccaccio, *The Decameron*, edited by G.H. McWilliam, Penguin (2003)

Boitani, Piero (ed.), *Chaucer and the Italian Trecento*, Cambridge University Press (2010)

Chesterton, G.K., *Chaucer*, Lume Books (2015)

Cooper, Helen, *The Structure of the Canterbury Tales*, Duckworth (1983)

Mann, Jill, *Chaucer and Medieval Estates Satire*, Cambridge University Press (1973)

Martines, Lauro, *The Social World of the Florentine Humanists, 1390–1460*, University of Toronto Press (2011)

Seymour, Michael, 'Manuscript Portraits of Chaucer and Hoccleve', *Burlington Magazine*, vol. 124, no. 955, 1982, pp. 618–623.

Strohm, Paul, *The Poet's Tale: Chaucer and the Year that Made the Canterbury Tales*, Profile Books (2015)

Guide to some of the less well-known ancient characters mentioned

Aeschines (389–314 BCE) – Athenian statesman and orator, known for the beauty of his voice. He probably came from a poor but respectable background. He spent some time as an actor before becoming a soldier and diplomat.

Amyntas III (420–370 BCE) – father of Philip II of Macedon.

Antipater (400–319 BCE) – Macedonian statesman and general. He was the man left in charge of Macedonia while Alexander campaigned. He was Aristotle's lifelong friend and correspondent.

Antipater of Thessalonica – author of epigrams and governor of Thessalonica at the end of the first century BCE.

Apellicon of Teos (probably died c.84 BCE) – rich book collector. He is supposed to have bought the surviving manuscripts of Aristotle and Theophrastus' works from Neleus' descendants and taken them away and filled in some of the gaps caused by damage and damp with his own version of what he thought was missing.

Arcesilaus (315–240 BCE) – philosopher and head of the Academy.

Artaxerxes II (404–358 BCE) – son of Darius II. His official title was King of Kings of the Achaemenid Empire. The Greeks called him Artaxerxes Mnemon because of his astonishing memory.

Athenaeus of Naucratis – Greek rhetorician and grammarian who lived in the second and third century CE. Author of *The Deipnosophists* (*The Philosophers at Dinner*), a long account of an imaginary banquet. He is supposed to have been strangled to death by peasants who broke into his house at night and killed him because he refused to stop writing.

Axiothea of Phlius (flourished c.350 BCE) – a female student of Plato's at the Academy.

Coriscus of Scepsis – philosopher, brother of Erastus and father of Neleus, who inherited Theophrastus' library.

Curtius Rufus – Roman historian writing probably in the first century CE, author of the *Histories of*

Alexander the Great. Nothing else is known of him than this.

Demetrius of Phalerum (350–280 BCE) – philosopher and statesman, pupil of Theophrastus'. He was made governor of Athens by Cassander, Antipater's son, who ruled Macedonia and Southern Greece up until about 317 BCE. Demetrius was exiled and defamed for debauchery by his enemies, in 307. He left and went first to Thebes and then to Alexandria where he lived as a philosopher until he died.

Demosthenes (384–322 BCE) – Athenian orator, statesman and professional speech writer. Made his own maiden speech at the age of twenty, in a bid to claim what was left of his inheritance. His statues make him look intense and undershot. He is supposed to have died after being finally defeated in court, having taken poison from his own pen, rather than be captured and put to death.

Diogenes the Cynic (404–323 BCE) – the first of the Cynic philosophers. There is an interesting anecdote in the *Life of Diogenes* (DL 6.22), which quotes Theophrastus on how he came to live so hand to mouth on the streets of Athens. 'Through watching a mouse running about', says Theophrastus in the lost Megarian dialogue, 'not looking for a place to lie down in, not afraid of the dark, not seeking any of the

things which are considered to be dainties, [Diogenes] discovered the means of adapting himself to circumstances.'

Diogenes Laertius (180–240 CE) – Greek, writing during the time of the Roman Empire, in the third century. Author of the *Lives and Opinions of Eminent Philosophers.*

Dion of Syracuse (408–354 BCE) – brother-in-law of Dionysius I of Syracuse and a disciple of Plato's. He was banished by Dionysius II, his nephew, who was suspicious of his ambition and his power. He went to Athens, where he lived until 357, when he returned to Syracuse to claim back his confiscated estates, and where he was assassinated.

Dionysius II of Syracuse (c.395–343 BCE) – Greek ruler of Syracuse and son of Dionysius I.

Erastus – Platonic philosopher and brother of Coriscus.

Harpalus – Macedonian noble and companion of Alexander the Great. His lameness prevented him from being much use in battle and so he was given an administrative post as treasurer, living with his Athenian concubine in Babylon, and passing his time adding Mediterranean plants to the Hanging Gardens. Later he was betrayed by Theopompus, who wrote to Alexander complaining of his behaviour – among other things, for attempting to deify his dead concubine. He escaped to Athens, possibly with some money that wasn't his, where he appealed for protection.

Hephaestion (356–324 BCE) – Macedonian noble and general in Alexander's army. He was Alexander's lifelong beloved and second in command. When he died suddenly at Ecbatana, Alexander petitioned the oracle at Siwa to have him made divine. His pyre was sixty metres high, its platforms variously piled with ships with golden prows and ornamental bulls and lions. His ashes were then taken to Babylon, with Alexander himself driving much of the way, where funeral games were held in his honour.

Hermias of Atarneus (died c.341 BCE) – philosopher, tyrant and possible eunuch, who invited Aristotle to Assos to set up a school. He was Aristotle's kinsman by marriage, through Pythias who was his niece or protégée, or possibly (if he wasn't a eunuch) daughter.

Herpyllis of Stagira – Aristotle's mistress, after Pythias died, and mother of Nicomachus.

Isocrates (436–338 BCE) – Greek rhetorician and Sophist, acquainted in his youth with Socrates. He fell on hard times and had to make his living teaching for money and writing speeches.

Lastheneia of Mantinea – Greek female student of Plato's at the Academy. She dressed as a man and was possibly the lover of Speusippus. There must have been several female philosophers whose names have been lost. An Epicurean called Leontion, sometimes described as 'a prostitute', wrote elegant criticisms of Theophrastus in Attic Greek, according to Cicero and Pliny, both of whom were astonished that a woman would dare to – or even would be able to – do such a thing.

Melantas – Theophrastus' father.

Menander (c.342–c.290 BCE) – pupil of Theophrastus' and playwright. Father of the Athenian New Comedy. He was known as 'o Kalos' (the good, or possibly the beautiful). He was variously described as 'cross-eyed but of nimble mind' (Suidas) and 'anointed with perfume, effeminate in dress, walking with delicate and languid steps' (Phaedrus, *Fabulae Aesiopiae* V). He died by drowning in the sea while swimming off Piraeus, where he lived.

Mentor of Rhodes (c.385–340 BCE) – a Greek mercenary who rose to become Persian satrap of the coast of Asia Minor.

Neleus of Scepsis – son of Coriscus and pupil of Theophrastus'. Theophrastus possibly hoped he would become Scholarch of the Lyceum after him and so left him its library.

Nicanor – a diplomat and friend of Aristotle's from Stagira who had served under Alexander in Asia.

Nicomachus – Aristotle's son, loved by Theophrastus. His mother was Herpyllis, a slave girl whom Aristotle lived with after his wife Pythias died.

Olympias (c.375–316 BCE) – daughter of Neoptolemus I, king of the Molossians, a tribe from Epirus in northern Greece. She was Philip of Macedon's fourth wife and the mother of Alexander the Great.

Parmenides (flourished c.515 BCE) – Greek philosopher born in Elea in southern Italy. Founder of the Eleatic School and father of metaphysics.

Phanias – Greek philosopher, compatriot and friend of Theophrastus'. Born at Eresos on Lesbos. His works, almost all of which are lost, seem to have been commentaries on the works of Aristotle and Theophrastus. His work on plants seems to be concerned mainly with those used in cultivation. He was a gardener.

Philocrates (flourished c.340 BCE) – Athenian statesman and diplomat. Brokered the unpopular Peace of Philocrates with Philip of

Macedon, after the fall of Olynthus. Subsequently, he fell out of favour, seen as being corrupt, and was condemned to death in exile.

Philodemus of Gadara (c.110–30 BCE) – an Epicurean who studied under Zeno of Sidon (not Zeno of the paradox, who was earlier and an Eleatic) and then moved to Italy. His philosophical works were thought lost until some of them were found preserved in the ash at Herculaneum in the eighteenth century.

Plutarch (c.46–119 CE) – Greek historian and philosopher, born at Chaeronea near Delphi where, in the last years of his life, he was priest of Apollo. He is best known for his *Parallel Lives*, which was a biographical account of pairs of famous Greeks and Romans, and for his *Moralia*, a book of essays on ethics.

Praxiphanes – Peripatetic philosopher and pupil of Theophrastus. He came from Mytilene on Lesbos and is supposed to have founded his own school which numbered Epicurus among its pupils. His main contribution to philosophy was in the subject of grammar, of which discipline he is thought, with Aristotle, to have been the founder.

Ptolemy Philadelphus (c.309–246 BCE) – son of Ptolemy Soter, he was the second of the Ptolemaic pharaohs of Egypt. He was responsible for making the Library at Alexandria, for which he acquired, or had copied, huge numbers of books.

Ptolemy Soter (367–282 BCE) – Macedonian companion of Alexander the Great and one of his generals. He wrote a lost eye-witness account of Alexander's campaigns. On Alexander's death, when the empire was split between five of the most trusted generals, he became regent of Egypt and later its first Ptolemaic pharaoh. He founded the Peripatetic School at Alexandria and possibly also the Library.

Pythias – kinswoman of Hermias of Atarneus, or possibly his adoptive daughter, and first wife of Aristotle. She is supposed to have made her own studies in biology and embryology but nothing of hers has survived.

Pytho – Greek statesman and diplomat, pupil of Isocrates. He led the embassy to Philip whose aim was to mend the Peace of Philocrates. When it failed, he was discredited.

Sappho (c.630–570 BCE) – Greek lyric poet from Lesbos, known as the Tenth Muse.

Speusippus (c.408–339 BCE) – Plato's nephew. He became head of the Academy on Plato's death.

Strabo (63 BCE–24 CE) – Pontic Greek (i.e. born in what is now Turkey), geographer, historian and philosopher, best known for his *Geographica*.

Strato of Lampsacus (335–269 BCE) – Greek philosopher, tutor of Ptolemy II. He specialized in the natural sciences and became Scholarch of the Lyceum when Theophrastus died. His work was rediscovered by Spinoza in the seventeenth century because his system lent itself to the pantheism that Spinoza was beginning to develop.

Theocritus of Chios – philosopher and rhetorician, pupil of Metrodorus, who himself was a pupil of Isocrates. He wrote maxims or citations, according to Diogenes Laertius who gives him a brief entry in Book 2 of the *Lives and Opinions of Eminent Philosophers*.

Theopompus (c.380–315 BCE) – Greek historian and rhetorician. Born on Chios, he was a pupil of Isocrates' and is known, among other things, for his huge *History of Philip II*, which ran to 58 books.

Xenocrates (c.396–314 BCE) – Greek philosopher and mathematician. Pupil and devoted disciple of Plato, he became Scholarch of the Academy after Speusippus. He was a man of legendary virtue and sobriety.

Acknowledgements

Over the more than ten years of trying that it took to frame what I saw as Theophrastus' story, I became a kind of Ancient Mariner, pouring out an insistent but often incoherent account in the direction of whichever friend or family member I could find. My thanks for their patience and their encouragement and their continued professions of interest go to all those who suffered the glittering of my eye. Chief among these were my parents, my siblings, my children, and my friend Kim Wilkie, who discussed Theophrastus with me over many years, as we walked round his newly planted wood, so that sometimes it felt as though a book could take as long as a wood to grow. Andrew and Cornelia Baines provided me with the scientists' take and spurred me on with their questions year after year. In particular, they provided, through Andrew's own teaching on scientific rhetoric, the feeling of an unbroken tradition.

To my agent Caroline, for always listening and for not hurrying me, I owe a great debt.

Hugh Barnes, Michael Dodson and Joanna Zenghelis put me up on Lesbos, drove me round and round the island, walked with me to find the fritillary that has Theophrastus' name, searched for Pella and generally threw themselves into my project with the most generous enthusiasm and energy.

Robert Pitt explained to me about Ancient Greek epigraphs and changed the way I saw literacy levels among the Athenians with his account of bored shepherds.

Many people, at different stages, read the many versions of the manuscript. My thanks go to Sam Brown, Helena Drysdale and Oana Aristide for their insight and their thoughtful criticisms. I would like to thank my mother and my sister Alice for saving me from the whimsicality of trying to write Theophrastus letters, and I'd like to thank my son Ivo, and my brother William, for the meticulous attention of their repeated readings. I'm particularly grateful to Ivo for his notes and to William for solving the problem of the book's ending.

The writers of the Zen writing group – Anne Aylor, Oana Aristide, Elise Valmorbida, Roger Levy, Rob Carroll, Anne-Marie Neary, Gavin Eyers – helped me brainstorm a title. Sarah Chatwin was an invaluably beady-eyed and brilliant copy-editor who patiently steered me free of much sloppiness and inconsistency. Alan Craig at Atlantic masterfully took on the problem of setting the pictures across two pages. To all at Atlantic, my sincere thanks. And most of all to James Roxburgh, the best editor a writer could imagine, for your ability to read and re-read always with the same fresh attention and for your ability to see the book I'm trying to write, thank you a second time.

Finally, to Rupert, for this and much more, thank you. This book is for you.

Index

Index

Demaratus, 291
Demetrius of Phalerum, 182–3, 217,
    281, 282, 284
democracy, 4, 24, 41, 117, 124
Democritus, 144, 168
Demosthenes, 24, 41, 42, 114–19, 121,
    224, 262, 263, 276
  Aeschines' trial, 123–9, 216–17
  Hermias' death, 142, 143
  Macedonia, views on, 114–19, 121,
    123, 262, 263
Demotimus, 291
Dickens, Charles, 232
Diogenes the Cynic, 28–9, 31, 140, 180,
    280
Dion of Syracuse, 52–3
Dionysius, son of Dion, 53, 102
Dionysus, cult of, 146, 272
Dionysus I of Syracuse, 52, 121, 130
dissections, 91–2
dissemination of knowledge, 92–3,
    218–30, 232–3
Divine Comedy (Dante), 240
Don Quixote (Cervantes), 167
dreams, 169
drunkenness, 116, 131, 125, 136, 146,
    169
Dürer, Albrecht, 222–3

eagles, 79
Egypt, 10, 22, 75, 117, 130, 132, 141,
    182, 187–92, 269, 284
Eliot, George, 228, 254
Eliot, Thomas Stearns, 229–30
Elis, 117
elm, 76, 89
embryos, 92, 133
Empedocles, 168
endangered plants, 90
England, 13–17, 167, 207, 211–12, 297
  Casaubon, works of, 224–5, 228, 233
  Chaucer, works of, 170, 235–54
  Hooke, work of, 70–72

Sidney, works of, 233–4
English language, 241–4
Enquiry into Plants, An (Theophrastus),
    90
enthusiasm, 169
Ephebes, 28, 42
Ephesus, Anatolia, 49
Epicureans, 186
Epicurus, 280
Epidaurus, 155
epilepsy, 169
Epirus, 113
Erastus, 55–6
Eresos, Lesbos, 22, 74, 98
Eridanos river, 282
Erinna, 97
eristic tradition, 133
Ermou Street, Mytilene, 44, 45, 48
Eros, 172
Etesian winds, 41, 91
ethics, 145, 213, 215
Ethiopia, 78, 100
Euboea, 117, 148, 276, 280
Eubulus, 54–5
eunuchs, 54, 143, 171, 172
Euripides, 119, 280
Euripos canal, Mytilene, 44, 45, 48, 283
Eurydice, 12–13, 299
Eve, 176
Every Man in his Humour (Jonson), 233
Evia, 69

fainting fits, 169
family, 96
first principles, 30, 58–60, 168
five senses, 155
flesh, 169
Flora, 80
Florence, 220–22, 240, 245, 252
forensic speeches, 169
Four Quartets (Eliot), 229
France, 158–60, 240
French language, 243

Index

kingly power, 169
klepsydra, 124
Knossos, Crete, 16
Koh-i-noor mountains, 273
de La Bruyère, Jean, 227
Laertius, Diogenes, 91, 149, 168, 170, 179
Langland, William, 241
Lastheneia of Mantinea, 96
Latin, 241, 242, 243, 252
law, 135, 168, 169
Lemnos, 144
Leodamas, 144
Leontion, 280
Lesbos, 3, 4, 7, 8–11, 22, 44–9, 54, 69, 74–106, 148
    Assos, relations with, 60, 62
    democracy in, 24
    spring in, 84
Lewes, George, 228
lime trees, 89
Linnaeus, Carl, 100
Lionel of Antwerp, Duke of Clarence, 237
liquefaction, 169
literacy, 25
Lives of the Philosophers (Diogenes Laertius), 31, 149
logic, 168
Loudias river, 131
love, 169, 170
lust, 172
Lyceum, Athens, 180–81, 183, 186–7, 217, 264, 268, 276, 280, 282, 284
Lyco, 180
Lycurgus, 276
Lykabettos, 91

Macbeth (Shakespeare), 167
Macedonia, 40–43, 100–106, 113–49, 268–76
    Amphipolis annexation, 114, 116, 120, 121

Aristotle in, 100–106, 117, 131–49
Athens, relations with, 40–43, 114–31, 144–5, 275–6
Byzantium, invasion of, 148, 262
court life, 146
Demosthenes and, 114–19, 121, 123, 262, 263
Hermias' death, 141–3, 145
Isocrates and, 119–23
Olynthus invasion, 41–2, 102, 105, 113, 125
Persia, relations with, 117–18, 141–3, 263, 268–76
Thrace, conquest of, 136, 148
Mandelstam, Osip, 196
mandrake, 79–80
Manes, 283
manna ash, 89
marine biology, 199–203
marriage, 170–73, 246
mathematics, 26, 168
Medici family, 221
Megara, 91, 117
melancholy, 169
Melantas, 74
Melantes, 290, 291
Melos, 23
Menander, 48–9, 215, 281
mental derangement, 169
Mentor of Rhodes, 141–2
Messenia, 131
Metaphysics (Aristotle), 58
Metaphysics (Theophrastus), 58, 76, 88
metaphysics, 30, 59–63, 168
meteorology, 91, 264
method, 80, 168
Methone, 114, 117
Methymna, Lesbos, 22, 62
Metrodorus, 291
Michaelmas daisy, 86
microscopes, 70–72
Mieza, 132, 136, 138, 140, 148, 282
Miller's Tale, The (Chaucer), 246

Index

phantoms, 153, 169
Philip II, King of Macedon, 40–43, 55,
    101–6, 113–36
    Amphipolis annexation, 114, 116,
        120, 121
    Aristotle, relationship with, 100–106,
        117, 131–2, 148, 149, 263, 276
    Athens, conquest of, 262–3
    Bucephalus, relationship with, 138
    Byzantium, invasion of, 148, 262
    death, 263
    Demosthenes and, 114–19, 121, 123
    drinking habit, 136, 146
    Hermias, relationship with, 141–3
    Isocrates and, 119–23, 130, 133–4,
        141
    Olynthus, invasion of, 41–2, 102,
        105, 113, 125
    Persia, relations with, 117–18, 141–3
    Speusippus and, 130
    Theopompus' biography, 212–13
    Thrace, conquest of, 136, 148
Philippica (Theopompus), 212–13
Philocrates, 116, 117, 121, 123
Philodemus of Gadara, 94, 218
Philosophers at Dinner, The (Athenaeus),
    182, 280
philosophy, 168
Phocis, 117
photographs, 154–60
photosynthesis, 80–81
Phryno, 125
Piers Plowman (Langland), 241
Piraeus, 3, 9, 10, 28, 42, 46, 49, 52, 210,
    268
Pirckheimer, Willibald, 222–3
plants, 75–91, 137, 211–12, 282
    descriptive terms, 87–8
    endangered, 90
    ground preparation, 89
    medicinal properties, 89
Plato, 7, 10, 26–30

Academy, 7, 10, 26–36, 53–6, 73,
    130, 185, 268, 280–81
Aristotle, relationship with, 32–4,
    38–9
beauty, views on, 140
cave allegory, 27
death, 38–9
Diogenes, relationship with, 29
Dion, relationship with, 52–3, 102
eristic tradition, 133
first principles, 30, 59–60
forms, views on, 27, 29, 33, 36
Hermias, relationship with, 55–6
Republic, 96
Sicily, visits to, 52–3, 102
Socrates, relationship with, 52, 57
Sophists, views on, 120
Timaeus, 26
travels, 52
women, views on, 96
wonder, views on, 34
Xenocrates, relationship with, 52, 53,
    104
pleasure, 168, 169, 170
Plutarch, 134, 139, 147, 188, 272
Pnyx, Athens, 298
politics, 135, 169
Polycritus, 144
Polystratus the Tyrrhenian, 281
Pompey, 188–9
Porthmus, Euboea, 117
Poseidon, 81
Pothos, 172
Potidea, 117
pottery, 6, 172
Praxilla, 97
Praxiphanes, 95
Praxiteles, 290
printing, 222
Progymnasmata, 219
proskynesis, 273
Proust, Marcel, 154

Index